Segregation by Design

Segregation by Design draws on more than 100 years of quantitative and qualitative data from thousands of American cities to explore how local governments generate race and class segregation. Since the early twentieth century, cities have used their power of land use control to determine the location and availability of housing, amenities (such as parks), and negative land uses (such as landfills). The result has been segregation – first within cities and more recently between them. Documenting changing patterns of segregation and their political mechanisms, Trounstine argues that city governments have pursued these policies to enhance the wealth and resources of white property owners at the expense of people of color and the poor. Contrary to leading theories of urban politics, local democracy has not functioned to represent all residents. The result is unequal access to fundamental local services – from schools, to safe neighborhoods, to clean water.

JESSICA TROUNSTINE is an associate professor of political science at University of California, Merced. She is the author of *Political Monopolies in American Cities: The Rise and Fall of Bosses and Reformers* (2008), which won the American Political Science Association's Prize for Best Book on Urban Politics. Trounstine served as President of the Urban and Local Politics Section of APSA from 2014 to 2015. Her research examines subnational politics and the process and quality of representation.

Segregation by Design

Local Politics and Inequality in American Cities

JESSICA TROUNSTINE
University of California, Merced

CAMBRIDGE
UNIVERSITY PRESS

CAMBRIDGE
UNIVERSITY PRESS

University Printing House, Cambridge CB2 8BS, United Kingdom

One Liberty Plaza, 20th Floor, New York, NY 10006, USA

477 Williamstown Road, Port Melbourne, VIC 3207, Australia

314–321, 3rd Floor, Plot 3, Splendor Forum, Jasola District Centre,
New Delhi – 110025, India

79 Anson Road, #06–04/06, Singapore 079906

Cambridge University Press is part of the University of Cambridge.

It furthers the University's mission by disseminating knowledge in the pursuit of
education, learning, and research at the highest international levels of excellence.

www.cambridge.org
Information on this title: www.cambridge.org/9781108429955
DOI: 10.1017/9781108555722

First published 2018
Reprinted 2019

Printed in the United Kingdom by TJ International Ltd. Padstow Cornwall

A catalogue record for this publication is available from the British Library.

Library of Congress Cataloging-in-Publication Data
NAMES: Trounstine, Jessica, author.
TITLE: Segregation by design : local politics and inequality in American cities /
Jessica Trounstine.
DESCRIPTION: New York : Cambridge University Press, [2018] | Includes
bibliographical references and index.
IDENTIFIERS: LCCN 2018009866 | ISBN 9781108429955 (hardback : alk. paper) |
ISBN 9781108454988 (pbk. : alk. paper)
SUBJECTS: LCSH: Discrimination in housing–United States. | Segregation–United States. |
Race discrimination–United States. | Local government–United States.
CLASSIFICATION: LCC HD7293 .T735 2018 | DDC 363.5/10973–dc23
LC record available at https://lccn.loc.gov/2018009866

ISBN 978-1-108-42995-5 Hardback
ISBN 978-1-108-45498-8 Paperback

For Brian

Contents

Figures

Tables

Acknowledgments

This book began in 2008 as a debate with Brian, my then partner, now spouse, while we were on a walk by the ocean in Half Moon Bay, California. We argued over the extent to which private control of coastal land would generate unequal access to the beaches and whether or not this was an important public policy concern. As this seemed like a straightforward question about control of local public goods, I went looking for evidence to support my perspective in the political science literature. I found unsatisfying answers. As I ventured into the puzzle, I realized that I had to wrestle with more essential questions about the relationship between land use control and inequality first. This book is the result of that quest. Throughout the process, Brian's views of the world, his unwillingness to adopt my perspective without evidence, and his unyielding support of my career made this work both exciting and possible. And it is to him that I dedicate this book. I am grateful for the life we have built and for the mooring that our marriage has provided in the journey.

In writing a book one incurs many debts. This is especially true when the writing of the book takes more than a decade. The project changed course numerous times. There were many false starts. Thankfully, I have brilliant and generous friends who have offered feedback every step of the way, graciously hosted talks on the research, and read many, many drafts.

The project was profoundly affected by comments from and conversations with Sarah Anzia, Irenee Beattie, Josh Clinton, Courtenay Conrad, Melody Crowder-Meyer, Ryan Enos, David Fortunato, Shana Gadarian, Tom Hansford, Matt Hibbing, Mirya Holman, Karen Jusko, Shawn Kantor, Vlad Kogan, Neil Kraus, Matt Lassiter, Gabe Lenz, Amy Lerman, David Lewis, Rob Mickey, Nathan Monroe, Rebecca Morton, Steve

Nicholson, Tom Ogorzalek, John Patty, Emily Ritter, Jacob Rugh, Celine Schafer, Kurt Schnier, Betsy Sinclair, Joe Soss, Lester Spence, Werner Troesken, Deborah Trounstine, Mary Trounstine, Phil Trounstine, Nella Van Dyke, Alex Whalley, and Katie Winder. Thank you all.

Two of my mentors from graduate school, Amy Bridges and Zoltan Hajnal, have continued to offer detailed feedback and advice long after their official job was complete. Clarence Stone, Daniel Hopkins, and Eric Oliver read the entire book and offered tremendous insights. The LIPS team, Sunshine Hillygus, Maggie Penn, and Tasha Philpot, kept me sane and helped turned my rambling thoughts into publishable ideas. Several colleagues provided data that were vital to the project: Sarah Anzia, Daniel Hopkins, Clayton Nall, Jonathan Rothwell, Allison Shertzer, Chris Tausanovitch, Jeff Tessin, Tom Vogl, and Chris Warshaw. Research assistance by Saniyyah Lateef, Stephanie Nail, Tanika Ray-chaudhuri, Kau Vue, and Chelsea Wood was essential.

Rafaela Dancygier not only read and commented on multiple drafts of everything from prospectus to complete manuscript; in 2016, she coord-inated a book conference on the manuscript at Princeton University. Funding for the conference was generously provided by the Mamdouha Bobst Center for Peace and Justice. Chris Berry, Claudine Gay, Elisabeth Gerber, Marty Gilens, Kevin Kruse, Nolan McCarty, and Ismael White all read the first version of the manuscript and, in (painstaking) detail, told me how to fix it. Chris Achen, Amaney Jamal, Doug Massey, Tali Mendelberg, and Omar Wasow also contributed incredible feedback at the conference.

My editor, Sara Doskow, has been cheering me on since this project was just a vague notion. Her support and guidance have been invaluable.

Prologue

Written by Jessica Trounstine and Darick Ritter
Illustrated by Darick Ritter

I

Introduction

Fear ruled everything around me, and I knew, as all black people do, that this fear was connected to the Dream out there, to the unworried boys, to pie and pot roast, to the white fences and green lawns nightly beamed into our television sets.

– Ta-Nehisi Coates, *Between the World and Me*, p. 28

City services sustain, prolong, and even save lives. In the latter half of the nineteenth century, urban populations and economies were booming. But so too were their filth, disease, and divisions. By 1900, infectious and parasitic diseases killed nearly eight in every thousand residents, accounting for more than 45% of all deaths (Tippett 2014) and more than 60% of deaths among children (Guyer et al. 2000). In some cities, 30% of babies would not live to celebrate their first birthday (Meckel 1990). But between 1900 and 1940, the overall mortality rate in the United States declined by 35% (Linder and Grove 1947), and the infectious disease mortality rate declined by 75% (CDC 1999, adapted from Armstrong et al. 1999).[1] Estimates indicate that between one-quarter and one-half of this decline can be attributed to the development of public water and sewer systems – systems that were financed, built, and maintained not by the federal or state governments, but by cities.

Across the United States, local public works significantly reduced outbreaks of diseases such as cholera, typhoid fever, diarrheal diseases,

---

[1] Total mortality declined from 17 per 1,000 persons to 11 per 1,000 persons.

and malaria (Cutler and Miller 2006; Troesken 2004).[2] Over time, the growth of municipal fire and police forces, street cleaning and refuse disposal, childhood vaccination and physical examination programs, regulation of food supplies, and the implementation of building codes all worked to prolong life expectancy (Condran and Cheney 1982; Haines 2001; CDC 1999).

But such benefits were neither inevitable nor universal. Although all major cities would eventually come to provide basic services, development was uneven. Nearly fifty years separated the delivery of publicly accessible water in Philadelphia and Boston (Cutler and Miller 2005). At the turn of the twentieth century, some cities spent as little as $100 per resident on services, while others spent more than $900. And, from the beginning, poor and minority neighborhoods received fewer and lower-quality services. They were less likely to be connected to sewers, to have graded and paved streets, or to benefit from disease mitigation programs.[3]

Today, the quality of public goods in the United States remains highly variable. Some people have access to good schools, well-paved and plowed roads, sewers that rarely overflow, public parks with playgrounds and restrooms, adequately staffed police and fire forces, and clean water. Others do not have access to these resources. As the epigraph by Coates illustrates, the availability of the American Dream for some, has for the entirety of American history, depended crucially on the denial of that Dream to others.

The quality of services one experiences in the United States is largely a function of the neighborhood in which a person resides. When the poor and people of color are concentrated in residential locations apart from wealthy and white residents, we say that a place is segregated. It is segregation that permits unequal access to public goods and services. Yet, the extent of segregation varies from place to place, and throughout the United States patterns of segregation have changed dramatically over time. This book asks how segregation becomes entrenched, why its form changes, and

---

[2] The dramatic improvement in mortality from the implementation of water and sewer systems required the development of filtration and treatment techniques, which were not immediately available when the systems were first built.

[3] This book explores race and class divisions in local politics and residential locations. There are many ways one might go about defining these groups. As explained in more detail in Chapter 3, I focus on divisions between whites and nonwhites and between homeowners and renters. I use the terms "minority" and "nonwhite" interchangeably. I also use the terms "black" and "African American" interchangeably.

what the consequences are. I argue that local governments have generated segregation along race and class lines. Striving to protect property values and exclusive access to high quality public goods, the preferences of white property owners have been institutionalized through the vehicle of local land use policy, shaping residential geography for more than 100 years. In the early part of the twentieth century when cities began their rapid ascent, local governments systematically institutionalized discriminatory approaches to the maintenance of housing values and production of public goods. They created segregation. These institutions persist, narrowing options for some residents and creating and recreating inequality and polarization today.

Between 1890 and 2010, the spatial scale of residential segregation along race and class lines changed (Logan et al. 2015; Reardon et al. 2009; Lee et al. 2008). In the late 1800s, whites and people of color, renters and owners, poor and wealthy were separated from each other in small clusters, so that residential segregation occurred on a block-by-block basis. By the middle of the twentieth century, segregation patterns had transformed; residents became segregated neighborhood by neighborhood. Throughout the postwar period, segregation between whole cities arose as the nation suburbanized. In recent decades, this city-to-city segregation has remained remarkably persistent despite decreasing neighborhood segregation. Because political representation is geographically determined, these changing patterns have had profound political consequences, generating opportunities for exclusion and increasing polarization. Local governments have been instrumental in driving and shaping these patterns.

Segregation is *not* simply the result of individual choices about where to live. Neither racial antipathy nor economic inequality between groups is sufficient to create and perpetuate segregation. The maintenance of property values and the quality of public goods are collective endeavors. And like all collective endeavors, they require collective action for production and stability. Local governments provide this collective action. So, supported by land-oriented businesses, white homeowners have backed a succession of maneuvers to keep their property interests and public benefits insulated from change – even as cities have grown, aged, redeveloped, suburbanized, and adjusted to industrialization. Battles over the control of urban space have always been the primary driver of city politics. At stake is the quality of life accessible to residents and markets available to commercial interests. The result has been *segregation by design*.

CHERRY HILL AND CAMDEN

An example from southern New Jersey illustrates changing patterns of segregation, rising inequality, and the role of local governments in producing these patterns. Camden and Cherry Hill are similarly sized cities, both just across the Delaware River from Philadelphia. Camden is home to two Superfund (toxic waste) sites; Cherry Hill is home to none.[4] In Camden only 1.7% of state roads had good pavement in 2004,[5] compared with 35% in Cherry Hill.[6] Camden has twenty-two combined sewer overflow outfalls (where raw sewage and storm water may be released to the surface during wet weather), while Cherry Hill has zero. Camden offers no electronic waste recycling and no yard waste collection; Cherry Hill provides both. In 2012, Camden's water supply ran so low that residents were required to boil water for consumption and were prohibited from watering their gardens.[7] Cherry Hill has a clean, plentiful water supply. Cherry Hill Public Library has more than 400,000 circulating materials, more than 300 adult programs and classes, and 67 public computers.[8] In 2011, Camden shuttered the doors of its main library and handed control of the remaining two small branches to the county.[9] Cherry Hill offers sixty-three recreational facilities (parks, art centers, tennis courts, and so on) for its residents and supports thirteen different swim clubs.[10] Camden has twenty-five parks and eight community centers.[11] Between 2007 and 2012, Camden's city budget declined by about $245 per resident, while Cherry Hill's increased by about $12 per capita. Clearly, living in Camden is unlike living in Cherry Hill. So, how did Cherry Hill and Camden get to be so different?

The story begins with a focus on Camden at the turn of the century. In 1900, Camden had a population of nearly 76,000 residents. The city boasted 55 miles of sewers and 79 miles of water mains, and about 38% of the city's streets were paved – figures that suggest that Camden's development was right in line with national averages. Also similar to

---

[4] www.epa.gov/superfund/search-superfund-sites-where-you-live

[5] www.state.nj.us/transportation/works/njchoices/pdf/camden.pdf

[6] Personal communication with New Jersey Department of Transportation. The NJDOT provided data from the NJDOT Pavement Management System by email. Available from the author by request.

[7] www.nj.com/news/index.ssf/2012/06/camden_residents_advised_to_bo.html

[8] www.chplnj.org/about/documents/2015%20Annual%20Report%20-%20FINAL.pdf

[9] www.nj.com/news/index.ssf/2011/02/main_branch_of_camden_public_l.html

[10] www.cherryhill-nj.com/Facilities   [11] www.ecode360.com/8508679

other cities were Camden's levels of race and class segregation, which were generally low. By the turn of the century, Camden was home to two well-established free black communities: Fettersville and Kaighnsville (Garwood 1999). Established in the 1830s and 1840s, these communities were comprised of small lots and affordable to people of modest incomes, many of whom were African American. One of Fettersville's neighborhood churches, the Macedonia African Methodist Episcopal Church, was a stop on the Underground Railroad. Although the majority of Camden's black residents lived in Fettersville and Kaighnsville, both neighborhoods were predominately populated with white, working-class residents.

According to the 1900 US Census, the wards representing Fettersville and Kaighnsville were about a quarter African American. For a city in which African Americans only comprised 8% of the total population, it is clear that blacks were not evenly spread across the city. But the extent and scale of black segregation would increase dramatically over time, climbing more than 50% in the first half of the twentieth century.

In 1930, Camden was a bustling central city. It had more than 118,000 residents and spent nearly $950 (in 2012 dollars) per capita on municipal expenditures – well above the national median. Cities with high levels of service provision, such as Camden, were more likely to have high property values, high tax rates, and high rates of homeownership compared with cities with smaller city budgets. And they were much more likely to be early adopters of land use regulations because they were more invested in protecting their high values and good services, ensuring that both were delivered to the residents with the most political power – white property owners. Camden first authorized zoning in 1928 and, like other early zoning adopters, moved quickly to ensure that land use policy was used strategically to "conserve the value of property" and protect the interests of white home-owning residents (Cunningham 1965). Thus, from early in the twentieth century, Camden's segregation was state-sponsored.

Figure 1.1 shows that by 1940, the black concentration exceeded 50% in the central part of the city, even though African Americans only made up 11% of city residents. After generating this segregated community, Camden's city government proceeded to underprovide services to and locate public nuisances in its black neighborhoods (Helzner 1968a, 1968b; Silvotti 1968).

As was the case for many large cities, the stress of the Great Depression left Camden with an enormous burden of vacant and uninhabitable properties, a disproportionate number located where black residents lived (Allen 1942). And so Camden became one of the earliest recipients of

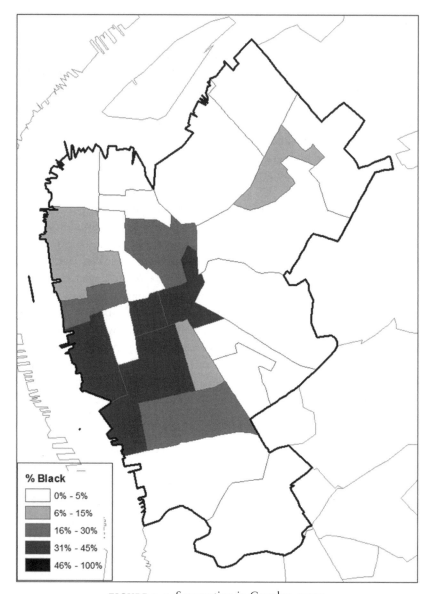

FIGURE 1.1 Segregation in Camden, 1940

federal slum clearance and public housing funds in the 1930s (Pommer 1978). In 1938, two public housing complexes were erected – one for whites and one for blacks. When the program was expanded in the 1940s, two more projects were built – also segregated. Unsurprisingly, the projects were placed in communities based on the demographics of their occupants, and the neighborhoods around each became increasingly segregated (Williams 1966a). Later, when Interstate 95 was run through the city, "an attempt [was] made to eliminate the Negro and Puerto Rican ghetto areas," destroying parks and homes, and increasing density in the remaining segregated black and Latino neighborhoods (New Jersey State Attorney General report, quoted in Rose and Mohl 2012, p. 108).

So it was that the creation of Camden's segregated neighborhoods echoed the creation of segregated neighborhoods throughout the United States. Camden city government used zoning laws, the placement of segregated schools and public housing, and slum clearance to create and enforce residential segregation between whites and African Americans, as well as between renters and homeowners.

Starting around the time of the World War II, the city faced desegregation pressures on several fronts. As of 1944, no black children attended white elementary schools in Camden, despite a state-level anti-segregation law that was passed in 1881 (Wright 1953; Jensen 1948). When the National Association for the Advancement of Colored People (NAACP) sued the district, officials responded that black parents had simply not requested attendance at their neighborhood schools. So, the NAACP took out ads in the *Camden Courier-Post* to convince parents to do just that. In 1947, hundreds of black children enrolled in previously all-white schools (Wright 1953).

School desegregation was just one of the first of many signs of racial transition in Camden. In 1951, the city witnessed its first biracial contest for city council when Dr. Ulysses S. Wiggins, president of the Camden NAACP branch, was nominated on the Republican ticket (Negro Runs for Camden Council Job 1951). He lost; but in 1961, Elijah Perry became the city's first African American city council member (Riordan 1996). In 1954, the New Jersey Supreme Court ordered public housing to be desegregated, and the first black families moved into white buildings in 1966 (Williams 1966a, 1966b). Although contested elections and moves toward the desegregation of public housing represented progress, deep racial disparities in municipal service provisions persisted, and people of color demanded equal treatment from the city government. In 1969 and 1971, the city erupted in violent race riots, touched off by police brutality against black and Latino residents.

The little hamlet of Cherry Hill boasts a much different history. Although Cherry Hill was incorporated as a municipality in 1844, like most would-be suburbs, it remained a small, undeveloped agricultural community in the first few decades of the twentieth century. In 1940, Cherry Hill had a population of just under 6,000 residents, 91% of whom were white and 9% black (NJSDC 2000; Barnes 1936). Not only small, it was economically weak, having defaulted on its bond obligations and been placed in receivership by the state government during the Depression (*Shay v. Delaware* 1939; Cammarota 2001). But after the war, while housing and schools in Camden were integrating, Cherry Hill's population and economy exploded, as was true of suburbs throughout the nation.

Drawn to places like Cherry Hill by the attractiveness of low-cost, federally insured mortgages, the development of new homes and new employment opportunities in outlying communities, and easy commuting along newly built federal highways, the nation's suburbs grew rapidly and homebuyers moved to the periphery (Nall 2018). But, due to a combination of restrictive covenants and racist lending policies in both the public and private mortgage markets, the opportunity to build a life in the suburbs was only made available to whites (Rothstein 2017; Jackson 1987). During the thirty-year period following World War II, Cherry Hill witnessed a tenfold population increase – nearly all white. Meanwhile Camden lost 13% of its residents.

Figure 1.2 shows the share of the total population living in rural areas, central cities, and suburbs over the twentieth century. The graph reveals that the pace of suburbanization increased sharply during the postwar period so that by 1970, a plurality of the population lived in suburbs.[12] The homeownership rate increased at the same time. This latter fact explains the driving force behind exclusionary zoning adopted by suburban communities. White homeowners in places such as Cherry Hill, intent on raising property values and maintaining exclusivity in their public schools, aggressively shaped the future of their residential communities.

As Camden rushed to utilize more than $30 million in federal redevelopment funds to revitalize its flagging urban center, Cherry Hill was busy implementing zoning restrictions that effectively prohibited the development of low- or even moderate-income housing (Cammarota 2001). These economic zoning practices effectively kept out people of modest incomes, but also maintained the racial homogeneity of the city and

---

[12] Rural here refers to populations outside any metropolitan area. A suburb is an area inside of a metropolitan area, but outside the central city. City refers to the central cities of metro areas. www.census.gov/prod/2002pubs/censr-4.pdf, p. 33 www.census.gov/hhes/www/housing/census/historic/owner.html

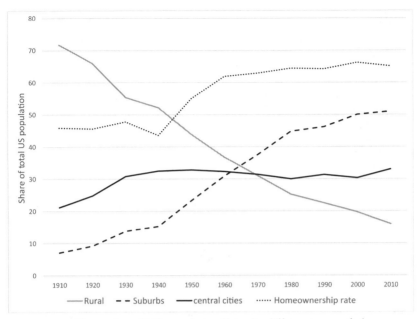

FIGURE 1.2 Share of total US population living in different types of places
Sources: Demographic Trends in the 20th Century, Census 2000 Special Report; Population Reference Bureau: Reports on America, 2011; Housing Characteristics, 2010 Census Brief

schools. In 1975, black residents of Mount Laurel, New Jersey (a suburb close to Cherry Hill both geographically and demographically), along with several local chapters of the NAACP, won a class-action lawsuit challenging Cherry Hill's type of exclusionary zoning. As a direct result of this decision, Cherry Hill was required by the state to zone for thousands of low-income housing units. The city declined to do so. As of 2015, Cherry Hill continued to face litigation for its failure to zone for affordable housing.[13] As is true in many places throughout the United States, exclusionary economic zoning cannot be disentangled from race. One activist argued, "[M]any residents carried racist feelings about affordable housing, fearing it would attract poor blacks and Hispanics" (Leonnig 1989, p. 42).

Figures 1.3 and 1.4 reveal how segregation between Camden and Cherry Hill changed between 1970 and 2010. In 1960, Camden was 76% white. This had declined to 60% by 1970. The maps show that although Camden's population of color had grown, in 1970 the city still had several exclusively white neighborhoods. These white neighborhoods

[13] www.cherryhill-nj.com/DocumentCenter/View/2562, p. 8.

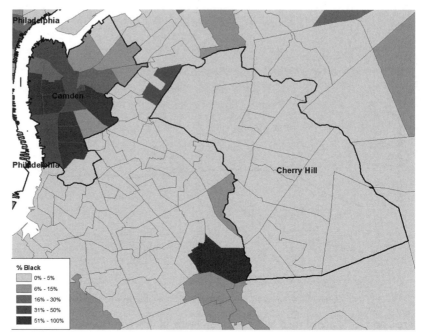

FIGURE 1.3 Segregation in Camden and Cherry Hill, 1970

had *completely* disappeared by 2010. In 2010, a greater share of segregation occurs between Cherry Hill and Camden than within them.

For the most part, the people who left Camden during the postwar period and those who moved to Cherry Hill were largely white, middle- and upper-class. As of 2014, about 39% of Camden's population owned their homes, 5% were white, and the annual median household income was $26,000. In Cherry Hill, 80% owned their homes, 75% were white, and the median household income was $89,500.[14] In 2012, per capita taxes in Cherry Hill were double Camden's. Camden simply cannot afford to offer the services that Cherry Hill provides.

But it is important to note that no one could have predicted the vast inequality between Camden and Cherry Hill in 1900 or even 1940. Indeed, Camden would have seemed poised to remain a regional economic engine and home to the area's premier amenities. Writing in 1886, George Prowell proclaimed:

[14] www.census.gov/quickfacts/table/PST045215/3410000,3400712280,00

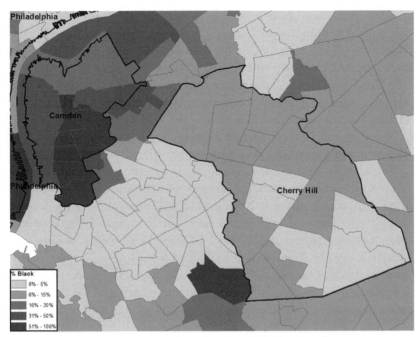

FIGURE 1.4 Segregation in Camden and Cherry Hill, 2010

[C]ould the first settlers upon the site of [Camden] now look upon the industry and energy that have asserted their power in the rumble of ponderous machinery, the whistle of the high-spirited iron horse, the hum and whir of revolving wheels, the stately magnificence of some of the public institutions, the comfortable homes and beautiful streets and the improvements in the modes of life and living, they would feel gratified that their children's grandchildren ... are so bountifully favored in this land of freedom and independence. (Prowell 1886, p. 407)

Today's segregation along race and class lines between Camden and Cherry Hill and the resulting inequality in access to public goods was produced by local public policy. It is a pattern that was replicated many times over throughout the United States, driven by white property owners' obsessive concern with property values and public goods, and carried out by local governments.

In the early decades of the twentieth century, homeownership rates in the United States were already much higher than in many other advanced democracies. In 1914, 10% of households in the United Kingdom owned their homes (House of Commons Research Paper 1999). In the United

States the figure was about 45%.[15] Even as of the late 1940s homeownership rates for France and Germany were only about 31% and 27% respectively (Kohl 2014). For most families, the home was (and is) the single largest component of household wealth (Knoll et al. 2014). Not only homeowners, but all property owners, land-oriented businesses (like real estate agencies), and local governments reliant on property taxes had a strong incentive to protect and enhance the value of property. In a world of limited resources, they also had a strong incentive to politically control the distribution of public goods increasingly offered to city dwellers.

Yet, homeownership and political power were not equally available to all urban residents. In 1900, the homeownership rate among whites was more than double the rate among blacks (Collins and Margo 1999). Chinese and Japanese immigrants were barred from owning property completely in many states, and the vast majority of blacks, Asians, and Latinos across the country were prohibited from voting (Keyssar 2000). Thus, as America became an urban nation, it was white property owners who dictated the policies of local governments. They used their power to pursue segregation. White economic advancement was built on the backs of people of color. By invoking the power of land use regulation and zoning, city governments promoted the generation of property wealth through segregation and unequal allocation of resources, institutionalizing prevailing race and class hierarchies.

In cities across the country, "Chinatowns" (McWilliams 1964, p. 105), Sonoratowns (Torres-Rouff 2013, p. 139), and "Darktowns" (Silver and Moeser 1995, p. 130) were walled off by public policy and violence condoned by police. Local governments then systematically underinvested in these neighborhoods, denying them adequate sewers, paved roads, garbage collection, or public health initiatives. By the onset of the Second World War, city governments had become proficient segregators. When millions of dollars were spent renewing and rebuilding urban communities, segregation was reinforced and deepened.

The consequences are irrefutable. Segregation causes higher poverty rates for blacks and lower poverty rates for whites, lower high school and college graduation rates among blacks, higher imprisonment rates, and higher rates of single-motherhood among blacks (Ananat 2011; Burch 2014; Cutler and Glaeser 1997). Segregated neighborhoods differ significantly with respect to "crime, poverty, child health, protest, leadership

---

[15] www.census.gov/hhes/www/housing/census/historic/owner.html

networks, civic engagement, home foreclosures, teen births, altruism, mobility flows, collective efficacy, [and] immigration" (Sampson 2012, p. 6). These differences, Patrick Sharkey (2013, p. 21) explains, are "*not* attributable primarily to factors that lie within the home or within the individual," but rather to the place itself, passed down from generation to generation.

Neighborhood disadvantage is also causally related to black/white income inequality, lack of employment stability among blacks, and larger gaps in cognitive skills between blacks and whites (Sharkey 2013). Cohen and Dawson (1993) show that neighborhood poverty undermines blacks' attachment to and involvement in the political system. Chapters in this book reveal that segregation leads to racial political polarization and underfunding of public goods. Cumulatively, these results suggest that both growing up and living in disadvantaged places, while they may not wholly determine one's fate, leave little margin for error. "Mobility out of the poorest neighborhoods," Sharkey (2013, p. 35) says, "may be even less common than mobility out of individual poverty." Perversely, home ownership for people of color in this environment can serve to limit mobility rather than enhance it. These inequalities, Sampson tells us, are "durable and multiplex but not inevitable or natural" (p. 99). They were created by local policy.

In the first half of the twentieth century, advantaged and disadvantaged neighborhoods resided within the political boundaries of large central cities. In the second half of the century, when the suburbs captured most of the population growth, the physical and – more importantly – political distance between advantage and disadvantage widened. Today, the most advantaged places are located outside of central cities altogether so that disadvantaged residents have no direct role to play in decisions about building affordable housing, expanding public transportation, or diversifying schools. In these advantaged places, development is restricted and residents are politically conservative; they vote at higher rates for Republican presidential candidates, support low taxes, want limited spending, and see inequality as the result of individual failings.

CONTRIBUTIONS TO EXISTING LITERATURE

Segregation by Design places race and racism at the center of local politics, local policy, and local outcomes; something several foundational works in the literature have neglected to do. In *Who Governs*, perhaps the founding tome of the field, Robert Dahl (1961) argues that city politics is inherently pluralistic. Influence in local politics is diffusely distributed and policy outcomes are the result of varied, competing interests. "Whenever a sizable minority ... is determined to bring some question to the fore," Dahl claims, "the chances are high that the rest of the political stratum will soon begin to pay attention" (p. 92). In a detailed case study of New Haven, Connecticut, Dahl finds power in the vote. Equality at the ballot box trumps social and economic inequalities. Dahl asserts that, "in comparison with whites, Negroes find no greater obstacles to achiev[ing] their goals through political action" (p. 294). *Segregation by Design* reveals this to be a profoundly untrue statement. Inequality is embedded in the very fabric of cities, and is produced and reproduced through the political process. While Dahl was conducting his research, the New Haven city government was busy shoehorning black residents into segregated neighborhoods. In 2011, New Haven was the still most segregated city in Connecticut.

In his famous treatise on the limits of city politics, Paul Peterson (1981) also fails to analyze the ways in which inequality is baked into the structure of cities. Peterson argues that housekeeping services (e.g., police and fire departments) are "widely and proportionately allocated" (p. 45). In the neighborhoods where property is more valuable, he says, "[O]ne also characteristically finds lower crime rates, less fire damage, and cleaner streets." Peterson claims that these disparities are not the result of differential efforts by city departments, but rather the function of "environmental variables influenced more by local government zoning laws" (p. 45). Yet, nowhere in the book does Peterson probe his own claim that local land use policy provides the backdrop for the entire endeavor. As a result, the inequalities that land use policy creates are never interrogated.

Instead, Peterson claims that all city residents share a unitary interest in "maximiz[ing] their economic position" (p. 29). More specifically, Peterson means that "what is good for business is good for the community" (p. 143). Peterson argues that policies that enhance the local economy (e.g., developmental policies) are consensual. He says they are "opposed only by those few whose partial interests stand in conflict with the community interests" (p. 41). Peterson draws on the case of urban renewal to make this point. Indeed, it was the case that more vigorous pursuit of urban renewal increased property values, income, and population in the aggregate (Collins and Shester 2013). But at what cost? Thousands of homes were destroyed. Hundreds of neighborhoods razed. These burdens were not borne universally; they disproportionately impacted people of color and the poor (Anderson 1964; Wilson 1966).

This was not accidental or unintentional. Decisions about which neighborhoods to clear and which to protect were made by the same set of interests, with the same goals, that had designed residential segregation in decades past. In Peterson's telling of the events, when disrupted communities protested slum clearance, it was *they* who acted selfishly, while the proponents of urban renewal acted on behalf of the community.

Peterson is certainly not the first theorist to conflate white property owners' interests with the interests of the whole. In *City Politics*, Banfield and Wilson (1963) argued that conflict in cities was rooted in a fundamental struggle between the "public regarding" Anglo-Saxon Protestants and "private-regarding lower-class" immigrants (p. 329). By their account, when city governments pursued policies for white, native-born residents, it was for the good of the whole; meanwhile, immigrants demand favors and benefits to be enjoyed by *their* group alone. Similarly, the municipal Progressive Reform movement was premised on the notion that reform goals were equivalent to the city's interest (Bridges 1997). Every institutional change (e.g., nonpartisan elections, city manager form of government, at-large elections, etc.) promoted by reformers had an eye toward amplifying the power of those who supported reform and silencing the opposition (Trounstine 2008). Reformers justified their approach by claiming that city politics was a nonideological realm, one in which the needs of the community could be straightforwardly addressed by apolitical public servants. But giving policy-making authority to unelected bureaucrats did not eliminate underlying divisions in municipal politics; it simply served to magnify the voice of some residents over others. Reform rhetoric was a strategic move that legitimized white property owners' claims while delegitimizing the claims of renters, the working class, and people of color. It is no accident that "residents of Anglo, middle-class neighborhoods were both [reform's] beneficiaries and its strongest supporters" (Bridges 1997, p. 11). If city policy were actually universalistic, as Peterson and the reformers claimed, white property owners would have had no need to fortify suburban land use regimes in face of rising black power or school desegregation orders from the federal government as chapters in this book reveal.

Another giant in the field of urban politics, Clarence Stone, brings race front and center in his analysis of coalition politics (Stone 1989). In Atlanta, the site of Stone's research on urban regimes, black votes are needed by politicians to win elections, and so black elites can bargain for desirable policy outcomes. But the real power remains in the hands of those with the private resources to govern: typically the business community. Yet, Stone fails to consider how it is that white property owners maintain their dominance in local affairs over people of color despite formal political equality.

Other scholars have written profoundly and extensively about the role of race and class in city politics (e.g., Gosnell 1935; Pinderhughes 1987; Browning, Marshall, and Tabb 1986; Jones-Correa 1998; Kaufmann 2004; Owens 2007; Shaw 2009; Hajnal 2010). What I add to these conversations is a link between the political economy drivers of local politics, as distilled by Dahl and Peterson, and the fundamental role of race and (to a lesser extent) class in animating the choices of residents and political actors. In so doing, I follow in the footsteps of scholars like Adolph Reed (1999) and Lester Spence (2015), who argue that local development imperatives and protections of economic markets have driven social inequalities. My work builds on these approaches by offering broad, empirical evidence that the protection of property values and public goods motivates local land use policy and generates inequality and polarization.

This book also contributes to a number of dense literatures including work focused on segregation, public goods, attitudes toward outgroups, and political inequality. Although a great deal has been written on each of these topics, very little research engages more than one of these areas. For instance, Tiebout's (1956) seminal article arguing that consumer-voters pick communities that best satisfy their preferences for public goods ignores the role of race, segregation, and inequality in these choices and is silent about the ways in which public goods packages are developed. In order for anyone to vote with her feet, she must first find a place to live. We cannot understand sorting (either to obtain a tax/public goods bundle or to avoid other racial groups) until we understand the ways in which housing choices, property values, and neighborhood character are structured by local governments.

Other scholars (Alesina et al. 1999; Hopkins 2009) show that diversity drives down collective investment in public goods, but do not consider the ways that geo-spatial arrangements might affect this relationship. I show that diversity alone does not undermine public goods provision. It is only when cities are also segregated along racial lines that we see this effect. I argue that segregated places are politically polarized places. The gulf between whites and minorities in segregated places makes it less likely that they will find common ground in support of a bundle of taxation and expenditures, driving down collective investment. It is segregation, not diversity, that contributes to inequality.

Still others have shown that whites' desire for homogeneity has played a role in generating racial segregation between cities and school districts (Reber 2005; Baum-Snow and Lutz 2011; Boustan 2010). However, these works largely ignore the political mechanisms by which such preferences are realized (e.g., the development of zoning policies).[16]

Outside of (excellent) case studies focused on one to two metropolitan areas at a time (Danielson 1976; Hirsch 1983; Sugrue 1996; Kruse 2005; Lassiter 2006; Kraus 2000), to date most of the research analyzing the relationship between segregation and public policy has focused on national level programs like the Federal Housing Administration underwriting guidelines (Jackson 1987) or the Home Owners' Loan Corporation neighborhood investment ratings (Hillier 2005).[17] With such far-reaching effects, the focus on these programs has been well placed, but has also tended to obscure considerable subnational variation; while the case studies offer invaluable historical detail, they are unable to provide evidence of broader patterns of the effect of local policies on segregation. In short, although scholars have documented changing patterns in racial and class segregation, they have not demonstrated the ongoing role of city politics and local service policy in creating segregation and growing inequality. I show how patterns of local service delivery, zoning laws, and other local policies not only mirrored patterns of segregation, but also drove them – not only in the pre–civil rights era, but also in recent decades.

Although many scholars have suggested that segregation across neighborhoods or between cities and suburbs fosters inequalities in access to public goods (Massey and Denton 1998; Burns 1994; Dreier et al. 2004),

---

[16] Baum-Snow and Lutz (2011) analyze the effect of school district desegregation orders on suburbanization. So while they focus on the effect of a public policy, they are not concerned with policies that intentionally aided segregationist preferences.

[17] Important exceptions include Rothwell (2011), who analyzes the effect of low-density zoning on metropolitan area racial segregation, and Dreier et al. (2004), who suggest (although they do not provide direct evidence) that zoning and redevelopment affect economic segregation across cities. Cutler, Glaeser, and Vigdor (1999) find support for a theory of "collective action racism" prior to 1970. They show that housing prices for equivalent quality housing were higher for blacks than for whites, implying that whites acted collectively to limit black housing choices. However, the authors do not provide any analysis of the types of collective action in which whites engaged beyond speculating that restrictive covenants and racial zoning may have played a role. Importantly, Cutler et al. do not distinguish between collective actions that occur in the public versus private realm.

very little research offers systematic evidence of this intuition.[18] Other scholars have carefully documented the pernicious effects of segregation on individual-level outcomes (Ananat 2011; Cutler and Glaeser 1997), but have not offered a direct link between these outcomes and allocation of public goods. I offer quantitative and qualitative data showing that segregation across both neighborhoods and cities allows governments to disinvest in poor and minority communities, which produces unequal access to public goods. These results help to explain why social mobility is tied to place, as scholars like Sharkey (2013) and Sampson (2012) find, and demonstrate the consequences of public policy and segregation for larger patterns of inequality.

Much of the work investigating the determinants of segregation (both within cities across neighborhoods and within regions across cities and suburbs) argues or assumes that the important driver of racial segregation is prejudice – that is, attitudinal predispositions toward racial and ethnic minority groups. This is an insufficient account. It is insufficient, first, because racial segregation has not declined as precipitously as one would predict given dramatic changes in overt expressions of racism. I argue that the institutionalization of prejudice through local public policy makes segregation more rigid. Second, pure prejudice does little to explain the rise of class segregation. I argue that if we understand segregation as a mechanism to protect public goods and property values, increasing class segregation is predictable. Finally, a pure prejudice account leaves unexplored the basis for these predispositions. Beliefs about the acceptability of different demographic groups as neighbors (e.g., what we might take to be pure prejudice) were influenced by the distributions of public goods and battles over those distributions decades ago.

Contrary to some scholars' conclusion that the core problems of segregation have been alleviated, I show that segregation persists, that segregation has grown across cities, and that local government policies continue to play a central role in perpetuating segregation.[19] White, wealthy Americans are still trying to segregate themselves. And

---

[18] An important exception is Troesken (2001, 2004) who provides direct evidence of the relationship between segregation and public goods inequalities. He shows that cities with racial segregation were more likely to generate unequal access to municipal water and sewer connections in the late nineteenth and early twentieth centuries.

[19] Several recent headlines make this claim, such as "Glimpses of a Ghetto-Free Future" (Frey 2014), "Segregation Continues to Decline in Most U.S. Cities, Census Figures Show" (Lee 2015), and "The End of the Segregated Century: Racial Separation in America's Neighborhoods, 1890–2010" (Vigdor and Glaeser 2012).

local governments still tend to invest more toward whites and the wealthy. I build this argument through eight substantive chapters, and a conclusion that considers omissions from the book and forecasts the path forward.

CHAPTER SUMMARIES

Chapter 2 provides a framework for the study, describing the theory in detail and clarifying empirical predictions. Then, in Chapter 3, I provide an overview of changes in segregation and public goods spending over the course of the twentieth century. I begin with a broad synopsis of spending between 1900 and 1940. It reveals that cities increased expenditures on street paving and lighting, refuse collection, sewers, libraries, health, education, public safety, and recreation, and increased revenue from taxes. During this early period, cities became modern service providers.

Chapter 3 continues on to explore early patterns of race and class segregation. I show that racial segregation increased dramatically between 1890 and 1940, while class segregation increased marginally. Then, I turn to analyzing fiscal and segregation patterns between 1970 and 2011. I suggest that during this period, white property owners turned to suburbanization as their primary mechanism for protecting property values. After 1970, the dominant trend in both race and class segregation was increasing differentiation between cities. During this period, suburban governments grew more intensely than central cities, so by 2011 central cities accounted for a smaller share of total metro area spending than they had in 1970.

In Chapter 4, I provide the first piece of evidence directly linking the patterns described in Chapter 3 by showing that public goods considerations drove efforts to segregate in the early decades of the twentieth century. Acting in response to white homeowners and land-oriented businesses, local government policy explicitly sought to exclude people of color from white neighborhoods and poor individuals from wealthy neighborhoods. In empirical analyses, I analyze the factors that encouraged the adoption of zoning laws and the role that zoning laws played in the development of race and class segregation. I find that exclusion was most adamantly pursued in cities that had become significant providers of public goods, where property taxes were high (and, so, raising property values was attractive), and where political support for progressive reform was strongest. I supplement this analysis with qualitative evidence that reveals the many factors local governments utilized to promote segregation, including strategies like the siting of segregated public goods – such as parks and schools. Finally, this chapter reveals that zoning laws had their intended effect: early zoning adopters segregated more rapidly over the next several decades compared with cities without similar ordinances, and zoned cities witnessed greater inequalities in housing values.

Chapter 5 documents the unequal provision of public goods that early segregation allowed. Using historical case study evidence, I show that poor and minority neighborhoods consistently received worse public amenities like road paving and health clinics. I draw on detailed ward-level data from Baltimore, Boston, Chicago, and Philadelphia to show that sewer extensions were less likely to be built in neighborhoods with higher proportions of African American and renting residents. As a result, inequality in water and sewer access was greater in more segregated places. I show that these inequalities persisted. Using data on all tracts in all cities in the United States, I provide evidence that whites and minorities (and renters and homeowners) had differential rates of access to public sewers in more segregated places in 1970, 1980, and 1990. I argue that these inequalities in service provision affected the ways in which white and wealthy residents would come to view poor and minority neighbors. Daria Roithmayr (2014) notes, "[W]e see the strongest evidence of continuing discrimination in housing markets" (p. 18). This is because the roots of this bias are whites' conscious and subconscious beliefs about the effect of nonwhite and renter neighbors on property values and the quality of public goods – beliefs that were fostered by government choices at the turn of the twentieth century.

Chapter 6 provides evidence of municipal policy effects on segregation in the middle of the twentieth century. By 1940, segregation was entrenched, as were the unequal allocations of public goods. But patterns would change in the postwar period. In some places, segregation along racial lines increased, while in others it had already begun to decline (as it would everywhere after 1970). Class segregation began a slow ascent and then leveled off. As was the case in the first time period analyzed, local public policy played a role in these patterns. I provide evidence that cities that more vigorously implemented urban renewal programs grew more segregated along both race and class lines.

The second half of Chapter 6 shows that during the 1960s and 1970s, white homeowners in many cities lost the political power needed to police the borders of their neighborhoods and control the distribution of public goods. I argue that such changes made suburban living a more attractive option than living in homogenous neighborhoods within cities. I draw on varied evidence to show that the integration of public spaces and residential areas encouraged whites and the wealthy to move to the suburbs during the postwar period, which allowed for more control over political decisions and the distribution of public goods.

Chapter 7 analyzes the negative consequences of segregation within cities. Quite ironically, given early claims that segregation was the best solution to racial discord, I show that segregation is associated with deep race and class divisions that dominate city politics today. Polarization makes cooperation difficult, and I show that segregated cities have smaller city budgets and spend less on individual categories of expenditure such as roads, policing, parks, and sewers. Underinvestment means that city services do not operate well. Focusing on one measurable area of public goods provision, I demonstrate that sewer overflows are more frequent in segregated cities.

Between 1970 and 2000, a major change in segregation patterns occurred. Neighborhoods became more racially integrated within cities, but whole cities became more racially homogenous, increasing segregation between them. Class segregation across cities also increased during this period. Chapter 8 offers an analysis of the role of local political control in generating these changes. Using demographic and finance data from all metropolitan areas in the United States between 1980 and 2000, I show that larger budgets, higher spending on policing, and minority mayoral victories are associated with more segregation across city lines. Where whites maintained control, they were less likely to move to the suburbs. Throughout the postwar period, cities and suburbs alike moved away from explicitly racial strategies toward class-based tactics, such as large lot zoning and limiting multi-family developments, to ensure segregation. I show that more restrictive zoning by suburban cities increased both race and class segregation. As a result, suburban communities made decisions that profoundly affected nonsuburban residents while preventing them from participating in the decision-making process. In this context, representative government, policy responsiveness, and political equality became hollow concepts.

In Chapter 9, I focus on the effects of segregation for national-level politics. I draw on restricted-access General Social Survey data geo-coded to 1970 Census tracts to show that residents who live in neighborhoods that were whiter than the metropolitan area in 1970 are much more conservative than those who live in more integrated places. I argue that this conservatism is rooted in the battles over integration that occurred in earlier decades.

In the conclusion of the book, I pull the many pieces of evidence presented previously into a single framework and discuss what the future holds. I reiterate my main claim: local governments pursue segregation at the behest of politically powerful interests. This allows politicians to target public goods toward some residents and away from others, resulting in differential access to public goods. Segregation generates unequal political outcomes, which, in turn, reinforces segregation. By linking neighborhood-level segregation to suburbanization, I suggest that preferences for separation have changed in form but not intent over time. Going forward, we can expect additional change. Rather than seeking residential segregation, some individuals will choose to leave the public realm altogether – relying more heavily on private provision of services like education, policing, and park space. We have some evidence that privatization has increased even as many cities have become more integrated. The drive to protect property values, ensure good schools for children, and provide safe streets for families has remained a powerful force. Finally, I consider potential policy solutions to these seemingly intractable problems. I suggest that the one path forward is to utilize lessons from school finance reform (e.g., Lafortune, Rothstein, and Schanzenbach 2016) to guide state governments' approach to producing more equal access to a range of local public goods. Another remedy is to concentrate on YIMBYism (Yes-in-My-Backyard) – that is, urging integration of housing types and increased development. Undoubtedly, such strategies will require intense political will, mobilization, and voice in currently underrepresented communities. This is a tall order, but a more equal future depends upon it.

2

A Theory of Segregation by Design

Local government policy is a fundamental driver of race and class segregation in America. Through the regulation of land use, local governments manage the use of space. They decide what gets built, what doesn't get built, and where the building happens. Local governments also determine the types of public services provided, along with their amounts and distribution. As a result, local policies affect the value of property. Battles to control space and its attendant value fundamentally underlay and animate local political processes. The consistent outcome of these struggles has been residential segregation, which in turn has generated unequal access to public goods and services. Segregation is not organic or inevitable. Rather, it is a matter of design pursued through the political process, offering spoils to those with political power.

Theoretically, city policy can affect property values in a variety of ways. Most directly, cities can limit new housing or commercial property development, thereby driving up land values in places where demand is high. Alternatively, they can allow for more development. Without a concomitant increase in investment in public goods and services, new property development means that local goods and services are likely to become more congested, and some public services may reach a limit for expansion. Underperforming city services further limit property value growth.

But city policy can affect land values in other, less direct ways too. Cities can invest (or fail to invest) in infrastructure development, like road paving or sewer installations, which can increase (or depress) property values. They can locate public nuisances (garbage dumps, freeways) or amenities (parks) in particular areas, which can lead to decreases or increases in property value. Policies that decrease (or increase) the quality of city services can also depreciate (or increase) values. For example, reducing the number of firefighters per capita makes fire response times slower, which makes conflagrations more likely. Cities have the authority to determine the staffing levels of fire forces as well as the placement of fire houses. Thus, they can affect the quality of services overall and the quality of services in particular locations, which can affect property values.

Policies that affect the demographic makeup of the community can also affect property values. For instance, cities can zone for more or less multifamily housing, which can affect the average income of residents and the number of families with children. Demographic characteristics like these can affect both the value of property and the cost of service provision. A city that restricts the development of housing at the low end of income distribution (say, by implementing a one-acre minimum lot size requirement) will have a population with higher socioeconomic status and higher property values. Additionally, because parental socioeconomic status is the most important driver of school quality, a higher socioeconomic status will translate into better school quality, which will, in turn, be capitalized into property values.

Policies can also affect the cost of local services by dictating the share of land devoted to uses that generate more service costs than tax revenue, and vice versa (e.g., public housing versus an office park). Finally, policies can affect the look and feel of a community (e.g., by setting height limits or banning billboards), which in turn can affect demand for property.

Obviously, these are all theoretical propositions; offering empirical evidence of causal links is considerably more challenging. However, generally speaking, property owners *believe* that local policy affects the value of their investments (Helper 1969) and the quality of life attached to their parcels, making them keenly attentive to the local political environment (Fischel 2001). Property owners and land-oriented business typically win local political battles because they have the most immediately at stake and the most political power.[1] Thus, the story of local politics and

---

[1] Of course, at times property owners conflict with each other. Consider a developer who purchases a large parcel of land in a neighborhood of single-family homes. The developer determines that the most profitable use of the land would be luxury condominiums, but the homeowners argue that a tall building will increase traffic, block their views, change the character of their neighborhood, etc. Recent research (Einstein et al. 2017) shows that the winner in this battle will be determined by the ease of filing lawsuits to slow the developer and the ultimate profit to be gained. When lawsuits are easy and profit margins are slim, homeowners will win; otherwise, developers will fight to build.

segregation is one that intimately links development, property values, and homeownership.

Land speculation has long been a core feature of urban development (Warner 1987; Einhorn 1991; Nicolaides 2002). In the early period of city building (following the end of the Civil War and leading up to the Great Depression), investors everywhere purchased property and pressed local governments to improve services, thereby ensuring the value of their investment (Logan and Molotch 1987). Later purchasers of the land sought to defend those values by improving services and quality of life. Since the earliest period, whites have been able to buy property at higher rates than blacks, and have had much more choice in the location of that property (Collins and Margo 2011). As Nathan Connolly (2014) explains:

Contests over land allowed certain aspects of Jim Crow's culture to become America's culture – politically, economically, and at the level of the built environment. Acceptable governance in Jim Crow America required minimizing the discomforts of white Americans, protecting the political power of property owners, and ensuring that poor people continued to generate other people's wealth. Good governing also meant making "colored people" the principal bearers of difficult or unpopular policy choices. (p. 4)

This property apartheid generated policy inequities that (re)produce racial discrimination (Conley 1999). Because of the incentives to protect property values, even today many whites are willing to perpetuate inequalities that far exceed their individual expressed racism. The remainder of this chapter describes these processes in greater detail.

THE NEED FOR LOCAL GOVERNMENT

In the late 1800s, as industrialization brought thousands of migrants and immigrants into cities, people of color and the poor were spatially isolated, not by ward or census tract, but by building and street (Logan et al. 2015). What this meant is that although blacks, Latinos, and Chinese residents were unlikely to live next door to white homeowners, they *were* quite likely to live down the street. By 1940, segregation shifted to the neighborhood level (Cutler et al. 1999; Massey and Denton 1998), so that large swaths of many cities had become predominately black or white, and both poor and wealthy residents became increasingly clustered in most places. By the onset of the Second World War, every large city in America had parts of town where people of color lived and parts of town where the poor lived. Sometimes, but not always, these neighborhoods overlapped. Race and class segregation both increased by more than 50% between 1900 and 1940. These concentrating trends continued at a slower pace throughout the postwar period until 1970, when both race and class neighborhood segregation peaked. Neighborhood segregation by race has declined since 1970, but segregation by class has increased.[2] During the postwar period, segregation between cities increased and has remained stable since that time (Massey and Hajnal 1995; Farrell 2008; Fischer et al. 2004).

The continued high level of racial residential segregation in America has been tremendously well documented (see Charles 2003, Ross 2008, and Boustan 2012 for extensive literature reviews). A smaller, though still well developed, body of literature is focused on class segregation (see Bischoff and Reardon 2013 and Jargowsky 1996 for reviews). The links between race and class segregation also form a considerable literature. The debate over the fundamental causes of segregation is extensive and nuanced. Scholars have focused on two primary explanations: individual preferences for same race and same income neighbors (particularly among whites and the wealthy), and market explanations (e.g., differences in the socioeconomic status of different racial groups and the ability to pay for quality housing and transportation among the poor).

The roots of these explanations are classic models of individual choice. Thomas Schelling (1971) argued that extreme racial segregation could result from individual decisions about where to live, given even mild preferences for having neighbors of the same race. A small number of racially intolerant white residents can cause a neighborhood to rapidly transition because as each intolerant white resident is replaced with a black neighbor, whites with lower and lower levels of intolerance choose to leave, creating neighborhood-to-neighborhood segregation. Scholars have found support for Schelling's theory. Research on racial segregation largely concludes that white preferences for same-race neighbors are the driving force (Cutler et al. 1999; Bayer et al. 2007; Charles 2006).[3] Denton and Massey (1991), Krysan et al. (2008), and Emerson, Chai, and Yancey (2001) find that whites avoid black neighbors *because* they

---

[2] The precise pattern of class segregation depends on the measures used to indicate class. Income segregation has increased significantly since the 1970s (though it remains lower than racial segregation), while homeowner/renter segregation has increased by a smaller amount.

[3] A small amount of scholarship shows that black preferences for same-race neighbors contribute to segregation (Bayer, Ferreira, and McMillan 2007; Fossett 2006).

are black. Boustan (2010) shows that in northern metropolitan areas between 1940 and 1970, every black arrival from the South was associated with 2.7 white departures to the suburbs. Yet, these scholars do not interrogate the source of these prejudicial attitudes. Reed and Chowkwanyun (2012) argue that placing the cause of segregation in the lap of prejudice "inadequately anchors the story of race and residence within the urban political economy – the drive to accumulate, the relationship among value, race, and space, or the role of property as speculative capital" (p. 157).

Another individual-choice scholar, Charles Tiebout (1956), proposed that residents with similar preferences for taxation and public goods provision should sort themselves into cities with like-minded neighbors. To the extent that heterogeneous preferences for tax and spending levels (or ability to pay) overlap with heterogeneous demographics, they will also generate segregation.[4] Support for Tiebout's thesis has been more limited. Alesina et al. (2004) show that people are willing to give up economies of scale to avoid being in a jurisdiction with significant income heterogeneity, and Bayer, Ferreira, and McMillian (2007) reveal that households self-segregate on the basis of education. However, many scholars have shown that racial segregation patterns cannot be convincingly accounted for by black-and-white differences in socioeconomic characteristics, such as education, income, wealth, or family structure (Bayer et al. 2004; Erbe 1975; Massey and Denton 1987, 1998; Iceland and Wilkes 2006; Krysan et al. 2008; Emerson, Chai, and Yancey 2001).[5] Logan (2011) summarizes by explaining that racial segregation for blacks is due to the inability to "translate higher income ... into residential mobility" (p. 15). Ellen (2000), Yinger (1997), Taub et al. (1984), and Harris (1999) argue that whites use black neighbors as a proxy for neighborhood quality. That is, whites do not avoid black neighbors per se, but rather choose what they perceive to be better neighborhood amenities or neighbor characteristics – like wealth.

With only a handful of exceptions (e.g., Rothwell 2011; Pendall 2000), quantitative research on the causes of segregation ignores the context in which it occurs. Local policies and political battles are crucial for

---

[4] Banzhaf and Walsh (2010) combine Schelling's and Tiebout's insights into a single model that establishes that preferences over public goods and demographics are mutually reinforcing in the generation of segregation.

[5] Socioeconomic differences do explain a fair amount of the segregation of Latinos and Asians.

understanding *how* and *when* white and wealthy preferences for homogeneity and socioeconomic inequalities are translated into residential patterns.[6] The backdrop to individual choice is the type and value of housing that is available – factors that are determined by local governments.

More deeply, theories reliant on individual choices are subject to instability in the absence of collective enforcement mechanisms (Oates 1969, 1981; Fischel 1992). That is, for an individual to ensure that her neighborhood remains white and has access to a nice public park, she needs the cooperation of her neighbors. But neighbors may have individual incentives that undermine the achievement of other residents' collective goals. For instance, it can be extremely lucrative for a white homeowner to sell her home to a black buyer. This is especially likely to be the case when black housing options are restricted and the black population is expanding. As Hamilton (1975) explained, individual incentives can also undermine the Tiebout model. It makes fiscal sense for a resident who prefers high-quality public goods but is unable to afford high tax rates to locate the smallest, least expensive home in a wealthy city. The taxes this resident pays do not support the share of the public goods she utilizes, but she benefits from them nonetheless. In Hamilton's tale, this behavior could lead to wealthy residents chasing each other around to try and maintain exclusivity. In the first instance, the collective goal of maintaining the white neighborhood is undermined by sellers seeking the highest sale price. In the second instance, residents who do not pay the full cost of their share of benefits undermine the provision of public goods.

Governments can promote collective action by generating enforcement of collective goals – and here it is *local* governments that play the starring role, because they alone regulate land use. By invoking their powers of control over land and making choices about service provision, local governments can affect the aggregate demographic makeup of communities and the spatial distribution of residents and services, thereby generating and enforcing segregation. From the perspective of

---

[6] To be sure, scholars have extensively documented the private mechanisms that affect segregation (e.g., racial steering and mortgage discrimination). But even private mechanisms may be shaped by local policies and political concerns. For example, white beliefs about available amenities in poor and minority neighborhoods are, in part, the product of underprovision of public goods early in the twentieth century. Cutler et al. (1999) find that these beliefs contribute to whites' willingness to pay higher housing prices in whiter neighborhoods.

property owners, the goal of these policy choices is stability (or enhancement) of property values and the protection of public goods quality. Politicians also stand to benefit from segregation (aside from appeasing constituents). When segregation increases property values, city tax rolls also increase. Segregation can also be useful to politicians who benefit from a concentration of voters in a particular geographic location (Trounstine and Valdini 2008).

As North (1990) explains, the relative bargaining strength of different interests in any community will dictate the structure of its rules. Such rules, he tells us, are frequently devised to promote private rather than public interests (p. 48). The history of local land-use planning and service provision fits squarely within this theoretical perspective. Property owners (and those who derive their livelihood from property, like realtors and lenders),[7] seek both property value appreciation and protection from losses in value. Because tax levels, service quality, and neighborhood demographics are capitalized in property values (see Hilber 2011 for a review), property owners invest considerable energy into dictating local policy (Fischel 2001; Stone 1989; Logan and Molotch 1987).

In the United States, property owners have always been disproportionately white, and property value has been tied to the race of occupants and neighbors (DuBois 1935; Hayward 2013; Freund 2007; Merritt 2016; Rothstein 2017). Furthermore, as Bradford, Malt, and Oates (1969) argued, the quality of many public goods, like education and public safety, is predominantly affected by the characteristics of the residents themselves rather than inputs from the government. Unsurprisingly, schools are the single most important public good that homeowners seek to protect and enhance. Even owners without children in public school are attentive to school quality because they perceive it to affect their home's value. Although cities do not (for the most part) handle the funding of schools, they play a key role in maintenance of this public good by using land-use regulation to shape who has access to which local public schools. School districts control school finances, but they cannot zone. Together, these circumstances have given property owners a powerful incentive to regulate who lives where since the earliest years of

---

[7] Developers, while also obviously earning their livelihood through property, only sometimes have goals that are aligned with homeowners. In some settings, developers prefer fewer regulations on development (allowing them to build smaller homes on smaller lots or denser multifamily structures, for example), but in others they are strong proponents of restrictive mechanisms like large lot zoning and racial covenants.

urbanization. White property owners have long been concerned with excluding certain types of people from their communities.

Americans, particularly white Americans, have long had a racist, classist understanding of property values and who deserves public benefits (Connolly 2014). It was widely accepted that poor and minority neighbors negatively impacted property values and were less deserving of benefits than property owners and whites. Local policies like zoning and redevelopment serve these ends, and the result has been segregation along race and class lines.

The very first laws generating segregation were adopted in the first decade of the twentieth century to protect both property values and public goods exclusivity. Over the course of the next 100 years, when property owners were stymied in their attempts to create exclusivity by demographic shifts, loss of political control, or meddlesome governments seeking to promote equality, they adopted new strategies to achieve segregation, often increasing the spatial scale of exclusivity to achieve their goals.

First, industrialization and then the explosion of wartime economies pulled great numbers of working-class people of color to cities. Many black and Latino neighborhoods swelled, threatening to spill into white, homeowner communities. City governments were called upon to use policy levers like land-use regulations and zoning, as well as the placement of thoroughfares and public housing to consolidate, and then circumscribe, minority communities. By World War II, the United States was already a very segregated nation. All large cities had clearly defined neighborhoods inhabited by people of color, and others inhabited by whites (Massey and Denton 1988).[8] As a result of the economic collapse during the Great Depression and the subsequent material scarcity during the war, the nation faced a severe housing shortage during the 1940s. When increasing numbers of blacks moved from rural areas into cities, and from the South to the North and West, the boundaries of existing black neighborhoods were pushed to their limits. In the Southwest, the Latino population also swelled with wartime employment.[9] These pressures resulted in explosive social and policy conflicts along racial lines.

---

[8] On the whole, the United States, both rural and urban, was still overwhelmingly white in 1940. About 10% of the population was black, about 1.7% of the population could be considered Hispanic/Latino, and about 0.1% Asian. www.latinamericanstudies.org/immigration/Hispanics-US-1850-1990.pdf; www.census.gov/population/www/documentation/twps0076/twps0076.pdf

[9] Hundreds of thousands of Mexican descendants were deported during the Great Depression, so the overall Latino share of the population changed little (Ethington et al. 2001).

Because city governments had the power to zone, to permit development, and to locate nuisances – and thus to determine the value of property – these fights were central to city politics. As Self (2003) argues, "the effects of property [valuation] are far-reaching ... They structure all kinds of interactions – from where one can buy a home to where politics is organized, from how police interact with neighborhoods to where children go to school. The struggle for the postwar city was over no less than the power to control and organize space" (p. 18).

In response to postwar demographic changes, white homeowners sought to protect their neighborhoods (which they considered to be the reward for their hard work and frugality) from disruption and disorder. In the minds of many, pursuit of these goals required racial exclusivity. Sugrue (1996) reports that in Detroit, as elsewhere, "a majority of whites looked to increased segregation as the solution to [the] 'colored problem'" (p. 215). Whites, particularly those who owned their homes, believed that they had a right to certain neighborhoods and the public benefits (e.g., schools, safety) associated with those spaces. They believed minority demands for integration and court-ordered desegregation plans undermined this entitlement (Kruse 2005, p. 126). Whites justified exclusion with fiscal arguments, claiming that "since Negroes are so poor and pay virtually no taxes, they are actually not entitled to get more public services than the whites care to give them" (Myrdal 1944, p. 336). When blacks *did* receive benefits, it was believed that whites unfairly bore the financial burden of their support. To illustrate this point, Kruse (2005) quotes a segregationist poem that made the rounds in Atlanta in 1957:

> Po' white folks must labor, 'tween sun and sun,
> To pay welfare taxes whilst we has de fun,
> We doan pay no taxes, we doan make no goods,
> We just raise little niggers, way back in the woods. (p. 127)

Above all else, whites feared that integration would jeopardize their single largest investment: the value of their home (Helper 1969), as well as the quality of their neighborhood (Kruse 2005). Blacks were seen as undesirable neighbors, in part, because the features of their neighborhoods became associated with individual members of the racial group. Whites came to similar conclusions about Chinese residents in San Francisco and Latinos throughout the Southwest (Shah 2001; Abrams 1955; Torres-Rouff 2013; McWilliams 1964). This was the case despite the fact that people of color and renters experienced poor neighborhood quality due to a lack of low-cost housing options, paltry municipal services, neglectful landlords, and the overcrowding that resulted from segregation, not from their own doing.

Thus, the tight coupling between property values, public goods, and racial exclusivity was inexorably tied to the racism embedded in the real estate market (Hayward 2013) and the poor public goods that cities had provided to neighborhoods of color in decades past (Myrdal 1944; Torres-Rouff 2013). Kruse (2005) explains that "by the time white home-owners confronted racial transition at their neighborhood's borders, the American real-estate industry had completely embraced the idea that such racial transition would, without doubt, lead to a devastating decline in property values" (p. 60). Public policies like redlining and expulsive zoning,[10] and private actions like racial steering and white flight, would make this relationship true over the long run.[11]

Although many whites agreed on the desirability of residential segregation,[12] they were stymied by various hurdles. The Supreme Court had ruled racial zoning (the designation of certain neighborhoods as being inhabitable only by whites) unconstitutional in 1917, so a perfectly direct policy approach to residential segregation was not an option.[13] Instead, the preservation of white communities required collective action to prevent individual homeowners from selling or leasing to minority residents. As minority populations expanded and white homeownership rates sky-rocketed, hundreds of white homeowners' organizations arose in the 1940s, 1950s, and 1960s (Sugrue 1996; Kruse 2005).[14] These organizations were often created by real estate developers to protect the value of their investment. The protection of property values was a charge taken

---

[10] Expulsive zoning is the practice of siting industrial, semi-industrial, or other nuisances in neighborhoods of color to both preserve white neighborhoods and induce black movement into particular parts of the city.

[11] In the short run, blacks paid much higher prices than whites for comparable housing (Cutler and Glaeser 1997). This fact was what made it so lucrative for individual whites to abandon neighborhood protection and move to the suburbs. In Atlanta, Kruse (2005) analyzes the property values in a neighborhood that transitioned from white to black between 1950 and 1960, and finds that the property values rose 27% over this decade.

[12] In 1964, only 27% of white Americans supported general integration (Schuman et al. 1985).

[13] Many white neighborhoods also utilized violence to defend their borders (Meyer 2000; Hirsch 1983). Although tolerated (even encouraged) by the police and political establishment of some cities, murders and arson were technically illegal as well.

[14] In some cases, the link between segregationists and homeowners' groups was direct. For example, the head of Atlanta's West End Cooperative Corporation got his start in community organizing as the head of Klavern No. 297's Housing Kommittee (Kruse 2005, p. 54).

seriously by property owners. These (typically all white) "civic associations, productive associations, improvement associations, and homeowners' associations" (Sugrue 1996, p. 211) fought public housing developments in their neighborhoods, sought representation on planning boards, and battled open housing laws (Self 2003).[15] Importantly, they relied on racial restrictions in housing deeds (and racism in the real estate market) to maintain neighborhood exclusivity. But the Supreme Court ruled restrictive covenants unenforceable in 1948 (*Shelley v. Kraemer* 1948), and an open housing movement swept the nation. Then, in the 1950s, other tools of segregation came under fire as the court struck down separate-but-equal accommodations in a series of cases.[16]

By this time, nearly all cities utilized zoning in some fashion and many invoked the power of eminent domain to shape development through, for example, the permitting of multifamily housing, the razing of slums, and the placement of highways, public housing, and industry. In the past, white homeowners had successfully used these tools to configure residential demography (Nightingale 2006), but they became even more important in the face of new court decisions and the rising civil rights movement.[17] At the same time, racial violence continued to erupt. However, local elites were committed to maintaining peace in their cities (Ogorzalek 2018). So, to convince city governments to defend their turf, white neighborhoods needed to change their approach.

In city after city, white, middle-class homeowners turned away from claims based on racial exclusivity and began to press their demands in terms of rights – a tactic Sugrue (1996) terms "defensive localism" (p. 210).

---

[15] They also served as social organizations welcoming new neighbors and organizing block parties (Sugrue 1996).

[16] E.g., *Muir v. Louisville Park* 1953; *Brown v. Board of Education* 1954, 1955; *Holmes v. Atlanta* 1955; *Dawson v. Baltimore* 1955; *Rice v. Sioux City Memorial Park Cemetery* 1955; *Gayle v. Browder* 1956; *Burton v. Wilmington* 1961; *Johnson v. Virginia* 1963; *Simkins v. Cone Memorial Hospital* 1962; *Watson v. City of Memphis* 1963.

[17] Throughout this period, neighborhood organizations also sought to maintain the color line using private mechanisms as well. For instance, some organizations raised funds to repurchase homes sold to black families to sell them back to whites. They also pressured real estate agencies and lenders to refuse to sell to black buyers. Additionally, they set fire to homes on the market for black buyers and newly purchased homes by black owners (Kruse 2005; Sugrue 1996). The problem with such tactics is that they were always susceptible to a sort of prisoner's dilemma. It was incredibly lucrative for a single white homeowner to sell her home to a black family, and this idea made individual white owners skittish about neighborhood transition. Neighborhood organizations constantly urged owners to think of the common good rather than their bottom line, but frequently failed.

White residents fought for the "'right' to select their neighbors . . . the 'right' to do as they pleased with their private property . . . and the 'right' to remain free from what they saw as dangerous encroachments by the federal government" (Kruse 2005, p. 9). Local governments responded with neighborhood protection by pursuing "racial stability through spatial apartheid" (Lassiter 2006, p. 52). In the South, these arguments were the moderate path – a response to violent white supremacy on the right and integrationists on the left (Lassiter 2006; Kruse 2005). The fact that rights-based language gained ground in all regions of the United States meant that it offered a powerful basis for the rise of a national movement.

The discourse had several facets. Subscribers claimed support for racial integration in theory (so as to distinguish themselves from the ugliness of Jim Crow), but angrily opposed government intervention in racial uplift or equalization. In fact, desegregation was typically viewed in zero-sum terms: gains for blacks equated to losses for whites. Government attempts to produce equal outcomes were understood to be an elevation of minority rights above those of the majority, a form of "reverse discrimination" (Lassiter 2006, p. 123). Policy solutions to redress inequality were cast as the work of an insidious, "'liberal elite' made up of judges, intellectuals, and government bureaucrats" (Hall 2005, p. 5).

Further drawing on racialized beliefs about the distribution of tax burdens, neighborhood defenders argued that they should not have to pay for public benefits or welfare for those who did not contribute to the public pool. So when people of color demanded, and then the court ordered, desegregation of public spaces and residential communities, white residents demanded that city governments defend their neighborhoods through their land-use powers. In addition, whites urged the city government to eviscerate public budgets, eliminate bus lines, and close pools and public parks (Kruse 2005). Whites voted down bonds for civic improvements, abandoned public schools, and railed against an activist government. In the end, many of these residents would leave the city altogether – packing up their belongings and their newly appropriated ideology to move to the suburbs where they had much greater political control over neighborhood boundaries (Nall 2015; Boustan 2010).

Suburban growth largely happened for market reasons that were unrelated (or, at least, only tangentially related) to racial conflict in cities (Jackson 1985). As Chapter 1 revealed, by 1970, a plurality of the population lived in suburbs, and more than 60% of Americans owned their homes. As the pace of suburbanization and homeownership picked up, arguments surrounding neighborhood defense lost explicit racial designations of who contributed and who did not, and who had a right to high property values and good services and who did not. As Self (2003) explains, the move away from making overt racial claims was "intended to inoculate segregation and white privilege against charges of racism" (p. 268). This new language offered a "color-blind" approach to the maintenance of neighborhood boundaries. This rhetoric perpetuated the myth that residential segregation was a matter of economics and individual choice. White homeowners came to see segregation as the consequence of "meritocratic individualism" not fostered by public policy or law (Lassiter 2006, p. 1). Those who lived in segregated minority neighborhoods could thus be blamed for their condition, making them undeserving of social assistance.

Maintaining exclusively white neighborhoods in the central city was possible with the help of cooperative city governments. But it was much easier in the suburbs, where a combination of federal public policies and private actions made homeownership only available to white residents (Jackson 1987; Hayward 2013). As independent municipalities, suburbs have the power to regulate land use for all parcels within their borders. Local governments employ land-use regulations to manage the character of their communities. Consequently, regulatory environments vary significantly from place to place. Cities are capable of enacting minimum lot sizes so that all development must be located on a certain acreage of land, requiring developers to preserve open space in their development, determining the number of multifamily units that will be allowed within city limits, requiring developers to pay a share of infrastructure improvements associated with new development, offering short/long review periods for zoning changes and building permits, and involving few or many local actors in the approval and planning process. Gyourko et al. (2008) find that there is a strong, positive correlation between different regulations. If a city regulates in one area, it is significantly more likely to regulate in other areas as well. Einstein et al. (2017) provide evidence that the accumulation of regulations reduces the supply of multifamily housing by allowing residents opposed to development to delay the process and file lawsuits. Gyourko et al. (2008) also find that community wealth is positively related to regulatory environments. Places with high median home values, more college-educated residents, and higher incomes are most likely to police land use.

By 1970, neighborhoods (both within central cities and outside of them) that had maintained their whiteness despite the massive demographic shifts over the preceding thirty years had developed a distinctive, conservative approach to politics throughout the nation. Homeowners in these places expected low taxes; they rationalized racial segregation and inequality as the product of meritocracy; and they conflated white exclusivity with high property values (Self 2003; Lassiter 2006; Freund 2007). They couched their demands in terms of protection of individual property rights. In so doing, they drew on a long tradition of American conservative principles emphasizing economic individualism, limited government, and equality of opportunity, but not outcomes (Feldman 1988; McClosky and Zaller 1984; Kinder 1998). Matt Lassiter eloquently explains that "the ascendance of color-blind ideology [was dependent] upon the establishment of structural mechanisms of exclusion that did not require individual racism by [its] beneficiaries to sustain white class privilege and maintain barriers of disadvantage" (2006, p. 4).

Nearly forty years later, these neighborhoods continued to foster distinctive politics. Whether or not new arrivals to defended neighborhoods had been involved in the earlier battles, they came to "accept the politics born out of white flight all the same. They embraced a new middle class rhetoric of rights and responsibilities" (Kruse 2005, p. 245). The Republican Party came to embrace the neighborhood defenders. Starting in the 1960s and throughout the 1970s, Republicans positioned themselves as the party that would help whites to resist social change and impose order in their environments (Hetherington and Weiler 2009; Carmines and Stimson 1989). These ideals held sway in defended neighborhoods, and residents dutifully sorted themselves into the Republican Party.

The arguments appropriated in support of neighborhood defense in the 1950s and 1960s are still visible in politics today. In the 2012 presidential election, Republican nominee Mitt Romney proclaimed:

There are 47 percent of the people who will vote for [the Democratic incumbent] no matter what ... who are dependent upon government, who believe that they are victims, who believe the government has a responsibility to care for them, who believe that they are entitled to health care, to food, to housing, to you-name-it. That that's an entitlement. And the government should give it to them ... These are people who pay no income tax ... My job is not to worry about those people. I'll never convince them they should take personal responsibility and care for their lives. (Corn 2013)[18]

---

[18] More boldly, 2016 Republican nominee Donald Trump's first wife explained, "I have nothing against Mexicans, but they [come] here – like this 19-year-old, she's pregnant, she crossed over a wall ... She gives the birth in American hospital, which is for free. The child becomes American automatically. She brings the whole family, she doesn't pay the taxes, she doesn't have a job, she gets the housing, she gets the food stamps. Who's paying? You and me." http://nypost.com/2016/04/03/ivana-trump-opens-up-about-how-she-advises-donald-his-hands/

Like the homeowners' organizations of the mid-century, Romney's statement invoked a class-centered (not race-centered) view of deservingness. Forty-seven percent of the American public, Romney implies, pay no taxes and rely on government benefits for subsistence. Romney's claim that these noncontributors do not take personal responsibility for their lives recalls the meritocratic arguments white homeowners made in the past about their success and their neighborhoods. It is unsurprising, then, that defended neighborhoods have offered disproportionate support to Republican candidates and conservative policies in recent years.

To say that neighborhoods condition political views and actions is not novel. A great deal of research investigates contextual effects on public opinion and political behavior. A significant portion of this literature focuses on the community's racial composition.[19] Some scholars find that diversity produces tolerance (e.g., racial contact theory).[20] Others find the reverse: that large minority populations are related to racial intolerance and lack of support for spending on race-focused or race-coded policies (e.g., racial threat theory).[21] Scholars also find a negative relationship between diversity and support for taxation, spending, and public goods provision more generally.[22] I draw on both of these frames to argue that rights-oriented conservatism was fueled in an environment of racial threat (integration in the 1940s, 1950s, and 1960s), but became entrenched in an environment of racial isolation (whiteness of the neighborhood in the 1970s). Today, white conservatism at the individual level is associated with homogeneity, not diversity, in neighborhoods.

Just as it is not novel to propose that neighborhoods affect political behavior, it is also not novel to propose that modern conservatism and Republican voting are rooted in racial conflict (see Hutchings and Valentino 2004 for a thorough review). Indeed, it is uncontroversial to state that the civil rights movement was a catalyst for partisan realignment, as Southern Democrats abandoned the party championing the rights of

---

[19] Other work on context analyzes social networks (Eulau and Rothenberg 1986; Zuckerman 2005), partisan contexts (Ceaser and DiSalvo 2006), and economic contexts (Gay 2006; Books and Prysby 1991; Oliver 1999; Oliver and Mendelberg 2000).

[20] Allport 1954; Oliver 2010; Sigelman et al. 1996.

[21] Key 1949; Gay 2006; Huckfeldt 1986; Orey 2001; Taylor 1998; Bobo and Hutchings 1996; Blalock 1967; Alesina and Glaeser 2004; Tolbert and Hero 1996; Plotnick and Winters 1985; Enos 2016; Baybeck 2006.

[22] Alesina et al. 1999; Glaser 2002; Alesina and Spolaore 1997; Easterly and Levine 1997; Poterba 1997; Habyarimana et al. 2007, 2009; Putnam 2007; Cutler et al. 1993; Goldin and Katz 1999; Hopkins 2009; Vigdor 2004.

black Americans.[23] Since the 1970s, scholars have argued that white public opinion shifted mid-century, from a willingness to endorse Jim Crow–style race prejudice and biological racism to subtler, more symbolic expressions of racial resentment.[24] Additionally, we know that racial attitudes are strongly predictive of views toward redistributive spending,[25] and government policies that have become racially coded.[26] If an individual holds negative stereotypes of racial minorities, he or she is likely to oppose expenditures on functions like welfare, and even all government spending in some settings (Sears and Citrin 1982).

What I add to these debates is not a link between racial politics, public opinion, ideology, and party identification, but a new perspective on location. The marriage between rights-based conservatism and white perspectives on race was amplified in the crucible of city politics. And white neighborhood defense appears to have played a causal role in the development of a host of conservative political opinions that appear to be "nonracial" (Hutchings and Valentino 2004, p. 6).

THE GEOGRAPHY OF INEQUALITY

Political geography is comprised of nested units: neighborhoods within wards, wards within cities, cities within states, and states within the nation. When residential segregation maps onto political geography, political divisions become fused with race and class divisions. This has two important consequences. First, segregation generates inequalities between race and class groups because in a world of scarce resources, the politically powerful deny public goods to those who are politically weak. Segregation within cities and suburbanization across city lines has meant that the benefits experienced by racial and ethnic minorities and low-income individuals are inferior to the benefits experienced by whites and the wealthy. Second, segregation generates political polarization between race and class groups and, ultimately, inhibits cooperation.

Segregation generates inequalities because it allows political elites to target public goods toward supporters. At one time, public goods were

---

[23] Frymer 1999; Carmines and Stimson 1989; Miller and Shanks 1996.

[24] See, for example, Kinder and Sears 1981; McConahay 1982; Sears 1988; Kinder and Sanders 1996; Sears et al. 1997; Bobo 1983; Bobo, Kluegel, and Smith 1997.

[25] Bobo and Kluegel 1997; Sears 1988; Kinder and Sanders 1996; Rabinowitz et al. 2009; Federico 2005; Gilens 1999; Quadagno 1994; Luttmer 2001.

[26] Winter 2006; Valentino, Hutchings, and White 2002; Mendelberg 2001; Hurwitz and Peffley 1997.

segregated directly, through laws that dictated that whites and blacks (and often Native Americans, Latinos, and Asians) could not attend the same schools; sit in the same areas on public transportation; utilize the same parks, pools, libraries, or hospitals; be incarcerated in the same facility; or be buried in the same public cemeteries.[27] The legal segregation of public goods allowed city, county, and state governments to provide unequal funding for black and white schools, black and white hospitals, and black and white playgrounds – thereby generating unequal quality. This meant that blacks received inferior public goods compared with whites, regardless of where they lived. But by the middle of the twentieth century, public goods inequalities had largely come to be determined by residential segregation instead of racial segregation.[28]

This transformation occurred in part as a response to the 1896 decision *Plessy v. Ferguson*, which dictated equality in separate facilities. It was cumbersome and expensive to develop separate and equal services in diverse communities. The duplication of schools, parks, hospitals, and cemeteries for black (as well as Asian, Latino, and Native American) and white residents meant higher expenses (Wheildon 1947). Such costs arose not only from the establishment of facilities that would not have been needed if the facilities were integrated, but also from the loss of efficiency that the replication of equipment and personnel entailed.[29] Obviously, these costs were minimized when nonwhite facilities were severely under-funded (Myrdal 1944, p. 342), but in the wake of *Plessy v. Ferguson* and successive lawsuits urging cities toward equal (albeit separate) facilities, residential segregation became an attractive alternative. After the many mid-century court decisions striking down any separate facilities (e.g.,

---

[27] Jim Crow laws demanded or permitted segregation in settings far beyond the reach of public goods, including everything from seating in theaters and circuses, to marriage and sex, to the playing of checkers or dominos in private homes (Woodward 1955). Furthermore, laws mandating segregation were but one way in which the rights of racial and ethnic minorities were violated during this period. For instance, various laws barred minority individuals from testifying on juries against white defendants, denied them citizenship status, prohibited their access to certain professions, excluded them from owning land, and, of course, prevented them from voting.

[28] The choice between segregating public goods directly and segregating public goods via residential segregation was not confined to the South. Leon Litwack (1961) writes of the antebellum North: "legal and extralegal discrimination restricted Northern Negroes in virtually every phase of existence" (p. 64). More details on Jim Crow segregation in the North are provided in Chapter 4.

[29] One study of St. Louis's segregated school system found that 75% of the city's transportation costs in 1951–2 were spent transporting Negro schoolchildren who lived in outlying areas to colored schools in the center of the city (Russell 1954).

Brown v. Board of Education), residential segregation became the only remaining option (Wheildon 1947; Kruse 2005). In addition to being constitutional, residential segregation was also an efficient mechanism for producing inequalities across multiple public goods at once.

A similar transformation occurred in the postwar period, as neighborhood-level segregation was traded for city-level segregation. In 1948, when the Supreme Court ruled restrictive covenants unenforceable in *Shelley v. Kraemer*, white neighborhoods lost one of their most effective means of defense against integration. The 1968 Fair Housing Act further limited white collective action. As technological changes enhanced suburban service delivery and commute possibilities, and as the federal government subsidized homeownership outside of the central city, segregation across city lines rose. Moving outside of city boundaries allowed suburbanites to provide high levels of public goods for their residents without having to pay for services for nonresidents. For the privileged, suburbanization was an even more efficient mechanism of segregation than choosing separate neighborhoods within the city. As Hayward (2009) has argued, suburbs offered the opportunity to "engage in exclusionary zoning practices ... to opt out of supporting public housing ... and even opt out of supporting public transportation within the boundaries of their municipalities," all while allowing suburbanites to "pool their tax monies ... to provide schooling and other public services" (p. 149). In addition to offering efficiency, suburbanization also freed residents from having to fight for control of the city government. Indeed, suburban flight was encouraged by a loss of political power in the central city.

In many ways, these inequalities in access to public goods are precisely the goal of segregation's promoters. But a second consequence of increasing correspondence between political geography and demographic division is an increase in political polarization. Within cities, segregation generates stark divides between racial groups, leading segregated cities to underprovide public goods. But, even beyond city borders, segregation is consequential. The process of building and defending white homeowner neighborhoods created new ideological commitments to a meritocratic discourse that depicted inequalities as being the result of the free market, and choices made by black and poor residents, rather than the result of actions taken by government or white homeowners. The new ideology that was bred in defended white homeowner neighborhoods took root, growing into a modern conservatism that prioritized protection of property, self-reliance, and individual achievement (Self 2003; Lassiter 2006; Kruse 2005). Over the years, this conservatism has persisted, inculcating new neighbors with the same perspective.

EMPIRICAL EXPECTATIONS

The preceding argument generates several broad predictions, which I test in various ways throughout the coming chapters. First, I predict that some communities will be more likely to generate segregation than others: these are places that have high property values and valuable public goods to protect. Such places will be most likely to implement local policies like zoning, urban renewal, and restrictive land-use regulations. When communities seeking segregation are thwarted in their ability to generate exclusivity, they'll seek to change the spatial scale of segregation – moving to exclusive neighborhoods and exclusive cities in order to protect property values and restricted access to public goods. Second, I predict that these local land use policies work to generate segregation along race and class lines. Third, I predict that residential segregation generates inequalities in access to public goods. Finally, I propose that residential segregation will lead to political polarization in both local and national politics. No chapter or time period contains tests of all of these predictions, but together they tell a compelling story. For more than 100 years, property owners (and those who derive their livelihood from property) have urged local governments to enact policies that institutionalize segregation along race and class lines to protect their property values and control the distribution of public goods; I show that they have been incredibly successful.

I find that segregation along both race and class lines has been promoted by white homeowners and land-oriented businesses since the beginning of the twentieth century. Where these interests dominated city government, segregation grew more rapidly. I also find that as segregation increased, service investment in white homeowner neighborhoods increased. As whites lost control over the distribution of benefits, they moved to the suburbs and continued to expand service delivery. Today, a greater share of public dollars is spent by suburbs than by central cities. Finally, I reveal that in more segregated places political polarization is greater, and poor and minority residents have access to lower-quality public goods.

IMPORTANT CAVEATS

Schools

This is a book about segregation, but I do not provide an analysis of racial or economic differences between schools, or the effects of school segregation on individual outcomes. This will seem a glaring omission to many readers, especially because many pieces of my argument overlap with accounts offered by education scholars. The literature exploring inequality of educational opportunities is extremely dense and well developed (see Reardon and Owens 2014 for an overview). As Stephen Macedo (2003) writes, "Local control, when combined with local funding, and district-based assignment of pupils to schools, has created a geography marked by stark inequalities centered on class and race: a new form of separate and unequal" (p. 743). The arguments that I advance here complement and underscore much of this research. One might view this book as an extension of these arguments to the provision of *all non-school local public goods.*

My focus here is on the various policies that local governments use to generate segregation, and the consequences of segregation for local and national politics. The vast majority of the governments that I study do not play a direct role in the governance of schools or the provision of public education. That is, most cities in the United States do not spend money on educational services, and most public school students (about 85%) attend schools that are governed by school districts, not municipalities. One could approach school district politics as I have done for municipalities – analyzing decisions about the drawing of catchment zones, policies on busing, and the allocation of resources across schools in the same district. But this would require vastly different data than what I have gathered.

However, school enrollment and quality play a major role in individual decisions about where to live. Because school districts cannot control who lives within their borders these considerations are an important driver of the generation of exclusive land-use regulations in cities. So, while I do not analyze the politics of school districts, my argument takes school dynamics into account when analyzing the impetus for segregation.

The Intersection of Race and Class

A large body of scholarship probes the intricate relationships between race and class, racism, and classism. *Segregation by Design* does not analyze, in any satisfying way, the intersection of race and class. Rather, racial segregation and class segregation are measured as independent outcomes and causal factors. I find, generally, that I am better able to explain the causes and consequences of racial segregation. In part, this is because the data for measuring racial segregation are available for a longer time series and at a finer grain of detail than the data for measuring class segregation.

But the record is also clear that exclusion of other races has been a more powerful driver of these processes than exclusion of the poor. Indeed, I find that policies that produce class segregation are often motivated by a desire to generate racial segregation. Rothstein (2017) eloquently explains, "[A]n important and primary motivation of zoning rules that kept apartment buildings out of single-family neighborhoods was a social class elitism that was not itself racially biased. But there was enough open racial intent behind exclusionary zoning that it is integral to the story of *de jure* segregation" (p. 48).

As many scholars have shown (e.g., DuBois 1935; Roediger 1991; Bonilla-Silva 1997, 2009; Gotham 2000; Reed 1999; Freund 2007; Soss, Fording, and Schram 2011), we cannot understand the development of class *without* race. In short, poor and working-class whites in the United States have invested in alignment with higher-status whites, rather than aligning with poor and working-class people of color. At the same time, social class is "constructed and reinforced via political institutions" that are "deeply racialized" (Michener 2017, p. 93). The origins of this intersection are as old as the nation itself. W. E. B. Dubois (1935) explains:

> The political success of the doctrine of racial separation, which overthrew Reconstruction by uniting the planter and the poor white, was far exceeded by its astonishing economic results ... The theory of race drove such a wedge between the white and black workers that there probably are not today in the world two groups of workers with practically identical interests who hate and fear each other so deeply and persistently ... It must be remembered that the white group of laborers, while they received a low wage, were compensated in part by a sort of public and psychological wage. They were given public deference and titles of courtesy because they were white. They were admitted freely with all classes of white people to public functions, public parks, and the best schools. The police were drawn from their ranks, and the courts ... treated them with such leniency as to encourage lawlessness. Their vote selected public officials, and while this had small effect upon the economic situation, it had great effect upon their personal treatment and the deference shown them. (p. 700)

Whites of all classes have participated in the generation of racial segregation by creating opportunities for white exclusivity in housing. From a political standpoint, this meant that racial segregation always garnered a broader base of support than did class segregation.

According to Weaver (1946), although residential restriction against people of color originated in middle-income neighborhoods, over time "low income groups, in direct proportion to their insecurities, [became] more vehement in their opposition to the entrance of colored families" (p. 96). This is evidenced today by the fact that many neighborhoods contain a mixture of homeowners and renters, as well as varied income levels – even when they are dominated by a single racial group. As a result, statistically speaking, racial segregation has always been higher than class segregation. However, today, local policies that generate class-based exclusion are generally upheld by courts, while race-based exclusion is not. Additionally, income inequality has increased in recent decades. As a result, class segregation has risen and will likely continue to rise, even while racial segregation stagnates.

Data Hurdles

The data that I use to reveal the patterns described earlier in this chapter differ in important ways from previous research. Most scholars who analyze the determinants of segregation focus on either metropolitan-level segregation (e.g., Dreier et al. 2004; Jackson 1987) or neighborhood segregation (e.g., Massey and Denton 1998),[30] and on racial segregation (e.g., Charles 2003) or class segregation (e.g., Bischoff and Reardon 2013); however, these types of sorting are intricately linked. Class segregation and racial segregation are correlated, but they are not identical. Determining both the causes and consequences of segregation requires taking these linkages into account. The data that I have collected measure segregation both within and across cities, account for both race and class divisions, and cover city expenditures on a wide range of services during the entire twentieth century. This required the encoding of archival data, the generation of new spatial data using GIS, and the compilation of thousands of digitized observations from the United States Census. The comprehensiveness of the data allows for a more complete picture of the patterns of segregation over time and allows for an analysis of the factors that give rise to this variation.

Throughout my empirical analyses, I face profound causal challenges. In some cases, my analysis is plagued by reverse causality: did white residents move to the suburbs because the central city elected a black mayor, or did the relocation of white residents make it possible for a black

---

[30] Fischer (2008), Reardon, Yun and Eitle (2000), Fischer et al. (2004), and Rhode and Strumpf (2003) are notable exceptions. However, none of these authors analyzes the political causes or consequences of segregation.

mayor to get elected? In other cases, my analysis suffers from an inability to disentangle selection from treatment: does living in a homogenous white neighborhood make people more conservative, or do people with conservative views move to homogenous neighborhoods? In still other cases, my argument would be aided by evidence of strategy on the part of local elites, but none exists: zoning generates greater segregation, but could this have been an unintended consequence?

In each chapter, I describe the hurdles presented by the (lack of) data and my strategies for overcoming them. Generally, I seek to build a case for my argument using both detailed qualitative evidence and quantitative evidence from hundreds, or even thousands, of places. I often draw on the timing of events for evidence of causality, and, where I am able, I utilize instrumental variables to underscore my findings. In the end, I hope that readers will find the combination of approaches persuasive as a whole, even if they fall short individually.

3

Protecting Investments

Segregation and the Development
of the Metropolis

At the turn of the twentieth century, cities in the United States experienced intense demographic change. The first waves of African American migrants left the South for northern communities. Immigrants from Europe streamed across the borders until the onset of World War I and the subsequent implementation of restrictive immigration laws. By the middle of the century, the spatial distribution of residents was markedly different from what it had been fifty years prior, and patterns would change again over the ensuing fifty years. Until the onset of the Great Depression, expenditures by local governments also grew rapidly. It was during this period that the foundation for modern urban politics was laid across the nation. This growth in municipal spending continued unabated for the next 100 years. This chapter introduces the primary datasets used throughout the book. It also charts and links changes in both demographics and service provision in metropolitan America, showing that segregation in later periods is associated with high property values and investment in public goods at earlier points in time.

I begin with a presentation of data on the growth of expenditures during the first four decades of the twentieth century. I analyze demographic correlates of this growth, showing that homeownership, wealth, diversity, and density were all associated with expanding municipal governments. This, I argue, explains why property owners and land-oriented businesses pursued residential segregation: to protect property values and capture public goods. Next, I present the changing patterns of race and class segregation for these early decades. I show that cities with greater spending became more segregated. I then turn to an analysis of segregation between 1970 and 2010. During this period, the level at which segregation occurred shifted. Neighborhoods within cities became less segregated, while cities started to look increasingly different from one another. As the next several chapters will reveal, the changing level of segregation has had significant implications for the allocation of resources.

Throughout the book, my geographical focus is on metropolitan areas as they were defined by the US Census of Population and Housing in the year 2000. Metropolitan areas consist of one or more counties that are defined as having a core population nucleus (e.g., a big city), along with adjacent communities that are economically and socially integrated with that core. My data and analyses do not cover rural America. For my purposes, a city is an incorporated municipality within a metropolitan area. Cities have independent, general-purpose governments (typically a city council and often a mayor), and the authority to raise and spend money. How cities become incorporated, how they may raise money, and what they can spend their money on is dictated by state law. A neighborhood is a geographically defined subarea of a city, measured here as a census tract (or city council ward in the earliest years of census data).

Central cities and suburbs are both types of cities. I define the central city in a metropolitan area as the city with the largest population. Suburbs are all other incorporated municipalities in the same metropolitan area. Generally, suburbs did not really exist as powerful players in most metro areas until the middle of the twentieth century. Even as of 1940, only about 15% of the population lived in suburban communities, compared with 51% in 2010.

THE RISE OF URBAN AMERICA

In the year 1800, only 5% of the population of the United States lived in cities, and approximately 90% of the workforce was tied to agriculture. For the next half-century, this figure inched modestly upward, so that by 1850, 15% of population lived in urban areas.[1] After the end of the Civil War, the pace of urbanization (and industrialization) increased

---

[1] The Census determines whether a particular geographical area is urban based on population size and density. Rural territory is any area that is not urban. Starting in 1900, the census has defined urban areas as all places with at least 2,500 residents. From 1910 to 1950, urban areas only included incorporated places (e.g., cities) that met the size threshold. In more recent decades, the determination has been a combination of size and density; urban areas that contain at least 2,500 people have a density threshold of at least 1,000 people per square mile.

dramatically. By 1900, the nation was 40% urban, and in 1920 the census reported a majority urban nation for the first time. This trend continued; today the nation is approximately 85% urban.

As industrialization advanced, massive demographic shifts accompanied the economic changes. Cities began to fill with migrants and immigrants seeking work in new factories and service sectors. During this period, most workers commuted to their jobs by foot, limiting the distance residential neighborhoods could be located from places of employment. The result was massive overcrowding – as early as the first decades of the 1800s in some cities. Housing and sanitary capacities became overextended; epidemics and conflagrations were rampant. O'Connor (1984) offers a vivid description of early nineteenth-century Boston:

Within the heart of the old city ... things had deteriorated badly over the years ... Its meandering streets ... were hedged in by four and five-story houses that blocked out the sunlight. Pedestrians were in constant danger of being knocked down by stagecoaches, or bowled over by droves of pigs being hustled to market ... [An] abominable stench rose above it all. Not merely the oily fish smells from the docks, the briny tang of salt water, or the sickish odor of the mudflats at low tide. This was the repulsive reek of uncontrolled street refuse and untended garbage. To make matters worse, the city's sewerage system emptied out into the Town Dock. (p. 80)

Until about 1930, "state and local governments were *the* governments of most Americans" (McDonald and Ward 1984, p. 14). This was especially true with respect to fiscal affairs. To the extent that any government would have addressed the negative externalities associated with rapid urbanization, it would have been viewed as the responsibility of the city (and their parent states). Yet, throughout the first half of the nineteenth century, city governments were fairly limited in scope. The economies of early cities were largely commercial, and a dedication to privatism and the market generally dictated political affairs (Monkkonen 1988; Warner 1968; McDonald 1986). A large and meddlesome government was something to be suspicious of and few cities provided extensive public services. Government was run by (and services were often partially funded by) the wealthy – typically merchants. As Bridges (1984) explains of New York City in 1830s: "it is impossible to determine where government began and noblesse oblige (and the church) ended" (p. 72).

In most instances, services were handled by volunteers (e.g., fire brigades) or part-time, municipally funded workers (e.g., night watchmen); while city budgets provided contributions toward these services, city responsibilities were largely focused on regulating access to urban activities (like city markets). But by the end of the nineteenth century, city governments began to adopt a new orientation toward public goods provision, and city leadership began to shift away from wealthy merchants and toward career politicians. As a result, services came to be increasingly funded by city budgets, not charitable contributions. Monkkonen (1988) argues that city goals had been broadened by the 1890s to include:

Protecting private property (firefighting); suppressing crime; controlling behavior in public areas; building and maintaining streets and sewerage systems; aiding the poor, schooling children and sometimes adults; funding public libraries; providing recreation and entertainment; supporting a minimal level of health; temporarily assisting all persons incapable of caring for themselves ... ; enforcing public morality; expending direct financial aid to private capital ... ; and constructing not-for-profit public buildings in which to house these activities. (p. 218)

Historians do not agree on what caused the transition from the regulatory approach of antebellum governments to what Monkkonen calls the "service city" by the late 1800s. Yet, with one exception (Brown and Halaby 1984), scholars have not analyzed this development quantitatively in more than a handful of cities. Simply put, we lack systematic, quantitative knowledge of the factors that affected the development and expansion of city government at the turn of the twentieth century when significant variation was present. In 1902, for example, the median per capita expenditure of local governments in cities over the size of 25,000 (n = 160) was about $11, but the standard deviation was more than a third of that amount ($4). Some cities spent very little providing services for residents – others, a great deal. If city governments were once limited and weak, why did some choose to begin providing services for residents while others lagged behind?

The most common view is to understand the growth of city government as the necessary response to the negative externalities of increased population growth and density such as pollution, congestion, conflagration, crime, and disease (see, for example, Griffith 1927; Still 1948; Glaab and Brown 1967; Chudacoff 1975; Anderson 1977; Troesken 2004). Yet, the capacity to fund such developments through taxation and debt varied widely across cities (Dilworth 2005; Cutler and Miller 2006; Monkkonen 1988).[2]

---

[2] Research indicates that prior to the advent of the municipal bond market, cities were largely unable to invest in large infrastructural development.

Another essential driver of the development of municipal government was the desire to manage increasing racial and ethnic diversity in growing, compact cities. In an analysis of city relief spending in 1929, Cybelle Fox (2012) argues that native-born Americans and social welfare workers sought to Americanize foreign-born populations by drawing them into the reach of government. Tebeau (2003) shows that the development and expansion of fire services was an attempt to confiscate power from ethnic fire brigades, ensuring that firemen would be loyal to the city and not to their group. Similarly, Monkkonen (1988) argues that spending was a mechanism to manage conflict. As cities grew, he says, the bureaucracy of municipal government was invoked to manage conflict and Americanize newcomers as a substitute for small town interactions. In support of this thesis, Brown and Halaby (1984) find a substantial, positive relationship between city expenditures and the percentage of the city population that is foreign born. But contrary to these arguments, Goldin and Katz (2008) show that community *homogeneity* was key in the expansion of free public schooling. A large literature linking diversity and limited public goods provision underscores this finding (Alesina et al. 1999; Poterba 1997; Vigdor 2004; Hopkins 2009; Habyarimana et al. 2007, 2009; Miguel and Gugerty 2005; Miguel 2004; Algan et al. 2011; Fearon and Laitin 1996). But we still do not know if diversity drove or suppressed municipal spending in early American cities.

Additionally, during this period, middle-class residents' views began to evolve to expect more from governments in support of their pursuits (Yearly 1970; Myrdal 1944). McDonald (1986) suggests that property owners in particular wanted good public services, which led to high spending through debt. Others highlight the demands of newly minted professionals engaged in the private provision of services, who would benefit from public funding. Teachers pushed for public education; firefighters pushed for fire forces (Katznelson and Weir 1985; Tebeau 2003). Monkkonen (1988) highlights the growing role of planners, real estate developers, and professional bureaucrats who helped to build the Progressive reform movement (see also Hays 1964, Bridges 1997, and Tretter 2012 on Progressivism and growth). Throughout the 1800s and early 1900s, cities across the nation witnessed boom and bust cycles in land and property values (Glaeser 2013). Landowners, seeking stability and profits, sought to attract population and commercial enterprises to their community. Investing in public services and infrastructure (and intensive advertising of these investments) was a strategy many places used to grow. Property speculation and the public policies that promoted it would come to be a major driver of segregation.

CITY SPENDING DATA

To provide a description of historical expenditure patterns, I built a new dataset from a number of government sources that include data from the turn of the century to the Second World War. Starting from 1902, the US Census Bureau has been responsible for collecting data on the finances of local governments. With a few exceptions, the data have been collected annually for cities that meet a particular population threshold (which has varied over time). The Federal Reserve Archive (fraser.stlouisfed.org/) has digitized copies of the paper census reports up until the year 1941, and I encoded a series of relevant variables from these digital reports at five-year intervals.[3] Thus, I have fiscal data from 1902, 1907, 1912, 1917, 1923,[4] 1927, 1932, and 1937, as well as other governmental data from a number of early special census reports.[5] I encoded socioeconomic data from the Census of Population and Housing in 1900, 1910, 1920, 1930, and 1940. To be able to analyze the diversity of the population, I gathered data on the country of origin for all of the foreign-born residents in each city. Details on the coding of foreign-born groups are included in the appendix.[6] Linear interpolation was used to create intercensal estimates for all of the socioeconomic variables. In my largest sample, I have a total of 1,397 city-year observations, which includes data from 262 cities.

---

[3] The five-year interval was selected to match the interval that the Census of Governments used starting in 1952. From 1902 to 1903, the report was entitled "Statistics of Cities Having a Population of over 25,000." From 1904 to 1908, it was entitled "Statistics of Cities Having a Population of over 30,000." From 1909 to 1931, it was entitled "Financial Statistics of Cities Having a Population of over 30,000." From 1932 to 1941, it was entitled "Financial Statistics of Cities Having a Population of over 100,000." Collection of data on local governments was spotty between 1942 and 1952. The census resumed regular collection of data at five-year intervals starting in 1952.

[4] The report produced in 1922 was limited to very basic data and lacked many of the variables of interest. The 1923 report was used instead.

[5] These include the General Statistics of Cities: Including Statistics of Sewers and Sewage Disposal, Refuse Collection and Disposal, Street Cleaning, Dust Prevention, Highways, and the General Highway Service of Cities Having a Population of over 30,000 (1909); Municipal Electric Fire-Alarm and Police-Patrol Signaling Systems(1912); General Statistics of Cities: Including Statistics of Governmental Organizations, Police Departments, Liquor Traffic, and Municipally Owned Water Supply Systems, in Cities Having a Population of over 30,000 (1915); General Statistics of Cities: Including Statistics of Parks, Playgrounds, Museums and Art Galleries, Zoological Collections, Music and Entertainments, Swimming Pools and Bathing Beaches, and Other Features of the Recreation Service (1916).

[6] Appendix available online at http://faculty.ucmerced.edu/jtrounstine/research.htm.

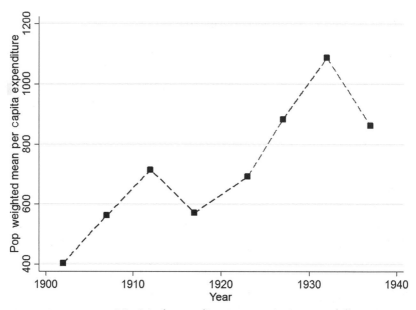

FIGURE 3.1 Municipal expenditures per capita in 2012 dollars

I begin with an analysis of total *per capita city expenditure*.[7] All data are shown in real (2012) dollars to make comparison to the modern period more straightforward. As Figure 3.1 shows, development of municipal budgets was rapid over this time period. The graph displays the population-weighted mean of per capita total expenditure plotted against time for all cities that had more than 30,000 residents in 1902. Table 3.1 shows inflation-adjusted (but unweighted) mean per capita spending and revenue on various categories over the same period.

The figure and table reveal that during this period, city expenditures grew across the board. In every category, from sanitation to safety, from health to highways, American cities became modern service providers. Spending slid during the time of the First World War and the Great Depression, but otherwise followed a steep upward trajectory. Over the next seventy years, growth continued. In 2012, per capita spending was literally ten times what it had been in 1902. Yet, even at the start of the period, growth was uneven – the means in Table 3.1 hide significant

---

[7] This measure includes all general expenses, expenditures on interest, and outlays for the municipal corporation.

TABLE 3.1 *Municipal spending in the early twentieth century: per capita expenditures in 2012 dollars*

Year	Inspections	Refuse Collection	Sewers	Libraries	Police	Fire	Health	Highways	Recreation	Schools*
1902	$1.3	$4.6	$3.7	$3.0	$28.9	$31.1	$4.8	$43.2	$6.5	$84.4
1907	$1.4	$6.7	$4.6	$4.4	$31.4	$35.4	$4.6	$38.7	$7.3	$96.0
1912	$2.2	$19.6	$5.0	$5.1	$33.3	$37.9	$6.2	$42.2	$10.1	$107.7
1917	$1.9	$16.1	$3.8	$4.0	$27.0	$29.2	$6.3	$32.6	$8.9	$97.5
1923	$2.4	$11.9	$5.1	$5.6	$36.1	$39.8	$9.0	$39.0	$11.9	$161.8
1927	$3.0	$14.1	$5.9	$6.7	$43.6	$45.2	$11.2	$43.4	$13.1	$202.3
1932	$3.9	$18.7	$7.7	$10.7	$63.2	$57.2	$17.7	$51.6	$22.3	$257.5
1937	$3.4	$16.1	$7.9	$10.7	$60.3	$53.5	$11.5	$43.4	$21.2	$233.0

* includes spending by school districts

variation. In 1902, some cities paved 100% of their streets and others paved none; some cities lit a majority of their boulevards, many more lit only their main street. Some cities already had professional police and fire forces; others still relied on volunteers. Some places provided sewers and water mains throughout residential neighborhoods; most did not.

To analyze the correlates of expenditure, I regress the natural log of inflation-adjusted *expenditures per capita* on several variables intended to capture explanations offered in the historical literature. Many scholars have argued that cities responded to pressing needs as they arose. While my dependent variable is measured as per capita spending, it is still possible that large and/or dense cities may have required higher levels of spending (if, for example, fires or diseases were more likely to spread in such places). Alternatively, large cities may have benefited from returns to scale, and therefore may have been able to provide services for a lower cost. To test for these possibilities, I include a measure of the *total population* (logged) and *density* (total population divided by total acres).

The analyses also include two different measures of diversity. The first is the share of all residents that were classified as *nonwhite* by the Census of Population and Housing.[8] The second measure of diversity is a Herfindahl Index of the foreign-born population.[9] There were fifty-two different foreign-born groups recorded by the census during this period (see the appendix). The resulting diversity index ranges from a low of 0.23 to 0.94, with a mean of 0.84,[10] indicating that the foreign-born population in the United States was extremely diverse.

As previously explained, property owners were among the most supportive of investing in new services (McDonald 1986). However, scholars also report a general tendency among the populace to rail against high taxes and profligate spending of city governments in the late nineteenth and early twentieth centuries (Bridges 1984). According to Monkkonen (1988), this belief was particularly pronounced among property owners.

---

[8] During this period, racial categorization was in flux (Roediger 2005), and the determination of race was made by census takers (Nobles 2000). However, generally speaking, the *nonwhite* category included blacks, Asians and Asian Americans, Native Americans, and sometimes Mexicans and Latin Americans. Persons of mixed race were typically identified as nonwhite.

[9] $Diversity = 1 - \sum_{f=1}^{F} \pi_f^2$, where π_f is the population share of the foreign-born group f and F is the total number of foreign-born groups.

[10] Making these categories comparable across censuses required some recoding. For instance, in 1930 and 1940, Irish immigrants were separated by northern and southern Ireland. I combined these categories to make the data comparable to the 1900, 1910, and 1920 censuses, which included only one category for Ireland.

To investigate the role of support for spending among owners, I include the proportion of housing units occupied by *homeowners*. To measure the wealth of the community, I include the *assessed value* of all property in the city. McDonald (1986) provides compelling evidence that this measure accurately captures the level of economic development in the city – which should correlate positively with ability to fund city services.[11] Finally, to capture the argument that the development of city services was driven by the emerging professional class (including land developers and planners), I add the share of adults employed as *professionals*.[12] Because I have missing data on a number of variables, I begin with a presentation of the results using only density and population as independent variables. I then add the remaining variables iteratively.[13] Summary statistics for all variables are available in the appendix, see Table A3.1. Table 3.2 presents the results.

The regressions reveal that the factors identified by historical research *do* correlate with expenditures. For instance, Glaab and Brown (1967) argue that industrialization and population growth generated demands that were fulfilled by city government, and Monkkonen (1988) argues that the need for social control through bureaucratization was greatest in large cities. The regressions indicate that places with large, dense populations witnessed higher spending per resident. In an alternate analysis, I add the number of fires per capita that cities experienced in 1902 and 1907. This variable is powerful. Increasing from the 25th to the 75th percentile (from 3 to 5 fires per 1000 people each year), increased spending by $50 per resident. Cities were clearly responding to the negative externalities associated with urbanization.

In support of the argument that cities used government to manage racial and ethnic conflict, I find an extremely powerful effect of both

---

[11] However, McDonald (1986) finds that when assessed values rose in San Francisco, politicians tended to lower tax rates, perhaps resulting in little difference in expenditure.

[12] The other occupational categories coded by the census during this period were trade, manufacturing, domestic work, and agriculture. In 1900, the category of professionals included actors, architects, artists, clergymen, dentists, electricians, engineers and surveyors, journalists, lawyers, literary and scientific persons, musicians, government officials, physicians, teachers, and other professionals.

[13] These variables are admittedly insufficient to capture all of the important differences across cities during this period. So, rather than attempt to explain variation across cities, I pursue a more modest goal: describe variation within cities over time. To do so requires that I use a city fixed-effects model for the analysis. This strategy overwhelms much of the variation present in the data, but allows for a more precise estimate of the effect of each of these contextual variables on spending.

TABLE 3.2 *Factors affecting citywide expenditure, 1902–37*

	Model 1			Model 2			Model 3		
	β	Std. Err	P > |t|	β	Std. Err	P > |t|	β	Std. Err	P > |t|
Population (log)	0.520	0.037	0.000	0.329	0.047	0.000	0.263	0.051	0.000
Density	0.016	0.004	0.000	0.013	0.004	0.001	0.010	0.004	0.011
% Nonwhite				0.838	0.412	0.042	0.821	0.409	0.045
Foreign-born diversity				0.893	0.322	0.006	0.702	0.326	0.031
Assessed value ($100 mill)				0.005	0.003	0.104	0.005	0.003	0.138
% Homeowners				2.672	0.385	0.000	2.030	0.423	0.000
% Professionals							3.197	0.934	0.001
Constant	0.045	0.421	0.916	0.332	0.481	0.490	1.275	0.559	0.023
N	1,397			1,051			1,040		
Number of cities	262			173			169		
R² within	0.175			0.301			0.315		
R² between	0.064			0.076			0.112		
ρ	0.681			0.608			0.567		

Note: Fixed effect for cities included, but not presented; DV is logged per capita expenditure.

racial and foreign-born diversity. Cities that had more nonwhite residents or a foreign-born population from many different places were bigger spenders – contrary to predictions that heterogeneity drives down public goods investment.

Finally, in support of *my* argument, cities with more capacity and demand (higher property values, more homeowners, and more professionals) also had larger budgets. These results are shown graphically in Figure 3.2. Panels show the marginal effect of each independent variable, holding all other variables at their mean value.

In this book, I argue that white homeowners sought to institutionalize the residential segregation of poor and minority residents to protect their property values and control the distribution of public goods. They were supported in this pursuit by land-oriented businesses. The pattern of relationships presented in Table 3.2 and Figure 3.2 begins to explain this impetus – particularly the positive correlation between property ownership, assessed value, percentage professionals, and municipal expenditures. Holding all other variables at their means, a city that was in the 25th percentile of homeowning, assessed value, and professionals (30% owners, $43 million in assessed value, 6% professionals) spent about $378 per resident. A city in the 75th percentile of all three measures (45% owners, $218 million in assessed value, 10% professionals) spent about $588 per person.

These relationships were circular. Local service provision was understood to increase the value of property. It was for this reason that the property tax was thought to be the most appropriate avenue for supporting local expenditures, as owners would be able to "recoup at least part of the levies in the form of higher real property worth" (Benson and O'Halloran 1987). Thus, property owners sought high levels of municipal services, which were expected to bring both direct benefits (from having access to clean water, paved streets, reliable firefighting, etc.) and indirect benefits through increases in property values. In turn, cities expected owners to fund public goods. Yet, even in the early twentieth century, owners were prone to believing that city governments were wasteful, and they often opposed increases in taxes. Residents wanted high-quality services, but were loath to pay for them.

Property owners' orientation toward both government and services was related to the emerging understanding of who should benefit from publicly funded improvements (Myrdal 1944). The cities with the fastest growing service provisions were also cities with high levels of racial and ethnic diversity. As Tretter (2012) explains, growth in municipal service

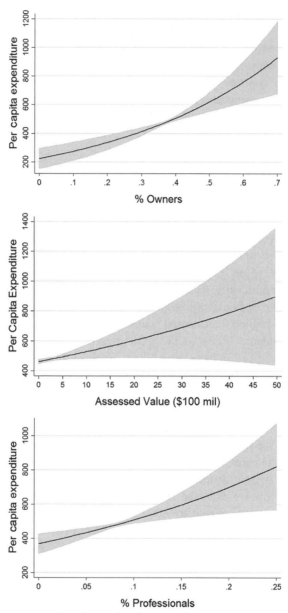

FIGURE 3.2 Correlates of early expenditure in cities, 1902–37

provision operated "within a framework of white supremacy" (p. 10). Controlling who accessed the new benefits was of utmost importance. During this period, the vast majority of blacks, Asians, and Latinos lived in places where they lacked the right to vote; and everywhere, foreign-born residents had to be naturalized before participating (Keyssar 2000). Thus, the preferences of these groups hardly played a direct role in formation of municipal policy. A white voter living in Birmingham in 1902 could be certain that, no matter how much money the local government raised in taxes, black residents would have little say in how that money was spent. The same was true for a San Franciscan thinking about his Chinese neighbors, and for an El Paso resident concerned with Mexicans in his city (Myrdal 1944; Chen 2000; Fox 2012). However, most public goods provided by cities were not targetable to individuals.[14]

When municipal governments provide streetlights and sewers, even those who are ineligible to vote benefit from these services. But residential segregation could limit equality of access. Segregation made targeting services – at least to groups, if not individuals – easier. As will be shown in detail in the chapters to come, segregation allowed city governments to collect taxes from poor and minority residents, but underprovide services to them – thereby holding down the total tax bill. Oates (1981) explains that for many important local services, such as education and public safety, the characteristics of residents are more important in determining the quality of the public good output than budgetary contributions. Thus, the generation of race and class segregation via policy enacted by local governments (such as zoning or urban renewal) was, in and of itself, a mechanism to improve municipal service provision. Segregation also ensured that the presence of poor and minority neighbors would not threaten property values. As the next section and chapters ahead will show, it was in those places where city spending was high that segregation was institutionalized through local public policy; such institutionalization was pursued most adamantly by white owners and developers of property.

---

[14] Municipal jobs, particularly when distributed as patronage, are an exception to this statement. However, despite early accounts to the contrary, the presence of political machines actually depressed spending (Trounstine 2008; Fox 2010; Brown and Halaby 1984). Thus, it appears to be the case that growth in municipal governments has never really been driven by the logic of patronage.

EXPLAINING AND MEASURING SEGREGATION

During this early period of municipal development, the nature of transportation and the needs of industry meant that even while they grew larger and more diverse, cities in the 1800s experienced low levels of segregation along race and class lines. At this time, the population of urban blacks was heavily concentrated in Southern cities.[15] In an early analysis of *The Negro Ghetto* (1948), Robert Weaver explained, "in the cities of the Old South, like Charleston and New Orleans ... most of the dwellings occupied by Negroes were either servants' quarters in the rear of the better houses or shacks on streets where low-income groups of whites also lived" (p. 8). In the north, Weaver says blacks "usually lived in clusters in racially mixed neighborhoods" (pp. 9–10). Detailed research on New York and Chicago by Logan et al. (2015) reveals that although northern blacks faced restrictive housing markets, they did not live in "predominately black neighborhoods" (p. 1062).[16] Because political representation is frequently defined at the neighborhood level, with low levels of neighborhood segregation, blacks and other minorities often benefited from public goods provided to white homeowners (Troesken 2004).

There are many different ways to measure segregation (e.g., the degree to which groups are disproportionately distributed across geographic space). Indices of segregation are typically correlated with each other, but capture different theoretical dimensions of separation, and, so, measure different things (Massey and Denton 1988). The two most commonly used measures are the index of dissimilarity and the index of isolation, which can be intuitively interpreted respectively as the proportion of a racial group that would need to move neighborhoods to generate an even racial distribution given the racial makeup of the larger community, and the racial makeup of the neighborhood in which the typical member of the racial group lives. While these are obviously meaningful dimensions of segregation, neither measure includes the most relevant information from a political perspective. In politics, what matters is not just how individuals from different racial groups are distributed across neighborhoods, but also how large each racial group is relative to others and how big of an impact each neighborhood might have on the vote. That is, we need a measure that

---

[15] My dataset includes demographics for 296 cities from the 1900 Census of Population and Housing. These cities housed about 1.2 million black residents, approximately 64% of whom lived in the South.

[16] They did, however, live in "*disproportionately* black ... neighborhoods" (p. 1062).

weights diversity by group size, and weights evenness by geographic units' population size. The *H* index developed by Theil (1972) meets these criteria.

Theil's *H* Index measures the difference between the diversity of the city and the weighted average diversity of individual neighborhoods. Diversity scores for each neighborhood and the city as a whole are influenced by the relative size of racial groups, while the overall index is influenced by the relative size of each neighborhood, giving more weight to larger than to smaller places. Both types of weighting are key to understanding the political implications of segregation. We should expect the effect of segregation to be most pronounced when minority groups are unevenly dispersed across geographic units *and* represent a substantial share of the population.

Theil's *H* has a number of other useful qualities. Importantly, for understanding city politics, Theil's *H* can be calculated for more than two groups at a time (unlike either the dissimilarity or isolation indices). Additionally, it is the only index that obeys the principle of transfers in the multigroup case: the index declines when a minority resident (theoretically) moves to a neighborhood with fewer minority residents (Reardon and Firebaugh 2002). Finally, as will be discussed in the next section, Theil's *H* is additive and can also be aggregated to higher levels or decomposed into its constituent parts.

Theil's *H* index is built from Theil's entropy score, which is a measure of diversity itself:

$$E = \sum_{r=1}^{R} (\pi_r) \ln \frac{1}{\pi_r},$$

where π_r represents the proportion of the population in racial group r (or class group r if the index is measuring class segregation). The higher the entropy score, the more diverse an area is.[17] The score ranges between 0 and the natural log of the total number of groups R. It is maximized when individuals are evenly distributed among the different racial groups.[18] $\pi_r = \frac{1}{R}$ for all r. Entropy is calculated for each neighborhood individually, and for the city as a whole.

The *H* index measures the degree to which the diversity in each neighborhood differs from the diversity of the city as a whole, expressed

---

[17] Where any group's share of the population is 0, the natural log is set to zero, as is the convention in the literature (Iceland 2004).

[18] A scatterplot relating a white/nonwhite calculation of *E* to percentage white is included in the appendix in Figure A3.1.

as a fraction of the city's total diversity and weighted by the neighborhood's share of the total population:

$$H = \sum_{n=1}^{N} \frac{P_n}{P_c} \left(\frac{E_c - E_n}{E_c} \right),$$

where P represents total population of neighborhood n or city c, and E is the entropy of n or c. H varies between 0, where all neighborhoods have the same composition as the entire city, and 1, where all neighborhoods contain only one group.[19] This H index serves as a key outcome to be explained throughout the book.

The dataset that I constructed to measure segregation is built from a number of different sources. The calculation of the H index requires data on population characteristics at the subcity level. Cutler et al. (1999) digitized subcity demographics on race and immigration for 178 different cities from the 1890–1950 censuses. To this, I add available data that I encoded on homeownership from the 1900 census, and data from the Elizabeth Mullen Bogue files (1975) on homeownership from the 1940 census.[20] For the 1970–2000 censuses, I rely on a product developed by GeoLytics called the Neighborhood Change Database (NCDB). The NCDB matches and normalizes census tract boundaries for each census year, allowing for direct comparison in demographic changes across time. Finally, I add data from the 2007–11 American Community Survey. These data allow me to create a panel dataset measuring segregation at the census-tract level for cities and metropolitan areas for more than 100 years.

Figure 3.3 plots the distribution of racial segregation scores in 1890 and 1940, using data for the eighty cities with populations of at least 25,000 and with at least 1,000 blacks as of the 1890 Census.[21] In

---

[19] In all analyses, neighborhoods are represented by census tracts, which are relatively stable, contiguous geographic areas containing approximately 4,000 people. Most studies of segregation (e.g., Massey and Denton 1998) use census tracts as a proxy for neighborhood (although this is not without debate; see, for instance, Logan et al. 2015).

[20] The data from 1900 to 1940 are collected at the ward level (political units for electing city council members). Starting in 1940, the census published tract-level data for some cities. Wards tend to be larger in area than tracts, and, therefore, suggest a smaller value of the segregation index without actually representing a lower level of segregation. To account for this, I adjust all ward-level estimates by a correction factor calculated using a set of forty-seven cities that reported both ward- and tract-level data in 1940.

[21] For all figures presented in this chapter, the two groups used to calculate the H index are whites and all others for years 1890–1970. For 1980–2011, the groups are non-Hispanic whites and all others. Throughout the book, I calculate the H index by tract-city-county-MSA

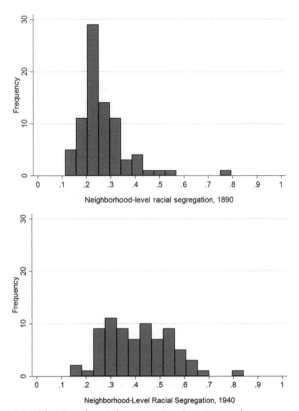

FIGURE 3.3 Neighborhood racial segregation in 1890 and 1940

Note: The white/nonwhite *H* index for 1890 is calculated using wards as the base population unit with a correction factor to make the data comparable to tract-level estimates. The *H* index for 1940 is calculated at the tract level where available and at the ward level otherwise. Data provided by Cutler et al. (1999) and Bogue (1975).

1890, racial segregation patterns were similar from place to place, and generally fairly moderate – although higher than some historical analyses indicate (Cutler et al. 1999). Both features had changed substantially by 1940.

(Metropolitan Statistical Area). This means that cities that cross county lines end up with multiple observations. This is necessary because census tracts are nested within counties – not cities. When presenting any analysis at the city level, I use the observation representing the largest share of the city population.

In all but a handful of cases, neighborhood-level racial segregation rose between 1890 and 1940 – on average rising 0.15, a change of about 65%. But the standard deviation is large at 0.13; some cities segregated much more intensely than others.

There are many ways to consider measuring class segregation. Throughout the book, I use two measures: the distribution of renters versus homeowners, and the concentration of households in the top income threshold.[22] The correlation between owner and wealth segregation is about 0.60. I rely primarily on the former measure for two reasons. First, it is available for the entire time period. More importantly, the existing scholarship indicates that it is property ownership – not wealth – that is the more important driver of local political participation and preferences (Fischel 2001; Oliver and Ha 2007). The downside of this measure is that, at an aggregate level, it is very resistant to change as the housing stock changes more slowly than demographics. Wealth segregation is a more straightforward measure of the residential divisions along socioeconomic lines, but it is only available starting with the 1970 census and is less directly affected by city policy.

To demonstrate change over time, Figure 3.4 presents data on the renter/homeowner distribution within cities. This figure reveals that class segregation started off much lower and was more consistent from city to city as compared with racial segregation, and increased a small amount (0.037) between 1900 and 1940.

To determine how segregation correlates with expenditure in the prewar period, I add to the segregation dataset the measure of *logged expenditures per capita* described in the previous section. Because segregation data are measured every decade, and expenditures are measured in years ending in 2 and 7, I interpolate spending data. I then lag spending by five years under the assumption that demographic sorting takes time to

---

[22] The census reports income categorically, not continuously; wealthy refers to the number of families in each census tract with incomes above particular thresholds for each census year. I use family, as opposed to household income because the NCDB does not report household income at the tract level. The thresholds were determined by calculating the average family income for all census tracts in the United States for each census year. The wealthy threshold represents the income bin with a starting point closest to the 90th percentile of this distribution. The thresholds for each census year are as follows: $35,000 for 1980, $75,000 for 1990, $100,000 for 2000, and $150,000 for 2011. All families with this amount of income or more are categorized as wealthy. Census tracts range from 0 to 100% wealthy, with a mean of 18%, a median of 13%, and a standard deviation of 16%.

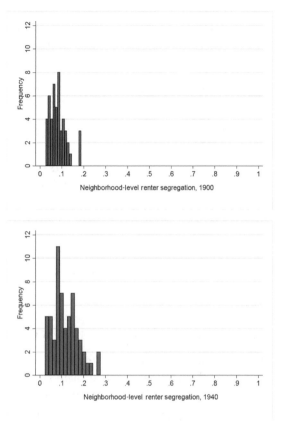

FIGURE 3.4 Neighborhood class segregation in 1900 and 1940

respond to budgets. I regress *racial segregation* and *renter segregation* on the lagged *expenditures* variable.[23]

The results presented in Table 3.3 indicate a positive correlation between spending and segregation. The R^2 suggests that about 30–40% of the variation in city segregation levels can be explained by variation in the budget. Places with larger budgets were more segregated five years later, compared with cities with smaller budgets up until the Second

---

[23] As in the previous section, I add fixed effects for cities. This fixed effect model analyzes the relationship between lagged expenditures and racial segregation over time within cities. This accounts for variation across cities on all other dimensions that might affect segregation and spending.

TABLE 3.3 *Correlations between spending and segregation, 1902–37*

	Racial segregation			Renter segregation		
	β	Std. err	P > |t|	β	Std. err	P > |t|
Expend. per capita, 5-year lag (logged)	0.100	0.010	0.000	0.026	0.003	0.000
Constant	−0.238	0.059	0.000	−0.052	0.018	0.005
N	368			179		
Number of cities	118			56		
R^2 within	0.292			0.383		
R^2 between	0.020			0.010		
ρ	0.802			0.931		

Note: Fixed effect for cities included, but not presented. DV is Theil's *H* index for race and renter segregation.

World War. For a host of reasons, this relationship would change going forward.

SUBURBANIZATION: ANOTHER FORM OF SEGREGATION

Teaford (1979) argues that two conflicting forces animated city development in the late nineteenth and early twentieth century. On the one hand, socioeconomic diversity generated an impetus for separation. As early as the mid-1800s, "the urban population was resolving itself into separate geographic spheres – factory zones, ethnic neighborhoods, upper-middle-class retreats, race track havens – and each zone sought local self-government as a means of protecting its own particular interests" (Teaford 1979, p. 23). This separation, Teaford shows, led to the explosion of newly incorporated municipalities. But, over the course of the next fifty years, many of these tiny new cities consolidated and/or were annexed into larger central cities for one primary reason: the provision of city services. Prior to 1900, suburban governments were simply unable to provide the quality of sewers, clean water, paved streets, uniformed police forces, and firefighting that was available in the central city. As a result, as cities became more diverse, the forces of separation pulled people into different neighborhoods – but not into different cities.

However, in the period following the Second World War, America began to suburbanize rapidly (Rappaport 2005). Scholars have detailed the role that automobile accessibility (Glaeser, Kahn, and Rappaport 2008), highway construction (Nall 2018), federal programs encouraging homeownership (Jackson 1987), changes in the building industry, and rising incomes (Margo 1992) played in the growth of suburbs. The vast majority of people who arrived in the bucolic, grassy neighborhoods filled with single-family homes were whites with incomes slightly (although not dramatically) higher than the median income of the central city (Cutler et al. 1999; Winsberg 1989). By about 1940, many larger suburbs were able to compete with central city service provision, thus increasing their attractiveness among residents, industries, and businesses interested in moving away from the center. As Teaford (1979) explains, "[W]hile the forces encouraging unity were weakening, the forces of separatism and disunion remained powerful" (p. 84). Thus, in the middle of the century, central cities stopped growing politically, and suburbs arose as powerful actors in the metropolitan universe (Teaford 1979; Danielson 1976; Miller 1981; Burns 1994). In 1970, more than half of all metropolitan-area populations lived outside of the central city, a figure that would grow to two-thirds over the next thirty years. The rise of suburbs decoupled residential spaces from job spaces and encouraged suburban residents to prioritize neighborhood amenities and property values in political decision making (Teaford 1979; Fischel 2004).

As they moved outside of the central city, suburbanites sought to protect their investments (high quality public goods and property values) in much the same way as their predecessors had: by institutionalizing segregation through public policies like land-use planning and zoning. Thus, the impetus toward separation in the latter half of the twentieth century played out across, rather than within, city lines. The level of segregation is of crucial importance to politics. When cities are not segregated by neighborhood, district representation ensures that all residents within a particular location are likely to be provided similar services. When a district councilor wins a public park for his neighborhood, all those who live nearby benefit. As the level of segregation shifts from blocks to neighborhoods, residents are more likely to lose representation. Still, though, when segregation occurs across neighborhoods within cities, it is possible for residents of segregated neighborhoods to affect the delivery of municipal services through the political process. If a heavily minority neighborhood lacks a public park, residents from this neighborhood might mobilize to try to elect a mayor or city council member who is responsive to their demands. But when segregation occurs across cities, heavily minority cities have no ability to affect the distribution of public goods from neighboring white towns.

To understand how segregation patterns have changed over time, I developed a measure that accounts for segregation both within cities and across them. To do this, I build on the measure of segregation presented in the previous section, using Theil's *H* index. Theil's *H* is suited to this purpose because it is perfectly additive for nested geographies (Reardon and Firebaugh 2002; Fischer et al. 2004). In my case, census tracts are nested within cities, and cities are nested within metropolitan areas. Residents can be segregated in two ways: across neighborhoods within cities, or across cities within metropolitan areas. My measure combines these two types of segregation.

As explained previously, the *H* index measures the degree to which the diversity (*E*) of subunits differs from the diversity of a larger unit. For each census year, I calculate *H* indices at the two levels that are of interest: within cities and across cities. Respectively, these measure the extent to which census tract diversity differs from city diversity (H_{c_t}) and the extent to which city diversity differs from metropolitan area diversity (H_{m_c}):[24]

$$H_{c\_t} = \sum_{t=1}^{T} \frac{P_t}{P_c} \left(\frac{E_c - E_t}{E_c} \right)$$

$$H_{m\_c} = \sum_{c=1}^{C} \frac{P_c}{P_m} \left(\frac{E_m - E_c}{E_m} \right),$$

where *P* represents total population of the tract *t*, city *c*, or metropolitan area *m*, and *E* represents the entropy of the geography ($E = \sum_{r=1}^{R} (\pi_r) \ln \frac{1}{\pi_r}$).

I combine the two indices to produce a total *H* index for the metro area, calculated at the tract level, H_{m_t}:

$$H_{m\_t} = \sum_{t=1}^{T} \frac{P_t}{P_m} \left(\frac{E_m - E_t}{E_m} \right) = H_{m\_c} + \sum_{c=1}^{C} \left(\frac{P_c}{P_m} \right) \left(\frac{E_c}{E_m} \right) H_{c\_t}$$

To illustrate the two levels of segregation, Figure 3.5 provides a representation of two metropolitan areas, each with three cities (a central

---

[24] Census tracts are perfectly nested within states and counties. However, in some cases, tracts cross city lines. In these cases, GeoLytics assigned the tract to the city containing the largest share of the tract population. In 2011, tracts are weighted by the share of population contained in each city. Observations are unique when defined by year, tract, city, county, and metropolitan area. Tracts located in unincorporated areas within a metropolitan area (even if they are denoted as places by the census) are combined as a single unincorporated unit. Tracts outside of metropolitan areas are not included in the analysis. I use Metropolitan Statistical Areas and, where possible, Primary Metropolitan Statistical Areas as the highest level of aggregation. I do not use Consolidated Metropolitan Statistical Areas, which are much larger.

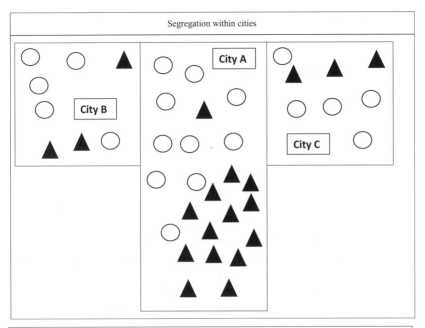

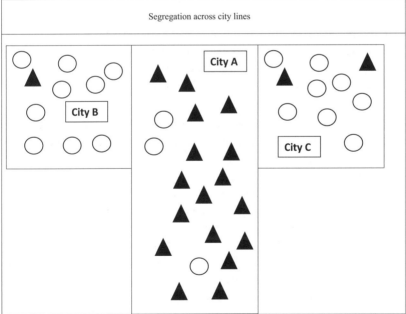

FIGURE 3.5 Segregation within city vs. across cities

city and two suburbs). In these images, cities are represented as rectangles and two different population groups (triangles and circles) reside in each city.

The upper panel shows a metropolitan area in which the two types of residents are segregated from each other in different neighborhoods within each city (indicating a high amount of segregation across tracts within the city, H_{c_t}). Each city in this panel has some triangles and some circles, and they live in different parts of town. The bottom panel represents a metropolitan area where group sorting is much more prevalent across city lines, as opposed to within them (indicating a high value of H_{m_c}). The cities in this panel are predominantly populated by either triangles or circles.

Chicago, Illinois, is a city in which racial groups are heavily segregated by neighborhood (like the top panel of Figure 3.5). The value of H_{c_t} in 2011 for Chicago was 0.379; the value of H_{m_c} (total segregation across cities) for the Chicago metropolitan area was 0.192. In the bottom panel, the cities of the metropolitan area are much more homogenous overall. The metropolitan area of Detroit, Michigan, is well represented by this picture. The value of H_{c_t} (within city segregation) in 2011 for Detroit was 0.220, while the value of H_{m_c} for the metropolitan area was 0.395.

How has metropolitan area segregation changed over time? The top panel of Figure 3.6 shows total metropolitan segregation measured at the tract level (H_{m_t}) since 1900, while the bottom panel shows the share of that segregation that was accounted for across cities rather than within them ($\frac{H_{m\_c}}{H_{m\_t}}$) from 1970 to 2011.

These figures reveal that by 1970, total metro area racial segregation had peaked and begun to decline, while class segregation began a slow ascent. The bottom panel reveals that between 1970 and 2011, neighborhood segregation was exchanged for city-level segregation along both race and class lines. As neighborhood-level segregation declined, city-level segregation has remained remarkably persistent. The figures also show that historically class segregation was much lower than racial segregation, but by 2011, the indices had converged substantially. The relationship between race and class segregation also increased over time. In 1990 (the earliest date for which I have data on all 330 metropolitan areas), the correlation between race and renter segregation was 0.19. It rose to 0.32 in 2011. The correlation between race and wealth segregation increased from 0.46 to 0.51 over this same period. The link between race and wealth segregation across city lines is even stronger; it was 0.70

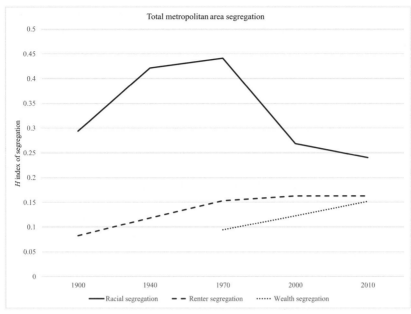

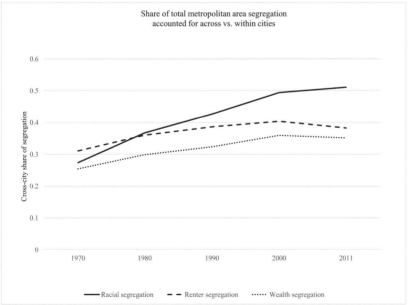

FIGURE 3.6 Changing metropolitan segregation patterns, 1900–2010

in 2011. This tightening link between race and class is driven by changes in both race and class segregation, both within and across cities. However, these remain distinct demographic patterns.

CONCLUSION

This chapter presented several important changes in the local political environment between 1900 and 2010. City services expanded dramatically during this period. The growth in urban public goods provision was driven, as expected, by property owners seeking to enhance the value of their land. At the same time, segregation along race and class lines also expanded dramatically – first within cities, and then across them. As the next chapters will show, segregation was driven by this same impetus to protect property values and access to the municipal services that owners had secured in earlier decades. Local governments would be the key to accomplishing these goals.

4

Engineering Enclaves

How Local Governments Produce Segregation

The last chapter revealed that segregation along both race and class lines grew in tandem with the growth of cities. Race, ethnic, and class enclaves developed as urbanization brought white migrants, African Americans, and immigrants to cities (Teaford 1979; Meyer 2000). At the turn of the century, the predominant pattern of segregation occurred building-by-building, block-by-block, and, sometimes, several blocks-by-several blocks, but typically not by neighborhoods (Logan et al. 2015; Meyer 2000). Many cities featured multiple racial, ethnic, and class enclaves (Kellogg 1982; Rabinowitz 1978). In Philadelphia, for instance, about 40% of the black population lived in central city wards (the fourth, fifth, seventh, and eight), but there were significant clusters of black homes in the fourteenth, fifteenth, twentieth, twenty-second, twenty-sixth, twenty-seventh, twenty-ninth, thirtieth, and thirty-seventh wards too (DuBois 1899). In Atlanta, blacks lived in "Shermantown, Mechanicsville, Hell's Half Acre, Bone Alley, and Pigtail Alley," as well as "Darktown ... Peasville ... and Jenningstown" (Rabinowitz 1978, p. 106). By 1940, neighborhoods had become much more homogenous. So, while the residential locations of people of color and the poor were nearly always restricted, the pattern of segregation changed during the years leading up to the Second World War. In this chapter, I argue that local governments played a key role in producing this change. Governments adopted zoning and other policies that created or reinforced segregation in service to business elites and white, property-owning constituents who were demanding a larger, more active city government.

In the very large social science literature on the causes and maintenance of race and class segregation, the contributions of local government are given limited attention.[1] Boustan (2012) concludes, "[T]he most important [factor in the generation of residential segregation] appears to be individual choices of white households" (p. 318). Hayward (2013) agrees, arguing that restrictive covenants were "a more significant mechanism of racial segregation" than local government activities (p. 59).[2] Other scholars combine private and public actions into a single theoretical construct. For example, Cutler et al. (1999) provide evidence of "collective action racism," which involves "specific policy instruments such as racial zoning or restrictive covenants prohibiting sales to blacks, or organized activities such as threatened lynchings or fire bombings that discourage blacks from moving into neighborhoods" (p. 476). Similarly, Dreier et al. (2004) associate racial zoning laws with biased real estate codes of ethics, racial steering, insurance redlining, and white violence, concluding that "racial segregation thus stems from the routine practices of the private real estate industry" and the spontaneous choices of urban residents "as well as from government policy" (p. 120).

The role of government was uniquely important and deserving of explanation. Using the state to promote restrictive collective action is qualitatively different from arranging segregation privately. Marshaling the power of city government institutionalizes prejudicial behavior and denies victims recourse. As Abrams (1955) explains, "[P]assions and prejudices ... unsanctioned by government ... exhausted themselves" (p. 206). But when democratically elected local governments developed policies promoting segregation, they became "instruments of oppression against minorities" (p. 207).

It is tempting to explain state-sponsored segregation as the inevitable result of racist attitudes among white residents. Troesken and Walsh (2017) offer an eloquent rebuttal to this argument:

There are, however, at least two problems with this simple, preference-based answer. First, to the extent that anti-black sentiments were widespread and generally held among white voters, an exclusively-preference-based answer suggests that laws promoting residential segregation would have been ubiquitous. Yet, the available historical evidence suggests that demand for formal segregation

---

[1] The contributions of the federal government, on the other hand, are well covered (Jackson 1987; Massey and Denton 1998).

[2] Of course, restrictive covenants required government action for enforcement. However, they could be generated without government involvement.

laws varied over time and across space ... Second, any answer to the question "why do we have laws promoting residential segregation" that relies solely on white preferences ignores the underlying economic processes that shaped demand for such laws. (pp. 2–3)

Understanding where and when local governments worked to create segregation along both race and class lines helps to clarify where segregation was likely to become entrenched and where it was more fluid, as well as provide insight into the factors that generate consequential local policy decisions.

In this chapter, I explore the factors that contributed to the adoption of zoning laws. I argue that zoning was enacted by political elites seeking to manage the distribution of public goods to their core supporters. To present that argument, I first offer a historical narrative detailing the adoption of zoning laws by municipal governments. Then, I present a quantitative analysis of these adoptions. I find that in cities with higher property taxes and larger budgets (where more was at stake), where Republicans (who led the municipal reform movement) had greater support, and where political participation was low (and thus more likely to be heavily skewed toward middle-upper class, native, white voters), zoning ordinances were more likely to be adopted. Finally, I analyze the effect of zoning adoption on future levels of segregation. I show that cities that were early adopters of zoning went on to become more segregated along both race and class lines than similarly situated cities without early zoning plans.

The dawn of the twentieth century was an exciting time for local government. Populations exploded as the Industrial Revolution took hold. In this environment, the limited, caretaker approach to city governance became suddenly and profoundly insufficient for maintaining health, order, and property. Monkonnen (1988) explains, "[C]ities could have chosen to ignore sewage, crime, unschooled children, and slow transportation by simply tolerating higher disease rates, offense rates, illiteracy rates, and traffic tangles" (p. 4). But city governments did not take that path. Instead, they worked aggressively to shape their social and economic environments. As Chapter 3 revealed, between 1890 and 1940, cities became modern – providing services like clean water, fire protection, police patrol, and road paving. It was in this environment that cities also began to seek control over space and residents' use of space through zoning and city planning. The end goal of this control, as was true of most Progressive Era reforms, was to improve the lives and opportunities for businesses and residents – more specifically, US-born Anglo residents (Tretter 2012; Woodward 1955; Toll 1969; Brownwell 1975).

As Monkonnen indicates, it was far from obvious that cities would assert control over their environments, but the rapid spread of slums, worries about skyscrapers blocking natural light, fears of conflagration, and concern about public health threats provided early inspiration for cities to invoke their policy power of regulation over nuisances (Toll 1969).[3] Reformers debated the correct policy solutions for these ills, recommending, for example, density restrictions (Woodbury 1929), stricter building codes (Power 1983), the removal of alley dwellings (Silver 1997), or policies, including increased public transportation, that would encourage suburban homeownership for the working class (Baar 1996). In many cases, typically at the urging of local chambers of commerce, city councils chose to pursue zoning – regulating the use, height, and area of buildings and land (Brownwell 1975).

Early on, zoning was frequently combined with general development plans for the city. Planners like Daniel Burnham and Frederick Law Olmsted (leaders of the City Beautiful Movement) sought to improve the squalid conditions in industrial cities by reducing densities and creating garden settings with tree-lined streets, wide boulevards, and central open spaces (Robinson 1916). To achieve these goals, planners advocated for local zoning measures that would allow for the restriction of tenement housing, the separation of housing from factories, and the building of public parks. But, while zoning became wildly popular, planning did not. The decoupling of zoning from planning was viewed negatively by some leaders of the early planning movement who thought the creation of homogenous neighborhoods would be likely to reinforce social divisions and inequality (Toll 1969). Of course, this was often precisely the goal of zoning supporters.

The rise of social Darwinism contributed to the attraction of zoning as a solution for burgeoning problems. Social Darwinists argued that the evolution of humanity would follow a process of natural selection in which the environment played a defining role. As a result, controlling the environment was of utmost importance (Toll 1969). A related body of literature came to understand race and the differences between racial and ethnic groups as biologically rooted – hence, immutable (Hayward 2013). According to this doctrine, the inherent inferiority of blacks and other

---

[3] A number of important court battles ensured that zoning would be constitutionally allowed for the promotion of health, safety, welfare, and morals, and did NOT constitute the deprivation of life, liberty, or property (see Hayward 2013 and Toll 1969 for overviews).

people of color (Native Americans, Chinese, Japanese, Mexicans, etc.), along with the preservation of "race purity," demanded "segregation and discrimination in recreation, in religious service, in education, before the law, in politics, in housing, in stores, and in breadwinning" (Myrdal 1944, p. 58). Additionally, scientific and medical experts, as well as politicians, believed that the unsanitary habits and homes of the poor and people of color spread epidemic disease (Shah 2001, p. 6). In combination, these new theories offered a convincing rationale for the creation of special districts to quarantine offending groups. By 1930, about half of all large cities in the United States had adopted comprehensive zoning plans.

Political leaders often used threats to public safety as a rationale for legislating segregation. New York's 1916 zoning law, the first comprehensive zoning ordinance in the nation, sought to limit the health threat posed by skyscrapers that blocked natural light and contributed to the spread of tuberculosis (Toll 1969, p. 154). Because immigrants and blacks were viewed as disease carriers, segregating them was a typical goal of zoning. In San Francisco, the first city to segregate explicitly on the basis of race, whites had grown increasingly paranoid that Chinese residents were spreading diseases like smallpox and tuberculosis, and, in 1890, enacted an ordinance that required all Chinese residents and their businesses to move, within sixty days, to the section of town that had been set aside for "slaughterhouses, tallow factories, hog factories, and other businesses thought to be prejudicial to the public health or comfort" (McClain 1996, p. 224). In Baltimore, segregationists agreed that "blacks should be quarantined in isolated slums in order to reduce the incidents of civil disturbance, to prevent the spread of communicable disease into nearby white neighborhoods, and to protect property values among the white majority" (Power 1983, p. 301).

The belief that zoning would create stability in property values was widely held and generated strong support from land owners, commercial organizations, bankers, realtors, and developers (Abrams 1955; Brownell 1975; Weiss 1987). Boston's first height restriction was passed in 1892 at the behest of downtown property owners who feared that the new skyscrapers would lead to an oversupply of office space and drive down property values (Kennedy 1992). In some places, this view had to be cultivated. In Los Angeles, for example, some developers were opposed to the city's 1908 zoning law because they worried it would inhibit growth (Weiss 1987). In other cases, builders and speculators objected to any limit on their liberty to earn profits from their land (Aoki 1992).

To combat such reservations, early supporters of zoning made sure to argue that their proposals would "enhance, not detract from property values" (Toll 1969, p. 150). Zoning could easily have been invoked to improve the quality and health of working- and lower-class neighborhoods and limit land speculation (as some of the early reformers argued it should); however, "political pressures from those less inclined toward broad civic improvement" won out (Silver 1997, p. 24). As Burnham and Bennet wrote in 1909, "the greater attractiveness" produced by municipal land-use control "keeps at home the people of means and taste, and acts as a magnet to draw those who seek to live amid pleasing surroundings. The very beauty that attracts him who has money makes pleasant the life of those among whom he lives, while anchoring him and his wealth to the city" (p. 189).

As zoning practices spread through the 1920s, emphasis on the enhancement of property values became the dominant argument; almost universally, it was believed that the wrong sorts of people residing, or even working, in an area could negatively impact property values. Abrams (1955) quotes an early real estate text that argued, "[P]roperty values have been sadly depreciated by having a single colored family settle down on a street occupied by white residents"; another text claimed a similar effect of "unassimilated aliens." Both prescribed "rigid segregation" as a solution, "no matter how unpleasant or objectionable the thought may be to colored residents" (p. 159).

Aside from adding wealth to property-owning and voting residents, city governments had a separate reason to protect and enhance property values – taxes (Lees 1994). An advertisement run by Fifth Avenue merchants in the March 5 and 6, 1916, editions of *The New York Times* argued that failure to support the city's new zoning plan would lead to "vacant or depreciated property," which would lead to "reduced taxes, leaving a deficit made up by extra assessment on other sections" (p. 5). Rising property values allowed municipal governments to grow without increasing tax rates. When property values declined, municipal officials faced the unwelcome task of raising tax rates or cutting the budget.

As municipal governments began to spend vast sums on improving the lives and environments of residents, ensuring that the right (white, wealthy) residents benefited from the new city services became of utmost importance. This goal was clear to observers at the time. Booker T. Washington (1915) explained that "the negro objects to being segregated because it usually means that he will receive inferior accommodations in return of the taxes he pays." Such objection stemmed from the belief that segregation would ensure that "the sewerage in his part of the city will be inferior; that the streets and sidewalks will be neglected, that the street lighting will be poor; that his section of the city will not be kept in order by the police and other authorities, and that the 'undesirables' of other races will be placed near him." Thus, Washington concluded, "[W]hen a negro seeks to buy a house in a reputable street he does it not only to get police protection, lights and accommodations, but to remove his children to a locality in which vice is not paraded" (pp. 113–14). Frequently, white elites made arguments that taxing whites to pay for black public goods (like schooling) was "an indignity." One delegate to the Louisiana Constitutional Debate in 1864, incredulous at the proposition, asked, "Shall we tear the slave away from his master and then force the master to educate him?" (Louisiana Constitutional Debate 1864). As a result, in many cities (see Chapter 5), black areas lacked municipal services, such as "paving, water, sewerage, lighting and garbage removal" (Knight 1927, p. 53; also Myrdal 1944).

Given that zoning was viewed as a way to both increase property values and maintain exclusivity in the distribution of public goods, it is unsurprising that southern cities made early use of zoning to hem in expanding black neighborhoods and create clear dividing lines between white and black residential areas. Of course, the development of racial zoning in the South was part of a much larger process of reconfiguring race relations after the Civil War. During the period of Reconstruction and Redemption, whites subordinated, exploited, and killed blacks; but, even in this context, the legal segregation of the races was not a foregone conclusion (Woodward 1955).[4] In fact, although Jim Crow laws were widespread, most southern cities did not legislate residential segregation directly.[5]

Blacks being able and willing to live in white neighborhoods was a necessary (although not sufficient) condition for the enactment of legislation. Baltimore passed the first racial zoning law directed at blacks in 1910 following the violent response of white residents to black migrants moving into previously all-white areas. Baltimore's ordinance prohibited whites and blacks from moving into city blocks occupied by a majority of

---

[4] One vivid example of the ways in which Jim Crow changed existing practice comes from New Bern, North Carolina. In 1913, the city aldermen passed an ordinance that required that all "colored bodies" buried in the public cemetery be dug up and moved to a segregated location (www.newbernsj.com/article/20140209/Opinion/302099914).

[5] Rabinowitz (1978) argues that the picture was different with respect to schooling. Here, segregation was immediate and unchanging after the end of the war.

members of the other race. Quite aware of the requirements of the Fourteenth Amendment, the Baltimore council argued (and the Maryland Supreme Court agreed) that because the ordinance placed the same limitations on both racial groups, it was not discriminatory (Racial Zoning by Private Contract 1928).[6] The vote of the city council fell along party lines, with all of the Democrats in support and all of the Republicans opposed.[7] Republicans were joined in their opposition by the entire community of black residents, white homeowners who lived in integrated neighborhoods, and some of the city's real estate brokers (Power 1983). Democrats were not just responding to their white voters in their promotion of segregation. Limiting black residential location also bolstered Democratic political power by ensuring that blacks would be packed into certain wards, thereby reserving the rest of the city for Democratic control (Rabinowitz 1978).

In some places, black political power slowed or inhibited the enactment of segregation ordinances (Rice 1968). In St. Louis, an effort to pass a segregation ordinance failed because it was opposed by a significant number of city elites (including most of the city's leading Republicans, labor interests, religious leaders, and newspapers). The National Association for the Advancement of Colored People (NAACP) and the Knights of Pythias lobbied the St. Louis city government tirelessly, and ultimately convinced twenty-one of the twenty-eight aldermen and the mayor to vote against it. In 1912, the city went so far as to station five police officers at the house of a black family to protect them from "possible attack by whites who resent what they term a 'Negro invasion' in their residential district" (The Ghetto 1912, p. 272). In a low turnout election in 1916, supporters of the segregation ordinance won a city referendum, and the city immediately began mapping the race of each city block (Meyer 2000, pp. 19–21). In Kansas City, Missouri, blacks had a modest amount of political power due to their ties to the Democratic Pendergast machine. Despite support from a significant segment of the city's white population,

---

[6] Although the Court agreed with the city's reasoning about the Fourteenth Amendment, it ultimately declared the ordinance unconstitutional because its provisions were retroactive, thereby representing a taking by the government (*State v. Gurry* 121 Md. 534 [1913]).

[7] Republicans were generally (tepidly) supportive of black rights in Baltimore, and between 1890 and 1931, six black Republicans served on the Baltimore city council (Greene 1979). Over the course of their careers, these councilors led the city council to provide significant contributions to Baltimore's black community, but none was able to defeat the segregated housing legislation.

a racial zoning ordinance never made it past the lower chamber of the city council (Meyer 2000).

Bacote (1955) reports that throughout the late 1800s in Atlanta, black support was frequently courted by white factions. For instance, in the 1891 election, black candidates were nominated for council positions in the first, fourth, and sixth wards on the Citizens' ticket (an antiprohibition faction of the Democratic Party). White factions did this when they were in danger of losing the election; in 1891, the antiprohibition Democrats were worried about a Populist victory. To prevent white factions from seeking black support in the future, the Democratic Party adopted the white primary in 1892, and the state of Georgia enacted a new constitution in 1908 that included a character requirement, a literacy test, and made property ownership a condition for registration (Bayor 1996). These changes severely restricted black participation, ensuring that white factions would rely only on white votes. The evisceration of the black electorate and black representation opened the way to the city's enactment of segregation ordinances (Key 1949; Kousser 1974; Woodward 1955).

Atlanta enacted a racial zoning ordinance on the heels of a violent race riot in 1906. The riot erupted after local newspapers alleged four unsubstantiated assaults upon white women by black men. According to Garrett (1969), the riot was ignited by the sight of black passengers riding next to whites on streetcars. A white mob killed and beat dozens of black Atlantans over the course of three days. A concerted organization effort among the city's African American population followed. White elites and politicians denounced the riot, and a public/private relief fund was even established for families of the murder victims (Garrett 1969). However, the riot also led many whites to conclude that "separation of the races is the only radical solution of the negro problem in this country" (*Charleston News and Courier*, quoted in *The New York Times*, September 30, 1906). Following the passage of the ordinance in 1913, all blocks in the city were assigned racial designations based on the race of the majority of current residents (Silver 1997).

Fighting racial zoning was one of the early nationwide causes to be adopted by the NAACP (Rice 1968; Meyer 2000), and due to the organization's work, in 1917, the Supreme Court ruled racial zoning unconstitutional in *Buchanan v. Warley*. In the *Buchanan* decision, the justices did not seek to protect the rights of black property buyers or to prohibit "amalgamation of the races," but rather to protect the right of white owners to "sell or lease their lands and houses to whomsoever they pleased" (Racial Zoning by Private Contract 1928, p. 531).[8] Nonetheless, the *Chicago Defender* (U.S. Supreme Court Kills Segregation Laws 1917) declared that the "hydra-headed monster of segregation ... was killed by the Supreme Court," and argued that the "decision [was] a direct slap in the face to white southern oligarchy." According to Rice (1968), it was also a "victory for moderate whites and Republicans" (p. 197).

Following *Buchanan*, many cities sought to enact constitutionally defensible racial zoning plans by turning to comprehensive city planning (Silver 1997).[9] In 1914, a racial zoning ordinance was proposed in Birmingham while the *Buchanan* case was already moving through the court. A group of black attorneys convinced the Birmingham city council that they could face a costly legal battle if the Supreme Court ruled against Louisville's ordinance. To prevent this, and to appease white demands for segregation, the council chose instead to adopt a comprehensive zoning plan in 1926 that included racial designations for different city zones (Connerly 2005). Atlanta's 1922 revision of the zoning ordinance combined zoning categories of land use and building regulations with racial designations. For instance, the city's master zone map noted that "unless otherwise designated on this map, all areas designated as dwelling house districts are also class H1 height districts and white race districts." Other areas were designated as "colored district and an apartment house district" or "colored district and dwelling house district."[10] In 1929, the zoning code was again revised, this time including a prohibition on occupying a home on a street where the majority of residences were occupied by persons whom the resident was forbidden to marry by law (Meyer 2000). Eventually, the court ruled against these ordinances, and by the 1930s segregationists had dropped the racial designations in favor of comprehensive zoning.

As the court struck down plans that endorsed outright racial segregation, the case for other forms of zoning had been building. A series of

---

[8] The Court found that the ordinance improperly restricted the rights of property owners to dispose of property. It did not challenge the separate-but-equal doctrine that was in place as a result of the 1896 *Plessy v. Ferguson* decision.

[9] San Francisco was the first city to utilize a form of use- zoning for a racial purpose. In 1885, the city enacted a set of regulations for laundries operating in residential areas in an attempt to keep Chinese residents (who owned nearly all of the laundries and typically lived above them) from white neighborhoods. The law was invalidated by the Supreme Court in the 1886 case *Yick Wo v. Hopkins,* in which the Court found that a law that is race neutral on its face may still violate the Fourteenth Amendment if administered in a prejudicial manner.

[10] cityloci.files.wordpress.com/2014/07/6-atlanta-19291954.pdf

judicial decisions established the bounds of permissible approaches to regulating the uses and size of buildings. For instance, the court determined that exercise of police power (e.g., the authority to regulate behavior and enforce order) "must be reasonably adapted to the purpose of protecting some interest of the community" (C.C.S. 1925, p. 417), and that nuisance regulation and other use restrictions "must bear a substantial relation to the public health, safety, morals or general welfare" (Monchow 1928, p. 323).

In many places, the debate over the adoption of zoning centered on the trade-off between limiting the rights of land owners to do with their land as they pleased and the goal of maintaining the "health, safety, moral and general welfare of the community" (Proposed Zoning System 1923, p. 13). The legality of zoning was settled by the Supreme Court's decision in *Euclid v. Ambler Realty Company*. In this 1926 case, the Court determined that comprehensive zoning would not require cities to compensate owners for losses in prospective land values, and zoning ordinance spread rapidly after this ruling.

Zoning adoption was also propelled by the Republican-led federal government. In 1922, under the direction of Secretary Herbert Hoover, the Department of Commerce issued a template for state enabling laws in the Standard State Zoning Enabling Act. The act was published in 1924, and a revised edition was released in 1926. Thus, while Republicans tended to oppose zoning in the South, they were frequently the drivers elsewhere. In Boston, Republicans were shut out of city government by the powerful Democratic organization, leaving them to pursue zoning laws through the Massachusetts state legislature instead (Kennedy 1992, p. 113).

The arguments surrounding the adoption of comprehensive zoning were broad but imbued with municipal Progressivism's race and class prejudices (Bridges 1997; Trounstine 2008). Zoning supporters argued that it was the most effective mechanism to protect "private restrictions in deeds" and "make the established character of any locality permanent" (Objects of Zoning Explained 1923, p. 35). Comprehensive zoning supporters highlighted benefits such as the "adequate provision of light and air," "stabilization [sic] and protection of property values," "protection and maintenance of the home and home environment," "to apply the most up-to-date methods of sanitation and hygiene," "simplifying the problems of street traffic regulations," and the prevention of congestion (Holliday 1922, p. 217). By separating industrial, commercial, and residential uses into separate districts – each with standard regulations regarding the use, height, and area of buildings – zoning would make "every town, city or village a more orderly, convenient, economic and attractive place in which to live and work" (Holliday 1922, p. 218). One key to ensuring high property values and orderly living arrangements was the ability of zoning ordinances to prevent noxious uses from polluting residential neighborhoods (Fischel 2001). Apartment buildings constituted one such noxious use.

In *Euclid v. Ambler* (1926), Justice Sutherland explained that the apartment house is often a "mere parasite, constructed to take advantage of the open spaces and attractive surroundings ... interfering by their height and build with the free circulation of air and monopolizing the rays of the sun ... depriving children of the privilege of quiet and open spaces for play enjoyed by those in more favored localities ... until, finally, the residential character of the neighborhood and its desirability as a place of detached residences are utterly destroyed. Under these circumstances, apartment houses, which in a different environment would be not only entirely unobjectionable but highly desirable, come very near to being nuisances" (pp. 394–95).

In allowing the protection of single-family home neighborhoods, *Euclid* laid the groundwork for the long-term shift from a country segregated by race to one that became increasingly segregated by income. In the early twentieth century, race and income were so strongly overlapping that denying apartment buildings in a neighborhood of single-family homes would also largely prohibit blacks and many immigrants from residency. Making this point, Bruno Lasker (1920), editor of *Survey Magazine*, asked:

Why, in this country of democracy, is a city government, representative of all classes of the community, taking upon itself to legislate a majority of citizens – those who cannot afford to occupy a detached house of their own – out of the best located parts of the city area, practically always the part with the best aspect, best parks and streets, best supplied with municipal services and best cared for in every way? Why does it deliberately "segregate" the foreign-born who have not yet become sufficiently prosperous to buy or rent a home under building regulations which preclude the possibility of inexpensive development and construction? ("Unwalled Towns," *The Survey*, Volume 43, 1920, p. 677).

Lasker suggested that the answer to his question was the dominance of politics by wealthy property owners who sought to employ "public power for the purpose of protecting sectional interests" ("The Issue Restated," *The Survey*, Volume 44, 1920, p. 278). Segregation enforced via zoning was a means to accomplish this end. In cities like Chicago, Kansas City, and Los Angeles, some of the most powerful voices in support of zoning were homebuilders and real estate boards who stood to gain monetarily from segregation (Gotham 2000). Between 1924 and 1950, the National Association of Realtors' code of ethics stated, "A Realtor should never be instrumental in introducing into a neighborhood a character of property or occupancy, members of any race or nationality, or any individuals who presence will clearly be detrimental to property values in that neighborhood" (Article 34 of Part III).[11] This perspective led to general support for the power of land-use regulation and zoning among real estate interests. Writing in 1924, Herbert Flint, a town planner from Cleveland, Ohio, explained that zoning plans should be developed by local planning commissions, populated with "those well-positioned in real estate, the law, banking, manufacturing and transportation; also representative citizens who would safeguard the interests of the homeowners" (What a Zoning Law Is and What It Does 1924, p. 44).

UNDERSTANDING THE ADOPTION OF ZONING

With such wide-ranging positive effects for powerful interests, it is easy to see why zoning became so popular. Yet, by the close of the 1920s, many cities had not yet adopted zoning plans. I have argued that zoning was a tool that enabled elected officials to generate segregation, increase property values, and make it easier to target public goods to certain constituencies, and that it was successfully implemented where zoning supporters had political power. To provide more systematic evidence of this argument, I collected data on all of the cities that enacted zoning ordinances between 1900 and 1930. I gathered racial zoning information from several reports, including Rice (1968), Connerly (2005), Silver (1997), and numerous issues of the NAACP's *Crisis Magazine*. To encode general zoning plans, I drew on an article published in *The American City* by Norman Knauss in 1929, which listed the years that zoning ordinances were enacted. Knauss reports sending a survey to all municipalities with the authority to enact zoning. His list includes 768 municipalities that reported having an ordinance. I coded the city year in which zoning was enacted as a 1, and years leading up to that date as a 0. Cities exit the analysis once they enact zoning. Cities that were included in the census but had no zoning law by 1929 are coded 0 for the entire time period.

[11] www.scribd.com/document/86952803/1924-Code-of-Ethics-of-the-National-Association-of-REALTORS

Zoning is my dependent variable. To these data, I merged city spending and demographic data culled from the census (which are described in Chapter 3).

My primary independent variables are per capita total *expenditure* and *property taxes*. I log the total expenditure variable because the data have a strong rightward skew. I expect both variables to be positively correlated with zoning. Where spending and property taxes were higher, local officials would have a greater incentive to protect the existing distribution of public goods and the total tax revenue. I argue that schools are the most important public good for homeowners to protect. So, in an additional analysis, I replace property taxes with local expenditures on *education*. Early censuses did not distinguish between education spending by cities and by school districts, so this measure represents combined spending for all local government entities. It is highly correlated with the property tax measure, and so I add it separately. I include two additional political variables: the county-level *Republican presidential vote share* (linearly interpolated for nonelection years), and county-level *turnout* of age-eligible voters.[12] Republican vote share is a rough proxy for the degree of support for regulatory policy, of which zoning was an example. I expect that greater Republican support will be associated with a higher likelihood of implementing zoning – except in the South where the Republican Party was the party most allied with black interests. A range of voting restrictions was in place throughout the time period under consideration, and I include the turnout of the age-eligible population to capture the permissiveness of the electoral environment. This measure is preferable to including state-level laws, like the poll tax or literacy test, because it allows for substate variation in the electoral setting. Generally, higher turnout is associated with greater participation of the poor and people of color (Hajnal 2010), populations that both tended to be opposed to zoning plans and stood to lose from their implementation. Thus, I expect that where turnout was higher, the likelihood of enacting zoning was lower.

A wide range of alternative explanations for the adoption of zoning was proposed by contemporary observers and later analysts of the movement, many of which are correlated with the political factors I seek to test. Writing about racial segregation laws, Woodward (1955) argues that the economic depression at the end of the 1890s led to "aggression against

---

[12] This denominator includes men over the age of 21 until 1919, and both women and men over the age of 21 in 1920 and later elections.

the minority race" (p. 81). To account for this possibility, I include a measure of the share of the total population that was *unemployed*, linearly interpolated from the Census of Population and Housing. Fischel (2004) claims that zoning adoption followed the invention of trucks and buses, which made it feasible for businesses and apartment buildings to be built in residential and suburban areas, away from rail lines. I include per capita spending on *roads*, which includes street paving, street cleaning, and street lighting to capture differences in vehicular accessibility. In the "History of Zoning," Gordon Whitnall (1931) explains that "the practice of zoning began ... when the concentration of population in cities began to be pronounced" (p. 2). The "urge for zoning," he goes on to say, "has arisen from the desire and the necessity to bring some order out of the chaos that has resulted from the anarchistic development of our cities." I include the *10-year rate of change* in total population and population *density* (persons per acre) to capture urbanization. To measure threats of disease and conflagration, I include per capita spending on *health care* and *firefighting*.

As described above, contemporary supporters of segregation ordinances often asserted the protection of white, single-family neighborhoods as the primary goal. To measure social threats I include the share of the population that is *black*, *foreign born*, and *renting* their homes. To capture the presence of noxious industry that might be better contained in a zoned city, I include the share of the employed population working in *manufacturing*. According to Connerly (2005) industrialists also preferred to maintain segregated cities to dampen the threat of union organizing across racial lines.

Many scholars (e.g., Woodward 1955; Myrdal 1944; Blumer 1958) understand segregation as a mechanism to bolster hierarchical racial control, as social distance may preserve the relative status advantage of whites. For instance, Wade (1967) argues that segregation was "rooted in the white's need for discipline and deference," and that it "provided public control to replace dwindling private supervision of the master over his slave" (p. 278). If this is the case, cities with existing patterns of segregation should be most likely to institutionalize the practice. It is also possible, however, that cities with high levels of segregation would have had no need for legislation (see Silver 1997 on Roanoke). To adjudicate between these two possibilities, I include a dummy variable coded 1 if the city had *segregated schools*. This variable is encoded from Johnson (2015), who characterizes states as requiring segregation, permitting segregation, prohibiting segregation, or with no segregation statutes.

My variable is coded 1 for states that require segregation, 0.5 for states permitting segregation, and 0 for all others. Bobo, Kluegel, and Smith (1997) argue that the political institutionalization of Jim Crow ideology was driven by the needs of the southern economy, particularly the exploitation of black agricultural labor. On the other hand, Godsil (2006) suggests that whites with a significant stake in retaining a large black laboring class may have opposed racial zoning, as such ordinances might lead black workers to leave the city. To account for either possibility, I include the share of the workforce employed in the *agricultural sector*. If the theory put forth by Bobo et al. applies to zoning, we would expect a positive relationship between agricultural dominance and zoning. We'd expect the inverse if Godsil is correct.

My observations represent 4,293 city-years from 240 cities.[13] Column 1 shows the base model with no controls. Column 2 replaces property taxes with school spending. Column 3 includes all of the above-described controls. In Column 4, I change the dependent variable to focus on racial and comprehensive zoning. Here, the dependent variable is coded 1 when the city adopts either race zoning or comprehensive zoning, and is coded 0 otherwise. In this analysis, I present an interaction between Republican vote share and region to show how party politics differed in the South. These results are presented in Table 4.1, and summary statistics are available in Table A4.1 in the appendix.

Table 4.1 offers strong support for my claim that cities with greater public goods expenditures and more property tax revenues were more likely to implement zoning ordinances. With all else equal, shifting from the minimum per capita expenditure (about $4) to the maximum (about $476) changes the probability of adopting a zoning ordinance from 0.004 to 0.15. Similarly, cities with the lowest property taxes per capita (about $2) rarely adopted zoning ordinances, while those with the highest taxes ($67 per person) had around an 18% chance of implementing zoning.

The results for school spending are even more powerful. At the minimum education spending level (about $0.57 per capita), cities had 0 probability of adopting zoning. This rises to a 28% probability at the highest level of school spending ($21/capita). Where turnout of the voting age

---

[13] All spending data are inflation adjusted and linearly interpolated. Census data are linearly interpolated as well. I run logistic regressions with errors clustered by city. I include fixed effects for region, which means that these comparisons are all within the same area of the country. That is, the regressions analyze the effect of city expenditures on the adoption of zoning in each of four regions: West, North, Midwest, and South.

TABLE 4.1 *Effect of local political factors on zoning adoption, 1902–37*

	Model 1			Model 2			Model 3			Model 4 Race and comprehensive zoning only		
	β	Std. error	P > |z|	β	Std. error	P > |z|	β	Std. error	P > |z|	β	Std. error	P > |z|
Expenditure, $ per capita (logged)	0.787	0.295	0.008	0.728	0.272	0.008	1.221	0.313	0.000	1.329	0.363	0.000
Property taxes, $ per capita	0.052	0.014	0.000				0.047	0.018	0.009	0.071	0.020	0.000
Education expend, $ per capita				0.237	0.031	0.000						
Presidential turnout	-2.094	0.753	0.005	-2.576	0.807	0.001	-2.803	0.817	0.001	-2.268	0.989	0.022
Republican vote share	5.133	0.671	0.000	4.421	0.688	0.000	5.306	0.808	0.000	10.808	3.28	0.001
% Foreign born							-5.043	1.767	0.004	-6.076	1.921	0.002
% Black							-0.870	1.966	0.658	-2.344	2.214	0.290
Highways $ per capita							-0.280	0.143	0.051	-0.256	0.144	0.076
Health $ per capita							0.251	0.327	0.443	-0.305	0.475	0.520
Fire $ per capita							0.197	0.175	0.262	-0.063	0.171	0.715
Density							-0.004	0.014	0.768	-0.007	0.015	0.629
% Renters							1.970	1.537	0.200	5.573	1.689	0.001
% Employed in manufacturing							3.073	1.357	0.023	3.713	1.513	0.014
% Employed in agriculture							6.047	1.539	0.000	7.135	1.645	0.000

(continued)

TABLE 4.1 (continued)

	Model 1			Model 2			Model 3			Model 4 Race and comprehensive zoning only		
	β	Std. error	P > |z|	β	Std. error	P > |z|	β	Std. error	P > |z|	β	Std. error	P > |z|
10-year pop. growth rate							−1.477	0.622	0.018	−2.363	0.679	0.001
School segregation							1.108	0.667	0.097	1.015	0.705	0.150
% Unemployed							5.319	2.738	0.052	5.548	3.164	0.080
Midwest	−0.621	0.265	0.019	−0.200	0.275	0.467	−1.401	0.368	0.000	0.148	2.364	0.950
North	−0.883	0.187	0.000	−0.391	0.252	0.122	−1.620	0.436	0.000	1.748	2.304	0.448
South	0.313	0.335	0.349	0.917	0.393	0.020	−1.573	0.816	0.054	4.023	2.386	0.092
North *Rep. vote share										−4.418	3.549	0.213
Midwest *Rep. vote share										−0.400	3.631	0.912
South *Rep. vote share										−7.896	3.574	0.027
Constant	−8.436	1.28	0.000	−9.004	1.305	0.000	−8.522	1.586	0.000	−15.411	2.619	0.000
N	4,293			4,286			3,514			3,701		
R²	0.123			0.154			0.173			0.170		

Note: Logistic regressions; robust standard errors clustered by city; DV is adoption of zoning ordinance in given year.

population was higher, zoning was less likely to be adopted. This result supports Toll's (1969) claim that "the demand neither for zoning nor for planning had grown out of any widespread outcry in the cities of the United States" (p. 199). Zoning adoption appears to have been led by the Republican Party, except in the South, where Republican voting strength limited the likelihood of adoption of comprehensive and racial zoning ordinances.[14] In additional analyses, I find that dominance by a municipal reform organization (Trounstine 2008) also significantly increased the likelihood of zoning adoption. These data fit the historical narrative presented above well.

Many of the control variables suggest interesting patterns. For instance, there is no evidence that larger racial and ethnic minority populations drove zoning adoption. This point should be underscored: the initial adoption of zoning was not driven by the threat or presence of large numbers of immigrants or people of color. Nor did greater threats to public health or conflagration increase the likelihood of zoning. Contrary to Fischel's prediction, zoning was not more common in cities with more spending on roads. Economic factors appear to have played a more important role. Zoning adoption was more likely in cities with higher unemployment and with greater shares of the workforce employed in manufacturing and agriculture. It was also more likely in cities with more renters (particularly in the case of comprehensive and racial zoning). This conclusion is bolstered by a secondary analysis in which I add a measure of renter segregation in 1900 for 42 cities. Where renters were more segregated from homeowners, zoning was much more likely to be implemented. This finding suggests that homeowners were more supportive of zoning measures when they lived in more defined neighborhoods they wanted to protect. It is also clear that zoning ordinances were much more likely to be enacted in places that already had school segregation in place. Where segregated schools were the law, cities were more likely to adopt zoning. In additional analyses, I find that cities with marked segregation at the turn of the century, particularly in the South, were also more likely to adopt zoning. These results support the contention that zoning was a mechanism used to reinforce existing racial hierarchies. In the next section, I provide evidence that this was precisely its effect.

---

[14] Cities with reformed institutional structures were not more likely to adopt zoning. In fact, nonpartisan cities were somewhat less likely to adopt. This effect is largely driven by cities in the South, where nonpartisan laws may have advantaged Republicans.

ZONING GENERATES SEGREGATION

As Chapter 3 revealed, race and class segregation existed prior to the introduction of public policy measures that would separate residents and land uses. The history of private mechanisms producing segregation is well understood (e.g., Jones-Correa 2000; Meyer 2000; Burgess 1994). Blacks, immigrants, and the poor tended to live in areas that were removed from native, white, middle-class residents for a variety of reasons. Rabinowitz (1974) explains, "[S]ome of the housing segregation was voluntary: Negroes sought proximity to their jobs, welcomed the freedom from white surveillance, and enjoyed the company of other blacks" (p. 98). More important was "black poverty, which limited housing options," and "white pressures to keep blacks out of their neighborhoods" (p. 98). Restrictive covenants – clauses written into property deeds specifying restrictions on the use of the property – were widely used to bar undesirable neighbors from occupying properties starting in the late 1880s (Fogelson 2005). Mortgage discrimination and real estate steering were institutionalized in the early 1900s (Helper 1969). However, Hayward (2013) explains that the problem with relying on black poverty or restrictive covenants to maintain segregation was that the market was susceptible to encroachment, requiring coordination and constant vigilance against potential violators (Brooks 2002; McAdams 2008). Marshaling the power of municipal governments to restrict land use offered developers and property owners the promise of a protected investment.

Evidence indicates that zoning adopted in the early 1900s followed patterns created by private actors (Burgess 1994; Tretter 2012). Writing in 1929, M. T. Van Hecke explained, "[Z]oning programs are frequently influenced by restrictions in deeds. Where a very substantial area has been set aside for a high type use through the medium of deed restrictions, and that area is sufficiently large and geographically distinctive, zoning officials ordinarily recognize the character of the development and classify that section accordingly, so that the objectives of the statutory and deed restrictions are the same" (p. 420). Both supporters and opponents of zoning argued that the new laws would simply reinforce patterns produced by the market. Supporters, like Robert Whitten, creator of Atlanta's post-*Buchanan* comprehensive zoning plan, claimed that zoning would serve to lessen racial antagonism and economic loss by making the future of development more predictable, as it enforced existing segregation patterns (Toll 1969, p. 262). Opponents suggested that zoning would add unnecessary (and, some argued, unconstitutional) regulations while restrictive covenants were perfectly suited to the job of preserving neighborhoods and property (Racial Zoning by Private Contract 1928; Ellickson 1973; Hayward 2013; Denzau and Weingast 1982; Berry 2001).

Aside from freezing private decisions in public policy, zoning also had the potential to generate race and class segregation through implementation. Ostensibly, zoning is undertaken in the interest of the city as a whole, but this "depends entirely upon the way in which the work is done" (Van Hecke 1929, p. 414). This is because zoning, as an administrative task, requires innumerable small decisions by municipal officers who may, consciously or unconsciously, bias outcomes toward some groups and away from others. E. T. Hartman (1925) explains, "[C]hief among the problems are the granting or refusal of permits in accordance with the law, the decisions of the board of appeals in appealed cases, and appeals from either or both by interested parties" (pp. 162–63). As is true of any regulation, zoning serves political purposes (Denzau and Weingast 1982). The discretion inherent in applying zoning laws meant that local officials could deny permits to builders who sought to house nonwhite or poor families, and/or make exceptions for developers serving white and upper-class residents (Bayor 1996; Meyer 2000). Abrams (1955) explains, "[T]hose who build for whites can get a modification pro forma. But the moment an unwelcome group appears, the officials stand firm" (p. 210). Until 1949, the Federal Housing Administration officially encouraged the use of zoning to generate race and class segregation (Stearns 1962). Valuators were instructed that "the best artificial means of providing protection from adverse influences is through the medium of appropriate and well-drawn zoning ordinances" (Federal Housing Administration 1936, *Underwriting Manual*, Part II, paragraph 227). Zoning was understood to protect locations "against declines in value or desirability" (Section 306[2]) by preventing the "infiltration of business and industrial uses, lower class occupancy, and inharmonious racial groups" (paragraph 229).

As Berry (2001) notes, providing evidence of the effects of zoning on segregation has proved challenging because zoning is ubiquitous today.[15] But, as the first section of this chapter revealed, in the first decades of the twentieth century, zoning adoption was variable. I use this variation to

---

[15] Berry (2001) takes advantage of the lack of zoning laws in Houston and their presence in Dallas to show that private controls – particularly covenants – produce the same outcomes as zoning laws.

show that early zoning adopters became more segregated cities – even accounting for the degree of segregation that existed when zoning laws were adopted. My dependent variables in these analyses are *change* in the level of *race* and *class segregation* between about 1900 and 1970. More specifically, I subtract the level of segregation at the earliest point in my dataset from the 1970 segregation of non-Hispanic whites and renters. The earliest measures for racial segregation are from 1890, 1900, or 1910. For renter segregation, the earliest measure is 1900 for most cities.[16]

My primary independent variables are drawn from the data described for Table 4.1. I expect that racial segregation will be most closely linked to racial and comprehensive zoning (as the historical discussion indicated), while class segregation will be tied to all forms of zoning. In the analysis of racial segregation, my independent variable is a dummy variable noting whether a city adopted either a race-based or comprehensive zoning ordinance in the period between 1900 and 1930. These *early zoning adopters* are coded 1, and cities that did not adopt racial or comprehensive zoning are coded 0. In the analysis of renter segregation, cities are coded 1 if they adopted any type of zoning ordinance between 1900 and 1930, and 0 otherwise. I control for the *change in city population* between the earliest point of measurement for each city and 1970. I do not add any additional controls because I have very few observations over the long time span. Table 4.2 presents these results.

The results in Table 4.2 are striking: cities that were early adopters of zoning ordinances grew more segregated over the next fifty years, compared with cities that were not early adopters. Around 1900, cities that adopted zoning had very similar racial segregation rates to non-adopting cities (0.265 for adopters and 0.287 for non-adopters). By 1970, cities that adopted early zoning ordinances had segregation levels about 10 points higher on average (0.489, compared with 0.390). Zoning also exacerbated renter segregation. Cities that were not early adopters saw about a 4% increase in renter segregation between 1900 and 1970, compared with an 8% increase in cities with zoning.

Furthermore, zoning had significant consequences for property value inequality (as its promoters had hoped). To measure property value

---

[16] I have data in 1900 for forty-nine cities. To increase the number of usable observations, I include the level of renter segregation in 1940 for fourteen additional cities. The correlation between renter segregation in 1900 and 1940 is .8676. The results are nearly identical (though less precise), using only the data from 1900.

TABLE 4.2 *Zoning's effect on race and class segregation, 1900–70*

	Change in racial segregation 1900–70		Change in renter segregation 1900–70	
	β	P > |z|	β	P > |z|
Early zoning adopter	0.135	0.001	0.036	0.061
Change in city population	0.000	0.002	0.000	0.000
Constant	0.057	0.099	0.026	0.181
N	89		63	
R²	0.198		0.222	

Note: OLS regressions; DV is change in segregation between 1900 and 1970.

inequality, I created a *property value Gini index* built from median home values at the census tract level in 1970. Cities in which all census tracts have very similar 1970 median home values have a low score on this measure, while cities that witness inequality in property values from neighborhood to neighborhood have a high score. Regressing the property Gini on the dummy variable for early zoning adoption, including state fixed effects, produces a coefficient of 0.09 (SE = 0.003). Cities without early zoning had an average 1970 property Gini of 0.04, compared with 0.13 among early zoning adopters. This difference is greater than a standard deviation on the Gini index. Additionally, more segregated cities have much greater inequality in property values, and this pattern worsens over time. Zoning led to significantly more inequality in home values.

Of course, zoning was not the only mechanism available to local governments to promote race and class segregation. One of the most successful strategies of directing residential locations without force was the placement of segregated amenities. Austin, Texas, was a pioneer in this practice. The city's 1928 comprehensive zoning plan found that "the Negroes are present in small numbers, in practically all sections of the city, excepting the area just east of East Avenue and south of the City Cemetery. This area seems to be all Negro population" (Koch and Fowler 1928, p. 57). So, the plan recommended that "all facilities and conveniences be provided the negroes in this district, as an incentive to draw the negro population to this area." This strategy would "eliminate the necessity of duplication of white and black schools, white and black parks, and other duplicate facilities for this area" (Koch and Fowler 1928, p. 57). Soon after the adoption of the plan, Austin's city council pursued this approach, providing a park, school, and sewer connections for African

Americans only in this one section of the city. The council went on to duplicate the strategy for Latinos (Tretter 2012). In the 1940s and 1950s (as I discuss in Chapter 6), the siting of segregated public housing followed a similar pattern.

Another tactic cities used to shape minority residential patterns was the use of eminent domain and the placement of public improvements. Abrams (1955) reports, "Sites abutting Negro developments have been acquired for railroad stations, incinerator dumps, urban redevelopment, public housing projects, roads, and similar improvements. These improvements sometimes tend to cut off the minority area from the rest of the city and stem the expansion of its living space" (p. 212). Such decisions became increasingly frequent as the federal government provided funds for redevelopment. As I show in Chapter 6, cities that spent more urban renewal dollars also became more segregated.

Cities also engaged in several strategies that enhanced and protected private decisions generating segregation. Chief among these was the refusal to deploy police forces to protect blacks from white violence when blacks sought to buy or rent homes in white neighborhoods. In many places, police routinely prevented the poor and people of color from setting foot in wealthy white areas at all (Meyer 2000; Myrdal 1944).[17] In some places, city governments took action to aid the effectiveness of private deed restrictions (Hirsch 1983). For example, the mayor of Baltimore established a special Committee on Segregation to help coordinate deed restrictions in white neighborhoods. The committee included the city's building inspector, representatives from the health department, real estate agents, and neighborhood improvement association members (Meyer 2000).

CONCLUSION

This chapter has provided the first pieces of quantitative evidence, along with qualitative historical references, to suggest that local governments influenced patterns of segregation by taking into consideration public goods provision, as well as the wishes of wealthy business elites and white property-owning constituents. Local governments institutionalized

---

[17] As was the case with zoning, the use of police to support segregationists was variable. For instance, Meyer (2000) reports several examples of police providing support for black residents in New York City, St. Louis, and Baltimore.

prejudicial behavior and promoted segregation through the use of zoning ordinances.

Political elites enacted zoning ordinances to generate growth and stability in property values and control the distribution of public goods in the city. They justified zoning and segregation legislation with the argument that the poor and minorities had habits that were harmful to public health. These policy goals were promoted by politically influential residents: white property owners who sought to defend their neighborhoods and commercial areas from those who could decrease the value of their investments. Local governments benefited from rising property values, as well, in the form of increased tax receipts.

Zoning was used as a tool to generate segregation along race and class lines. When cities restricted land use and the location of specific buildings, this created areas that were homogenous, leading to the reinforcement of inequality and social divisions. In 1917, the Supreme Court ruled racial zoning ordinances unconstitutional. In response, many cities turned their attention to comprehensive zoning plans and other forms of zoning that did not make racial segregation an obvious goal. New comprehensive city plans were fueled by continuing race and class prejudice, and influenced the long-term shift from racial segregation to segregation by income level.

The historical evidence presented in this chapter support the argument that local politicians used zoning as a mechanism to control the distribution of public goods, as well as to create and maintain high property values in their cities. Zoning was implemented effectively in areas where those in favor of zoning had political power to turn racial and class prejudice into legislation. Cities that were early adopters of zoning ordinances grew to be 10% more segregated over the following fifty years than did cities that were not early adopters. The results also illustrate that zoning ordinances doubled the amount of renter segregation. In early adoption cities, property values would also become more unequal by 1970.

Local governments used zoning ordinances as a mechanism to institutionalize, existing racial hierarchies and prejudice, and this practice has had long-lasting effects. Cities could have used zoning to enhance the life of all residents, instead local government officials tended to cater to the private interests of their supporters. They utilized policy tools – including the placement of segregated amenities, public improvements, eminent domain, and redevelopment funds – to protect and increase property values. The consequence of these practices was a generation of long-standing race and class segregation.

5

Living on the Wrong Side of the Tracks

Inequality in Public Goods Provision, 1900–1940

Throughout the first decades of the twentieth century, neighborhoods became increasingly homogenous along both race and class lines. By 1940, white/nonwhite segregation had increased by an average of 63%, while renter segregation increased by 54%.[1] Chapter 4 provided evidence that cities pursued race and class segregation in an effort to protect property values and allow for the delivery of public goods to constituents with political power – namely land owners, realtors, developers, and white homeowners. Segregation served this goal because both local public goods and local political representation have a spatial component. While it is difficult to deny particular households access to sewer lines or a local public park, it is much easier to deny particular neighborhoods. Thus, as segregation geography shifted, so too did public goods inequalities.

Nothing about the existence of residential segregation necessitates inequality in service provision, but residential segregation does make it easier to produce inequalities in service, if that is what city officials prefer to do. In fact, early planning advocates often argued that taking race into account when developing city plans was the key to protecting black communities and ensuring that they received "all necessary municipal services – paving, city water, sewers, electricity, fire, and police protection" (Knight 1927, p. 137). While it was clear that public facilities would be separate, some planners insisted that there would be "equal opportunities and facilities" (Racial Zoning by Private Contract 1928,

---

[1] As described in detail in Chapter 3, renter segregation remained at lower levels than race segregation throughout this period.

p. 526). In most places, though, inequality was the norm, as "housing segregation ... permit[ted] any prejudice on the part of public officials to be freely vented on Negroes without hurting whites" (Myrdal 1944, p. 618).

As Abrams (1955) explains, "[T]hough often merged into a single neighborhood, the ghetto was not always a slum nor the slum always a ghetto ... the slum-ghetto was created when those of a single ethnic minority group lived not only in a ghetto but also in bad housing" (p. 76). Local governments contributed to the development of slum-ghettos by providing worse city services to neighborhoods populated predominantly by certain groups. Myrdal (1944) explains that the argument offered in support of these unequal allocations was the (erroneous) belief that whites paid all of the taxes, and were therefore entitled to all of the benefits. It followed that "whatever [Negroes] get is a charitable gift for which they should be grateful" (p. 336).

Over the long run, this pattern of government behavior contributed to the development of negative stereotypes about the people who lived in the slum-ghetto; for example, that racial minorities or the poor "*cause[d]* the deterioration of the places in which they live[d]" (Hayward 2013, p. 64, emphasis in original). This is what Glenn Loury (2002) refers to as a "politically consequential cognitive distortion," because the disadvantage observed among a group of people is assumed to be "intrinsic to that group when, in fact, that disadvantage is the product of a system of social interactions," which then leads observers to be opposed to policy solutions or systemic reform (p. 26). It was in the early part of the twentieth century that the foundation for continuing inequality in the twenty-first century was laid. By building inequality into the physical landscape, cities added "unprecedented durability and rigidity to previously fragile and fluid [social] arrangements" (Torres-Rouff 2013, p. 257).

In Chapter 4, I provided evidence that political power in the hands of opponents could slow or inhibit the enactment of such policies. A similar pattern existed with respect to the distribution of benefits. In many cities, political participation of lower socioeconomic status groups and racial minorities limited the degree to which public goods were allocated unequally. When these groups were able to assert political power through voting strength or in official positions, they received more benefits from municipal governments.

Here, I show that between 1900 and 1940, neighborhoods that were identifiably poor or inhabited by minorities were allocated lower-quality services, including road paving, public health efforts, and sewer extensions. I draw on detailed data from Atlanta, Birmingham, Baltimore, Boston, Chicago, and Philadelphia to provide this evidence. Where relevant, I discuss mobilization efforts on the part of underserved groups that limited the extent of unequal allocation. I also show that in the case of sewer connections, this inequality persisted into the latter half of the century. Where minorities and renters were more concentrated (e.g., in more segregated cities), they were less likely to be connected to public sewers in 1970, 1980, and 1990.

A common argument promoted in the literature, as early as the 1930s, was that class, not race, was the more important determinant of inequality. A 1932 report commissioned by President Hoover stated, "These conditions of Negro housing in our cities are not the result of any willful inhumanity on the part of our society. On the contrary, they merely emphasize the present shortcomings of our individualistic theory of housing ... The Negro's housing problem is part of the general problem of providing enough housing of acceptable standards for the low-income groups in our society" (Johnson 1932, p. viii). Myrdal (1944) also argued that "in the North there is little, if any, direct discrimination ... What inequality there is in the Negro's consumption of public services in the North is due mostly to poverty, lack of education, and other disabilities which he shares with other lower class persons in the region" (p. 335). Thus, the belief that blacks endured worse conditions than whites solely because of their lower socioeconomic status was widespread. As will be shown throughout this book, this was not true in either the historical or modern period, regardless of the measures used or the region studied. Race and class exert powerful, independent effects on distributional outcomes, and frequently class segregation was the product of efforts to achieve racial segregation.

JIM CROW AND PUBLIC GOODS INEQUALITIES

Until the mid-1950s (and in some places long after), many southern (and some northern) cities generated inequalities in public goods by segregating access directly, and then underfunding nonwhite services. Of all of the public goods residents sought to secure, none was as important as schooling. As of 1947, all southern states, along with Arizona, Indiana, Kansas, and New Mexico, required or allowed the direct segregation of schools (Wheildon 1947). Until the mid-1930s, about 75% of public school revenues were completely locally derived

(Snyder 1993).[2] In the postwar period and later, federal government contributions rose. According to the data described in Chapter 3, localities spent an average of $103 (in 2012 dollars) per capita on schooling in 1902, representing about 35% of total expenditures. Per capita spending rose dramatically over the next twenty-five years (to $203 in 1927), but not as quickly as other expenditures. In 1927, schooling represented about 31% of local budgets. Until (and in some places even long after) *Brown v. Board of Education* was decided in 1954, racial segregation in schools was generated directly – that is, residential segregation was not needed to ensure that whites and blacks attended different schools. This was true in both the North and South. As one observer explained, "[C]ontrary to the general impression, this doctrine [of segregated schools] is of Northern and not of Southern origin. It originated in fact in the Quaker state of Pennsylvania and the abolitionist state of Massachusetts, and; although it repudiates any implication of a superior and an inferior race and insists on equal opportunities and facilities" (Racial Zoning by Private Contract 1928, p. 526). Litwack (1961) found that "by the 1830s, statute or custom placed Negro children in separate schools in nearly every northern community" (p. 115).

In 1912, the census reported expenditure data on schools separated by race in forty communities. Unsurprisingly, white schools were better funded than black schools. I estimate that these cities spent about $4

---

[2] Technically, most schools in the United States are governed by approximately 13,000 independent, single-purpose governments called school districts, rather than by cities. Not only are the governments that provide schooling and garbage services different entities, with separate budgets and separately elected officials, they do not often share the same boundaries. Today, only about one-quarter of cities over 50,000 people have boundaries that are coterminous with a single school district (Fischel 2010). However, the 1902 Census Statistics of Cities reports that "[i]n most cities [included in the report] the schools are under the control of the city government, or of a school district, practically coterminous with the city" (p. 21). In his study of modern district boundaries, Fischel (2010) confirms that older cities are much more likely to have coterminous boundaries. It is for this reason that I include a discussion of schooling in this section. The figures cited in this paragraph combine revenue and expenditure for the municipality and the district as reported by the census. However, it is not proper, even during this early period, to think of expenditures on schooling as being exchangeable with expenditures on other types of services. That is, increasing school spending did not directly impact funds available for policing, although one might imagine a theoretical budget constraint that the voters could impose on all governments. Due to a lack of clarity, both theoretically and statistically, for the most part, I do not consider school district revenue and expenditure as part of the municipal budget in the remainder of this book.

per white resident and about $2.6 per black resident (in 1912 dollars).[3] However, the ratio of spending in black to white schools differed by region. While northern black schools were not, as the *Virginia Law Register* implied, equally funded, it was the case that the disparities were greater in the South. For cities in the Midwest, the ratio was 0.846, compared with 0.685 in the Northeast and 0.573 in the South.[4] School enrollments were also lower among black children. For the 1902–3 school year, about 56% of black children were enrolled in school in southern states, compared with 72% of white children (DuBois and Dill 1911, p. 24). In some places with substantial black populations, no black schools were provided at all (Dubois and Dill 1911). Indeed, as Rabinowitz (1978) has argued, segregated schools actually represented an improvement in many communities because the alternative was complete exclusion – not integration.

Black schools had fewer teachers per child, shorter school years, and inferior physical infrastructure (DuBois and Dill 1911; Myrdal 1944). Teacher pay also differed substantially. For instance, in 1908 Georgia, the average teacher salary for whites was $45.47 compared with $26.37 for blacks (DuBois and Dill 1911). Despite similarly sized populations of white and black schoolchildren, Atlanta provided only fifteen black grammar schools in 1920, compared with more than forty grammar schools for white children. But not all white schools were treated equally. Schools serving poor whites (largely immigrants) were also "older, less well equipped and often more overcrowded" (Myrdal 1944, p. 338).

Everywhere, blacks paid property taxes that were used to support white schools. Myrdal (1944) explains, "[W]henever the proportion of Negroes in the population is high, and the standard of Negro schools is kept well below that of white schools, the white educational system can derive substantial gains from segregation. Segregation makes discrimination possible; discrimination means lower expenditures for Negro schools, and the

---

[3] I used linear interpolation to estimate the total white and Negro population in each city in 1912. The figure represents the total amount of funding for white and Negro schools reported by the census, divided by my population estimates.

[4] It is important to note that these data only represent a fraction of the communities with black schools or significant numbers of black school-aged children (see discussion on p. 122 in Financial Statistics of Cities [1912]). The forty communities included in this special census report spent less overall on schooling compared with other communities (about $3.6 per capita vs. $4.8 per capita). Compared with data reported in DuBois and Dill (1911), these figures appear to understate the discrepancy in funding between black and white schools.

white population thus gets a vested interest in separation" (p. 341). In 1917, the Negro-at-Large series sought to catalogue reasons for the increasing northern migration among southern blacks. The results of the organization's survey were printed in the *Atlanta Independent*. The third most important reason (after unhappiness with Jim Crow laws and disenfranchisement) dealt with inequality in school funding. The survey stated, "At present Negroes pay their proportion of taxes directly and a big portion indirectly through their rents, yet Negro schools receive in some cases less than 30 per cent of their just desserts" (reported in West 1976, p. 14). Although we lack measures of school quality during this period, it is reasonable to assume that underfunding black schools negatively affected the ability of teachers to deliver an educational experience as good as in white schools. In turn, this may have affected whites' beliefs about black students' and black teachers' capabilities.

However, the extent of inequality differed from place to place. DuBois and Dill (1911) report that in Washington, DC, where blacks sat on the Board of Education and held an assistant superintendent position, "there is no discrimination in the pay of teachers or in the requirements for teachers or in the course of study laid down" (p. 32). St. Louis and Baltimore both offered black high schools during this period. A 1954 study of inequality in education funding in St. Louis found that black schools were underfunded given their enrollment, but the difference was only about 5% and teacher pay was nearly identical (Russell 1954). In Atlanta, an active chapter of the NAACP sought to mobilize black voting power to improve public services in general and schooling in particular. In spite of a series of restrictions on voting (e.g., the white primary, poll taxes, etc.), the organization was able to register enough blacks to vote to sway some elections (Bacote 1955). In 1919, black Atlantans organized to defeat a bond package that would have solely funded white schools. So, in 1921, sponsors of the referendum sought black support in exchange for a black high school (West 1976).

Schools were not the only public good directly segregated during this period. Recreational facilities like parks, swimming pools, bathhouses, and golf courses were also designated for white use only in many southern cities. In Atlanta, blacks had three recreational sites, compared with twenty-two for whites (Kruse 2005, p. 75). In 1954, the Atlanta Urban League calculated that whites had access to one acre of parkland for every 155 residents, compared with one acre of park land per every 1,020 black residents. As a result, black parks witnessed severe overcrowding and much more rapid degradation (Kruse 2005). Myrdal (1944) writes, "[V]irtually the whole range of ... publicly administered facilities ... are much poorer for Negroes than for whites" (p. 335). A graphic from President Truman's Report of the President's Committee on Civil Rights (Wilson 1947, p. 88) makes the point visibly (Figure 5.1).

Although Jim Crow legislation was efficient at producing racial inequality, it was not perfect. As the Truman Report explained, "Following the *Plessy* decision, the Supreme Court for many years enforced with a degree of leniency the rule that segregated facilities must be equal. Gradually, however, the Court became stricter about requiring a show of equality" (Wilson 1947, p. 82). Separate-but-equal facilities increased costs dramatically (Myrdal 1944). Additionally, some public goods could not be segregated directly. Troesken (2004) argues that "because most cities and towns installed their water and sewer systems before 1920, during an era of relatively low residential segregation, it was difficult to construct systems that underserved African Americans without also underserving whites" (p. 91). As a result, he finds that the delivery of clean water and sewage disposal had a dramatic effect on lowering black mortality in the South. Furthermore, in some places, white public opinion had already begun to develop in opposition to overt racial prejudice, and blacks were able to make headway in pursuing integration. Boston desegregated its schools in 1855 after sustained protest by blacks and abolitionist whites (Mabee 1968). By 1947, eighteen states had enacted antidiscrimination legislation prohibiting direct segregation (Konvitz 1947). Even some southern cities (e.g., Atlanta) witnessed a significant local voice in opposition to Jim Crow (Kruse 2005). As direct segregation became untenable and the black population of these cities expanded, residential segregation, generated and protected by municipal land-use laws, became the obvious solution. Furthermore, unlike Jim Crow legislation, residential segregation permitted the separation of poor residents from wealthy residents in addition to the separation of residents of color.

INEQUALITIES GENERATED THROUGH RESIDENTIAL SEGREGATION

When the nonwhite or poor community was segregated residentially, systematic denial of services was possible. A mid-century analysis of "American Negro, Puerto Rican, and Mexican" housing in large cities found that:

Garbage collections, building inspections, street maintenance, and other city services are less satisfactory than in other areas. The abnormal number of rat

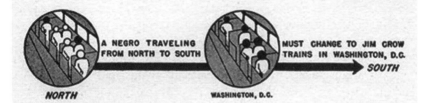

THE NATION'S CAPITAL
A SYMBOL OF FREEDOM AND EQUALITY?

A NEGRO TRAVELING FROM NORTH TO SOUTH

MUST CHANGE TO JIM CROW TRAINS IN WASHINGTON, D.C.

SOUTH

NORTH   WASHINGTON, D.C.

IF HE DECIDES TO REMAIN IN D. C. OVERNIGHT HE WILL FIND THAT:

HE CANNOT EAT IN A DOWNTOWN RESTAURANT

HE CANNOT ATTEND A DOWNTOWN MOVIE OR PLAY.

HE CANNOT SLEEP IN A DOWNTOWN HOTEL.

IF HE DECIDES TO STAY IN D. C.

HE USUALLY MUST FIND A HOME IN AN OVERCROWDED, SUB-STANDARD, SEGREGATED AREA:

NEGRO-OCCUPIED DWELLINGS

40% SUBSTANDARD

WHITE-OCCUPIED DWELLINGS

12% SUBSTANDARD

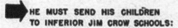

HE MUST SEND HIS CHILDREN TO INFERIOR JIM CROW SCHOOLS:

HE MUST ENTRUST HIS FAMILY'S HEALTH TO MEDICAL AGENCIES WHICH GIVE THEM INFERIOR SERVICES:

WHITES   NEGROES

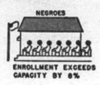

WHITE   NEGRO

CAPACITY EXCEEDS ENROLLMENT BY 27%

ENROLLMENT EXCEEDS CAPACITY BY 8%

●● HOSPITALS IN THE DISTRICT OF COLUMBIA EITHER DO NOT ADMIT NEGROES OR ADMIT THEM ON A SEGREGATED BASIS

FIGURE 5.1 Segregation in the nation's capital
Source: www.trumanlibrary.org/civilrights/srights2.htm

bites in Harlem, for example, may be ascribed not only to lack of proper upkeep but to the ready supply of uncollected garbage in the streets. Southern cities and some in the North omit street paving and sidewalks in Negro sections. In hills sections the residents try to fill gullies in the streets with broken masonry, worn-out linoleum, old tires, and other trash. (Abrams 1955, pp. 74–5)

In Birmingham, a committee of black professionals protested the city's 1923 segregation ordinance, saying that while blacks "would prefer to live to themselves," black neighborhoods, "are without the necessary sanitary arrangements, street improvements, lights, police protections, and the necessary comforts given other people in the municipality" (Connerly 2005, p. 44).

Among the most ambitious and expensive public goods that cities developed in the first decades of the twentieth century were the delivery of clean water and removal of waste through sewer systems. Sewer and water mains were built along major roads, and homes located along these lines would have had the opportunity to be connected to the system. Troesken (2004) suggests, in a detailed analysis of Savannah and Memphis, that segregation "facilitated efforts to underprovide African Americans with sewer and water systems" (p. 91). I build on Troesken's case studies by analyzing sewer and water extensions over time in four cities: Baltimore, Boston, Chicago, and Philadelphia. These cities all witnessed increases in racial and renter segregation between 1900 and 1940, and had data available on sewer construction.

To measure segregation, I calculated the H index (as described in Chapter 3) for Baltimore, Boston, Chicago, and Philadelphia using ward-level demographic data from the 1900, 1910, 1920, 1930, and 1940 Censuses of Population and Housing.[5] For racial segregation, I use whites and nonwhites as the groups in the calculation of the measure. For class segregation, I use renters and homeowners. Table 5.1 shows each city's H index in 1900 and 1940, measuring white/nonwhite segregation and renter/homeowner segregation.

My theory predicts that nonwhite and renter households would have been less likely to have access to water and sewer connections in more segregated cities. Unfortunately, I do not have the individual-level data to

---

[5] In order to make these scores comparable to modern data, I adjust the scores using a correction factor to make the ward-level estimates similar to the tract-level estimates used in later decades.

TABLE 5.1 *Segregation increased in the early twentieth century, H-Index 1900 & 1940*

	Race		Class	
	1900	1940	1900	1940
Baltimore	0.43	0.60	0.07	0.12
Boston	0.33	0.52	0.09	0.11
Chicago	0.46	0.84	0.09	0.15
Philadelphia	0.29	0.44	0.04	0.09

test this hypothesis. However, there are also aggregate implications of my theory: if elected officials were taking demographics into account when making decisions about where to build sewer extensions, we should witness an interactive effect between segregation and the demographics of a neighborhood. As segregation increases, it should be the case that the share of residents who are nonwhite or renters should have a more powerful, negative effect on new sewer extensions.

The data I use for this analysis were provided by the Center for Population Economics at the University of Chicago in the Historical Urban Ecological dataset (which is really a collection of many different datasets and maps). The dataset (Costa and Fogel 2015) includes ward boundaries for the four cities, listed earlier, between 1900 and 1930, and also includes a map of each city's sewer system. The sewer map includes the year in which different segments of the system were built. Using ArcGIS, I created counts of sewer segments in each decade for each ward and combined these counts with ward-level data from the Census of Population and Housing.

Observations are arranged by ward-census year. That is, each observation represents one ward in a city in a single year. The dependent variable in the analysis is the *total new segments* built in each ward before the next census. The key independent variables are the share of each ward's total population that is *black* and the share of occupied housing units that were *rented* (as opposed to owned). These demographic variables are interacted with each city's *H index of segregation* (for race and class, respectively) in a given census year.

I control for the *total new segments* built in the city in each decade to account for the slackening pace of sewer development over time. I include the *total segments* built in the ward at the completion of the sewer system to account for the variation in sewer needs across wards. I also control for the proportion of those total segments that were built at the beginning of each decade in the variable *percent built*. Finally, I account for the share of the ward population that is *foreign born* to account for the possibility that city governments were providing fewer benefits to immigrant neighborhoods (which would have correlated with renter neighborhoods).

An important alternative (and undoubtedly true) explanation to account for is that black and renting residents chose housing that lacked public services because it was less expensive. I do this by taking advantage of time. I explore the pattern of sewer line extensions in each decade between 1900 and 1940 given the racial makeup of each ward at the beginning of the decade. For instance, the total number of extensions built between 1900 and 1910 is regressed on the share of the ward that was black and the share that were renters in 1900. Because the dependent variable is a count of sewer segments, I fit a Poisson regression.

I was able to obtain data at the ward-level detailing racial makeup for every decade between 1900 and 1940, but data on renters is only available for 1900 and 1940. Because ward boundaries changed dramatically in some cities between these years, interpolation is not possible. Additionally, the census did not tabulate data on renters in 1940 for the city of Chicago. As a result, adding the proportion of renters to the models significantly decreases the number of observations. For this reason, I present the model without and with the proportion of renters.

The results, presented in Table 5.2, reveal a powerful negative relationship between the share of the ward that was black or renting and new sewer extensions in more segregated cities.

The data indicate that in more segregated cities, heavily black and renter wards were unlikely to receive new sewer lines. Figure 5.2 plots the predicted number of new sewer segments across the full range of black and renter population shares for the least and most segregated city-years in the dataset. The graph in the top right makes it clear that majority black wards see no additional investment in their sewer systems in highly segregated cities. A similar pattern exists for wards with increasingly large renter populations in cities that were segregated by class. In these neighborhoods, poorer residents and residents of color were unlikely to benefit from sewer expansion.

In integrated cities, however, the reverse is true: larger black and (to a more limited extent) renter populations increase sewer line extensions. This may seem puzzling at first glance – but it is not. Troesken (2004)

TABLE 5.2 *Segregation decreased access to sewers for blacks and renters, 1900–40*

	β	Std. Error	P > |t|	β	Std. Error	P > |t|
% Black *racial segregation	−21.643	1.347	0.000	−11.811	2.002	0.000
% Black	9.429	0.676	0.000	6.713	0.925	0.000
Racial segregation	1.874	0.082	0.000	−4.645	0.424	0.000
% Renters*renter segregation				−48.256	8.570	0.000
% Renters				3.654	0.765	0.000
Renter segregation				58.505	6.510	0.000
Total new segments in city	0.000	0.000	0.000	0.001	0.000	0.000
Total segments in city	0.000	0.000	0.000	0.000	0.000	0.000
% Built	−3.275	0.044	0.000	−2.740	0.062	0.000
% Foreign born	0.074	0.097	0.442	−0.411	0.198	0.038
Constant	2.611	0.048	0.000	0.651	0.521	0.211
N	541			271		
Pseudo R²	0.788			0.748		

Note: Poisson Regression; DV is number of sewer extensions added to ward in proceeding decade.

explains that the reason for this apparent generosity was self-preservation. He says:

[D]iscrimination in this arena was costly to white politicians and voters in at least three ways. First, given the networked structure of these systems it was difficult to deny service to African-American households and neighborhoods without also denying service to white households and neighborhoods … Second, in a world where blacks and whites lived in close proximity, "sewers for everyone" was an aesthetically sound strategy. Third, failing to install water and sewer mains in black neighborhoods increased the risk of diseases spreading from black neighborhoods to white ones. (pp. 9–10)

As a result, to the extent that sewer systems were built prior to rising segregation, variation in sewer system service did not disproportionately affect any demographic group. In Richmond, Virginia, neighborhood segregation actually declined between 1890 and 1930, and one contemporary observer wrote, "With the completion of the 1925 program practically the whole of Richmond was sewered and supplied with city water" (Knight 1927, p. 51).

In other cities, organized political action on the part of nonwhites and the poor mitigated inequalities. Bond passage in Atlanta required approval

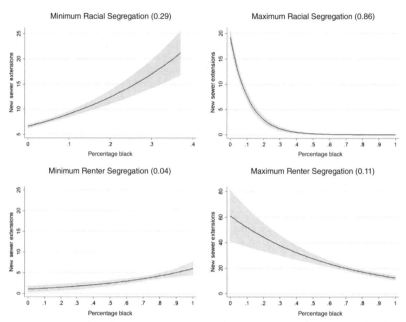

FIGURE 5.2 Predicted sewer extensions at the minimum and maximum level of segregation, 1900–40

of two-thirds of votes cast, and the two-thirds majority had to constitute a majority of registered voters; by simply registering and not turning out, African Americans could ensure defeat at the polls (West 1976; Bayor 1996). In 1919, black voters defeated a million-dollar bond package that was to provide "for improvement of waterworks, a motorized fire department, erection of a museum at cyclorama, and the construction of a crematory with electricity generating facilities," after being told that "blacks would receive no benefits from the measures" (West 1976, p. 13). When a new package was submitted to voters in 1921, it included $2,850,000 for water works and $750,000 for the viaduct (Qualify and Vote for Bonds 1921, p. 4). The mayor promised to appoint a special commission of black residents to advise the Bond Commission regarding the distribution of the funds (Qualify and Vote for Bonds 1921, p. 4). On election day, Atlanta's "colored citizens … voted for every improvement named on the ballot" (Qualify and Vote for Bonds 1921, p. 4).

In many cities, sewers were built at the behest of property owners and developers. This was the situation in Birmingham and Los Angeles. In cities with this type of process, landowners played a crucial role in the eventual sewer map. Because very few landowners were people of color, blacks in Birmingham and Mexican and Chinese residents in Los Angeles lacked the opportunity to request sewer extensions or connections. While it might seem reasonable to explain inequality in access as the result of these economic differences, cities had other means by which to compel development. In Birmingham, sanitation and building codes were ignored in black neighborhoods (Connerly 2005), and in Los Angeles the city council ordered sewers to be built at the "cost and expense of the several parties owning property along [one] route." However, they declined to compel sewer building in Sonoratown or Chinatown (Torres-Rouff 2013, p. 224; quoting Los Angeles City Council minutes, April 4, 1873). Because most Mexican and Chinese residents were renters, this refusal was a significant benefit extended to their landlords. As a result, in both cities, the absence of sewer and water service was concentrated in minority neighborhoods.

In this next section, I ask whether this unequal pattern of sewer development continued to affect minority and renting residents in the latter half of the twentieth century. In order to investigate this question, I draw on the GeoLytics Neighborhood Change Database, which matches and normalizes census tract boundaries between 1970 and 1990. This normalization allows for direct comparison of tract attributes across time. I use this database to construct the race and renter H index (as described in Chapter 3) for 4,566 incorporated municipalities and 800 unincorporated county areas.

The dependent variable in my analysis is the share of housing units in a given census tract that is connected to *public sewers*. My primary independent variables, similar to the previous analysis, are the share of the tract population that is *nonwhite*, and the share of households that are *renters*. These variables are interacted with each city's H index *of segregation* (for race and renters, respectively) in each census year. I control for the proportion of *wealthy families* in the tract (those earning incomes above the ninetieth percentile for a given census year: $15,000 in 1970, $35,000 in 1980, $75,000 in 1990), the total *city population*, and the total number of families connected to *public sewers* in the city. I include fixed effects for region and cluster the errors by city. The results are presented in Table 5.3 (summary statistics are in Table A3.2, available in the appendix).

TABLE 5.3 *Nonwhite and renter sewer access in segregated cities, 1970–90*

	β	Std. Error	P > |t|
% Nonwhite*racial segregation	−0.261	0.069	0.000
% Nonwhite	0.164	0.037	0.000
Racial segregation	0.122	0.035	0.000
% Renters*renter segregation	−2.643	0.854	0.002
% Renters	0.851	0.228	0.000
Renter segregation	1.631	0.418	0.000
% Wealthy	0.254	0.105	0.016
City population	0.000	0.000	0.000
City public sewer connections	0.000	0.000	0.000
Midwest	0.053	0.013	0.000
South	−0.040	0.012	0.001
West	0.017	0.012	0.171
Constant	0.327	0.161	0.042
N	146,102		
R²	0.327		

Note: OLS regression, DV is % of households in census tract connected to public sewer.

As was the case in the early period, between 1970 and 1990 renters and nonwhite residents continued to have inferior sewer access in more segregated cities. Of course, today, overall sewer access is high; the median census tract has 97% of homes connected to public sewers. The point demonstrated by this analysis is that both in the past and today, lack of access to public sewers is disproportionately concentrated among minority and renting residents.

Delivery of other public goods followed a similar pattern to sewer development. In 1900, 8,000 automobiles were registered in the United States; by 1940 the figure was 27.5 million.[6] But during this same period, actual spending on roads increased very little and dropped as a share of total budgets.[7] This meant that road-paving distribution was an intensely political decision, and different areas of the city were treated differently. One study of four Virginia cities reported "a general lack of paving in the Negro residential areas" (Knight 1927, p. 53). In Los Angeles, Torres-Rouff

---

[6] www.fhwa.dot.gov/ohim/summary95/mv200.pdf

[7] In a sample of eighty-four cities for which I was able to obtain data between 1902 and 1937, mean per capita road spending was $44 in 1902 (in 1912 dollars) and $43 in 1937. It reached a high of $51 in 1932. Road spending represented about 13% of city budgets in 1902 and about 8% in 1937.

(2013) explains, "[M]any paved streets ran through the Anglo residential neighborhoods and commercial center but abruptly yielded to dirt as soon as they crossed into Sonoratown and Chinatown" (p. 226). A 1958 study of Birmingham analyzed white and black blocks in a single working-class neighborhood, and found that about a third of the black blocks had unpaved streets on three or four sides, compared with only 6% of white blocks (Connerly 2005, p. 31).

As described in Chapter 1, mortality rates in cities during this time period, particularly the early years, were high. A budding public health movement sought to utilize government funds to address disease contraction and death. Cities created new public health departments, passed regulations regarding the storage and transport of milk, sent inspectors to stores and dairies, and engaged in large-scale fumigation efforts. In all of these activities, white and homeowner neighborhoods were treated more protectively than neighborhoods inhabited by people of color and renters. In 1915, the nationwide infant mortality rate was 57% higher among nonwhites than whites. One study of four southern cities determined that nearly one of every two black babies died (Meckel 1990, p. 142). Even still, black infants were "almost entirely" excluded from the "early part of the infant welfare campaign," (Meckel 1990, p. 142). A 1914 analysis of Baltimore's public health department by the US Surgeon General found that regulations were not enforced in the poorer parts of town. The report explained:

An inspection was made by me of the stores selling milk in two of the districts of the city. One was located on the outskirts of the city in a good neighborhood ... In every store the milk was sold in unbroken packages, was kept in a separate compartment of a large refrigerator and the conditions were as good as could be expected ... The other district visited was of a different type altogether. It was located in the slums, among the foreign population. Here all the milk was sold in bulk under the most insanitary conditions. To make regulations here is practically hopeless. There are but three things to be done – stop the sale of milk in such places, establish a municipally controlled dairy within the district, or prohibit the sale of anything but bottled milk in original packages. (Fox 1914, p. 37)

In 1901, the Baltimore Health Department (reported in HUE dataset by Costa and Fogel 2015) reported an assessment of water quality in each ward. Only one ward had water that was classified as "very muddy" (as opposed to clear, fairly clear, cloudy, or muddy). That one ward was 52% black. The same ward also had the lowest level of chlorination in the entire city. In fact, there was a powerful negative relationship between chlorine parts per million and the share of black residents in a ward. Figure 5.3 provides a scatter plot of the data.

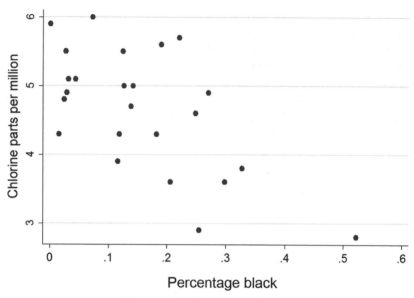

FIGURE 5.3 Chlorination of water in Baltimore wards, 1901

Figure 5.3 reveals that the wards where most of Baltimore's black residents lived had water that was much less likely to be treated with chlorine by the city government. A lack of access to chlorinated water was a direct cause of higher mortality rates in cities during this time period (Cutler and Miller 2006), and it seems reasonable to assume that it was also a direct cause of higher mortality rates in Baltimore's black neighborhoods.

Not only were services provided differentially, but many cities engaged in a practice Rabin (1990) calls expulsive zoning: the placement of negative uses in minority neighborhoods. Kruse (2005) explains that as neighborhoods transitioned from white to black, city officials would assume that property values would fall and the area would become a slum. "Accordingly, planners and zoning committees lowered their standards for the region and began approving projects they would have routinely rejected if the residents were still white" (Kruse 2005, p. 74). A 1932 analysis of housing in one New Orleans neighborhood reported, "The superintendent of the public school system used to live in this area but the white residents began to move out and then the city built a garbage incinerator over here, and all of the best whites moved out and the

Negroes moved in with the poor whites" (Johnson 1932, p. 19). In Birmingham, city planners zoned black neighborhoods in floodplains and in industrial areas (Connerly 2005). Myrdal (1944) reports that it was common to ignore criminal activity in black areas. As Muhammad (2011) explains, municipal authorities allowed crime to flourish in black neighborhoods as a service to white politicians and constituents. Doing so allowed whites access to prostitution, gambling, illicit alcohol, and drugs while protecting white neighborhoods from the criminality. Because such operations were "mostly owned, partially operated, and unofficially regulated by a largely white power structure" (Muhammad 2011 p. 227), the benefits were captured by whites, while the negative externalities of vice were borne nearly exclusively by blacks. These strategies created conditions that led later generations of planners to denote black areas as blighted slums, thus enabling the expulsion of blacks from these neighborhoods in redevelopment projects.

The historical record indicates that lower levels of segregation and more political power in the hands of blacks and the poor could mitigate such inequalities. Throughout the late 1880s, blacks held significant bargaining power in Atlanta city politics. Blacks were appointed to the nominating committees for city elected offices, and black votes were courted with promises of a black fire company, schools for black children, and street paving (Bacote 1955). After the white primary was struck down in 1946, blacks gained even more leverage in Atlanta politics. Black leaders had been pressing the city government for years to hire black police officers, "hoping to solve the problems caused by both the absence and the presence of white policemen" (Kruse 2005, p. 33), but their requests were ignored until they could marshal votes in city elections. In 1948, eight black patrolmen were hired (although they were only allowed to patrol black neighborhoods and could not arrest whites).

In Birmingham, many black neighborhoods formed active, dues-paying civic leagues to lobby the city government for improved services. While they won a few small victories (the first city-owned park for blacks, some street paving and lighting, fire hydrant installation, sewer extensions, and gas lines), they were mostly met with staunch resistance from the all-white government. One organization, the Harriman Park Civic League, waited for four months to get an appointment with the public safety commissioner, Bull Connor. When the meeting finally occurred, Connor literally turned his back on the presentation (Connerly 2005, p. 221). In the 1960s and early 1970s, as political power began to shift toward black residents, many of the requests brought by the civic leagues were finally addressed.

In Boston, Progressive Reformers attracted public support and won a series of institutional reforms between 1903 and 1913. Nonpartisan neighborhood organizations arose as powerful voices in municipal politics. The result was the consolidation of political power in the hands of middle-class homeowners (Connolly 2009) at the expense of working-class, white, ethnic immigrant constituencies, like the Irish. However, the city was fairly integrated residentially along both ethnic and class lines during these years; and so, while political power shifted hands and the agenda changed, when neighborhoods won improvements like street cleaning and repair, playgrounds, libraries, or improved police protection, they benefited all residents in the immediate vicinity, not just those with political power.[8]

Between 1914 and 1950, Boston was governed (on and off) by a staunch advocate of the poor and working classes: James Michael Curley. Curley was a machine-style politician, who was never able to consolidate a dominant citywide organization (Erie 1988). Many histories of this period note Curley's lavish attention to the city's "working-class, ethnic neighborhoods" (Connolly 2009, p. 146). But the census data from the period reveal that even the most heavily ethnic wards were actually fairly mixed. In 1930, for instance, wards ranged from 21% foreign born to 42%, and no ward housed more than 11% of the total foreign-born population. So, when Curley "ordered loans to clean and pave local streets, build a playground and bathhouse, and improve sewer and water serves" (Connolly 2009, p. 166) in the North End in order to woo Italian votes, non-Italian residents also benefited.[9]

Yet, in many cities, even when residents and activists mobilized to lessen inequalities, "segregation [became] the cornerstone of the elaborate structure of discrimination against some American citizens" (Hurwitz 1949, p. 128). Hayward (2013) explains that the "black ghetto [was] subjected to systematic disinvestment, while collective investments in new residential and commercial structures, and in 'public amenities,' such as parks and athletic facilities and well-built and well-equipped schools, [were] disproportionately channeled to places that were, first legally, then practically, restricted to those constructed as white" (p. 63). These

---

[8] Connolly (2009) argues that this shift in political power altered the agenda of city politics toward neighborhood improvement and away from issues that the working class prioritized, like union protections and wage and pension increases (see pages 115–20), while also decreasing participation among working-class voters.

[9] One scholar (Puleo 1994) estimates that in 1920, 95% of the North End population was Italian (p. 116). Without detailed data regarding the exact location of Curley's benefits, it is impossible to know the degree to which they served other populations.

inequalities contributed to a growing collective sense of whiteness and homeowner identity on the one hand (Sugrue 1996; Hayward 2013), and on the other hand, the hardening of stereotypes about the suitability of poor and nonwhite residents as neighbors.

White homeowners believed that individuals who shared demographic characteristics with those who lived in disinvested neighborhoods would bring slum conditions with them wherever they lived. In 1951 and 1953, Rose Helper conducted forty interviews with real estate agents in New York City and Chicago to learn about the "reasons for excluding Negroes from white residential areas" (Helper 1969, p. 18). She reported that the agents believed that "[white people] fear that their neighborhood will deteriorate if Negroes come because of their manner of living in other areas: they associate Negroes with the undesirable slum (dirt, noise, squalor, stealing, vice), something to be avoided if possible" (p. 79). Helper found that a fear of school integration (and the potential for a decline in school quality) was the main reason that whites refused to entertain the possibility of black neighbors. She concludes that "not the broker but the property owner or tenant – that is, the white American citizen and his conception of Negroes – is the basic problem in housing discrimination" (p. 294). Thus, to promote residential and school homogeneity, white homeowners sought continued governmental protection of their neighborhoods. Over the next several decades, they succeeded in this fight.

CONCLUSION

Between 1900 and 1940, America's cities became increasingly segregated along race and class lines. While renters and homeowners both became more concentrated, the most dramatic changes in segregation occurred between whites and people of color. These changes in residential living patterns changed the distribution of public goods. As cities became modern service providers, the allocation of public goods was intensely political. In the earliest years, when no neighborhoods benefited from paved streets or clean water, health and cleanliness did not differ dramatically from place to place. But as streets became sewered, paved, and lit, and as inspectors enforced building, sanitation, and health codes, some neighborhoods reaped the benefits while others "continued to contend with dirt roads and open cesspools" (Torres-Rouff 2013, p. 227). As Torres-Rouff (2013) explains, "[T]hese decisions produced a city that physically imposed inequality on its citizens" (p. 227). Such choices would be consequential for the future as inhabitants of these neighborhoods came to be associated with poor living conditions. Today, evidence indicates that segregation is maintained by white homeowners' willingness and ability to pay a premium to live among white, educated neighbors (Cutler, Glaeser, and Vigdor 1999). That they have the opportunity to do so is dictated by past and present land-use regulations generated by city governments.

6

Cracks in the Foundation

Losing Control over Protected Neighborhoods

By 1940, segregation patterns in cities were well established. The boundaries of minority neighborhoods were clearly defined and white prejudice against nonwhite neighbors was entrenched. As one Chicago realtor explained, "[Our] firm has a policy where they won't sell to a Negro in an area where Negroes are not resident ... the general public ... is not willing to accept the Negro as a neighbor" (Helper 1969, p. 41). During the buildup of the war effort in the early 1940s, massive demographic changes rippled through the nation. A great migration of African Americans moved to the North and West, and the war and agricultural industries attracted Latinos to cities and farms in the Southwest (Weaver 1948; McWilliams 1964). In the postwar period, swelling urban populations, along with preexisting segregation in housing markets, led to extreme overcrowding and slum conditions in poor and minority neighborhoods. In response, city governments utilized policy instruments like urban renewal and the placement of public housing to prevent minority and poor neighborhoods from expanding into white areas, and to protect property values for white homeowners. At the same time, tumultuous battles over racial integration (of neighborhoods, schools, buses, lunch counters, unions, etc.), the rising civil rights movement, and the passage of the Voting Rights Act threatened to undermine white homeowners' control of the political system, distribution of city services, and ability to police the borders of their neighborhoods (Sugrue 1996; Kruse 2005; Self 2003).

A great deal of insightful, detailed historical research studying the civil rights movement, segregation, and suburbanization has been written about the postwar period, and this chapter does not attempt to retell what we already know. Instead, here, and also in Chapter 8, I focus on the role of city politics in the generation of neighborhood segregation and suburban-ization. An important contribution of these chapters is to explore why, if the drivers of segregation and suburbanization are similar, do white home-owners choose one avenue of separation over another? Political control plays an essential role. When white homeowners lost the power to guard their neighborhoods and dictate municipal policy and public goods distri-bution, different patterns of segregation became attractive. First, I show that urban renewal was linked to increased race and class segregation in the postwar period. Then, I demonstrate that whites in racially segregated cities witnessed increasing threats to their political power, both electorally and, more specifically, with regard to housing policy. Finally, I provide evidence that federal pressures to desegregate public schools led to an increase in segregated neighborhoods, as whites sought to utilize residential segrega-tion to produce school homogeneity.

URBAN RENEWAL AND SEGREGATION

In 1932, more than 80% of local revenues came from property taxes. By the end of that year, nearly 750 homes would be foreclosed every day (Gotham 2000). City government revenue plummeted. Mayors sought relief from the federal government, organizing as the National Conference of Mayors and testifying in hearing after hearing about the dire need for federal subsidy (Ogorzalek 2018). As part of its response, Congress enacted housing legislation. With its first foray into this area, the 1934 Housing Act and establishment of the Federal Housing Administration (FHA), Congress had multiple goals: the reemployment of the construction industry, the shoring up of the financial sector, and the stimulation of home ownership. But these policies were also spurred by a commitment to residential segre-gation. As Gotham (2000) details, the major authors of the proposals under consideration were "leading officials in the real estate and lending industries" (p. 303), most of whom, by this time, had come to view race and class segregation as a stabilizer of property values and, therefore, made segregation a conscious goal of these policies. Thus, it should not be surprising that the FHA played a major role in the institutionalization of segregation, particularly in the suburbs throughout the postwar period (Gelfand 1975; Jackson 1987; Massey and Denton 1998).

However, the next piece of federal housing legislation to be enacted was a conscious turn away from these forces. The 1937 Wagner-Steagall Hous-ing Act sought to "provide financial assistance to the States and political subdivisions thereof for the elimination of unsafe and insanitary housing conditions, for the eradication of slums, for the provision of decent, safe, and sanitary dwellings for families of low income, and for the reduction of unemployment and the stimulation of business activity" (Wagner-Steagall Act 1937). To achieve these goals, the act established the United States Housing Authority (USHA) to "make grants and loans to local public housing authorities, to enable them to build, own, and operate housing projects for families of low income" and, importantly, to clear slums (Robbins 1937, p. 4). As such, the Wagner Act served as the first congressional effort to assist in what is now commonly referred to as "urban renewal" – local efforts to address the ravages of time, revitalizing the "urban built environment" (Avila and Rose 2009, p. 339).

Whereas the establishment of the FHA and passage of the 1934 Housing Act were aimed at assisting those who could afford housing in the private market, the Wagner-Steagall Act sought to "provide decent, safe and sanitary housing for that large group of our population who [could not] afford to pay enough to cause private capital to supply their housing needs" (Brabner-Smith 1937, p. 681). In addition to focusing on low-income residents, the Wagner Act also understood that "any realistic approach to clearing slums and rehousing low income families would necessarily include a large number of Negroes as tenants" (Weaver 1940, p. 150). Thus, the USHA created an Office of Race Relations directed by an African American, Harvard-trained economist, Dr. Robert C. Weaver (Meyer 2000).[1] Weaver's office was charged with reviewing applications for federal funds to ensure that "sound racial policy may be reflected in all projects" (Weaver 1940, p. 155). In a 1968 interview, Weaver recalled:

The Public Housing Program was perhaps one of the outstanding examples of equity of treatment as between white and black Americans ... In public housing we not only got approximately a third, as I recall, at one time of the units available to nonwhites – most of them were Negroes – we also got Negro managers, which was unheard of in places like Atlanta and Memphis and Jacksonville and in Miami. We were able in the North to get projects which were open to both Negroes and whites. This required some doing as early as 1937 to '38. These were the exceptions rather than the rules but they did occur. (Weaver Oral History 1968, p. 9)[2]

---

[1] Dr. Weaver was the first African American to earn an economics PhD at Harvard. He went on to serve as the first black cabinet member, as the Secretary of Housing and Urban Development.

[2] Available at http://transition.lbjlibrary.org/files/original/6404ca478ed6c3848eedaaf380a cdb45.pdf

Reviewing Dr. Weaver's tenure, *The Crisis* (the official publication of the NAACP) reported, "As a result of his efforts and the support of USHA officials, a more fair and equitable racial policy now exists in USHA than in any other branch of the Federal Government. On the basis of need, Negroes are enjoying equitable benefits from public housing" (National Defense Labor Problems 1940, p. 319).

However, despite the fact that "The United States Housing Authority ... tried to set ... desirable precedents in the field of practical racial relations" (Weaver 1940, p. 155), the seeds of segregation were embedded in the design of urban renewal – planted by the coalition that brought it to fruition.

The most important of these seeds was local control. J. W. Brabner-Smith, counsel for the Federal Housing Administration, explained in 1937 that the "problem is essentially local and should be decentralized as far as possible" (p. 681). Allowing local governments to decide what land would be cleared and where new housing would be built virtually guaranteed the continuation and exacerbation of race and class segregation, because white homeowners and land-oriented businesses controlled city governments and planning commissions and opposed residential integration along either race or class lines. Further, these interests quickly moved to ensure control of the new housing and renewal authorities created to direct and manage the process (Hirsch 1983; Sugrue 1996; Gotham 2001). Sugrue (1996) explains, "[L]ocal governments had the final say over the expenditure of federal funds, the location of projects, and the type constructed" (p. 60).

In Chapter 5, I provided evidence that city governments underprovided city services and practiced expulsive zoning – the placement of negative uses (like garbage incinerators) in poor and minority neighborhoods. The land values in these areas were low; the environment was degraded. As a result, they were considered blighted. In the early 1930s, local realtors and bankers assisted the federal Home Owners' Loan Corporation (HOLC) in mapping property values of every block of every city in the nation (Gotham 2000). The HOLC's low appraisal of neighborhoods of color and those with large numbers of renters is well known (Jackson 1987; Weaver 1948). These low ratings were used to justify slum clearance. In San Antonio, 82,000 Mexican Americans populated a four-square-mile neighborhood west of downtown. Many of the homes were wooden shacks or converted horse stalls. Tellingly, the neighborhood lacked paved and lit streets, parks, and sufficient sewer capacity (obviously the doing of the local government). Annual flooding created a breeding ground for mosquitoes (Fairbanks 2000). Neighborhoods like this – predominately populated with people of color and renters, particularly those close to downtowns or homogenous white neighborhoods – were the first to be cleared (Hirsch 1983; Sugrue 1996).

At the same time, to preserve property values and access to FHA loans (which required racial homogeneity), white homeowners vigorously blocked the building of low-income and multiunit housing in their neighborhoods (Weaver 1948; Sugrue 1996; Hirsch 1983). Weaver (1948) reports that even whites living miles away from proposed projects objected to their development on the grounds that their property values would be threatened. Sugrue (1996) asserts that proposals to construct public housing in or near white neighborhoods was the "most contentious political issue of the 1940s and early 1950s in Detroit" (p. 72).

Real estate developers, business organizations, and neighborhood associations pressured municipal elected officials everywhere to protect property values and the character of neighborhoods. Municipal land-use planning was instrumental in achieving these goals. Through slum clearance, decisions about highway locations, prohibitions on the building of multifamily developments, and, of course, the placement of public housing sites, city planning commissions (and their ilk) throughout the United States worked to entrench race and class segregation.

Nearly all new public housing was provided on a segregated basis – that is, whites and nonwhites were not to live in the same projects (Weaver 1946). To provide enough units for racial minorities, and given the few sites that were available for building, many of the public housing projects were constructed as high-rise buildings – which, even at the time, were understood to be less desirable for the successful integration of people in need (Weaver 1946). Thus, as neighborhoods with large populations of renters and people of color were razed, these residents were displaced into even more densely segregated communities. In both the decisions regarding clearance and the decisions regarding the building of replacement housing, local control generated increased segregation.

As is true of all large government endeavors, the coalition in support of the Wagner Act and its later revisions was a collection of diverse, conflictual interests. These interests can be roughly categorized as those who emphasized slum clearance versus those who sought "public low-rent" housing (Ickes 1935, p. 109).[3] The former included business interests who held property downtown and/or relied on a healthy economic market

---

[3] Although, of course, there was diversity within these broad groups; see Marcuse 1995.

downtown, as well as real estate elites, urban planners, homeowners, and local politicians hoping to increase the tax base.[4] As one journalist representing this slum clearance advocates explained:

[T]he housing problem is not merely one of replacing insanitary or unhealthful dwellings for large numbers of our people. More importantly, it involves the whole problem of progressive neighborhood decay, which for years has been eating like a cancer at the heart of every great city in America. The victims of this cancer are not only slum dwellers. In greater number these victims are taxpaying, home-owning families in neighborhoods from humble to well-to-do in all parts of the country. (Lewis 1937, p. 189)

On the other side were those concerned about the extreme housing shortages among lower-income residents, severe overcrowding plaguing minority neighborhoods, and the influence of slums on community disorder (Dean 1949).[5] This group included many low-income and working-class residents, people of color, organizations like the NAACP, institutions like the Chicago Defender, unions, and social workers (Meyer 2000; Gotham 2001; Federal Housing Bill 1936).

From the outset, slum clearance supporters, like the National Association of Real Estate Boards, were opposed to direct government provision of housing (Gotham 2001). However, much of the land that local elites viewed as blighted and sought to redevelop was residential, and the areas were often physically quite large. Razing the houses and assembling parcels required eminent domain, which (by law) needed a clear public purpose. Public housing offered this justification, but only when local authorities engaged in the taking – thus necessitating local control. In *United States v. Certain Lands in the City of Louisville* (1935) the 6th Circuit Court ruled that the condemnation of land for slum clearance by the *federal* government was unconstitutional because it did not constitute a use necessary to carry out the powers delegated to Congress. The Housing Act of 1937 thus moved to decentralize housing administration – requiring local housing authorities to be established to receive loans and grants from the federal government and engage in slum clearance and public housing construction (Freedenberg 1941). Public housing advocates worried that local control over site selection and construction would exacerbate segregation (Meyer 2000), but without support from the slum clearance interests, public housing would have collapsed nearly as soon as it started for lack of funding (Marcuse 1995).

---

[4] See Zipp 2012; Ringelstein 2015; Avila and Rose 2009; Gotham 2001; Sugrue 1996.
[5] See also Zipp 2012; Meyer 2000; Hirsch 1983.

When the Wagner-Steagall Housing Act was revised and expanded in 1949 and 1954, power shifted toward the interests favoring slum clearance and segregation. Because the crisis of the Great Depression had abated, slum clearance was much more popular with voters and elites than was public housing (Fairbanks 2000; Zipp 2012).[6] As Gotham (2001) explains, these revisions "represented the culmination of real estate industry lobbying efforts to curtail the production of public housing, create local redevelopment authorities with broad powers of eminent domain, and provide generous public subsidies for private redevelopment" (p. 297). By the time the last funds were allocated to local governments in 1974, the program had operated for more than twenty-five years as a mechanism to maintain and deepen segregation; it was termed the "successor-weapon to the restrictive covenant and the racial zoning ordinance" (Abrams 1950). According to Collins and Shester (2013), urban renewal cumulatively resulted in the clearance of 400,000 housing units and 57,000 total acres; 300,000 families were displaced, about 54% of whom were nonwhite.[7] But, as we saw with racial zoning in Chapter 4, there was great variation in the local pursuit of urban renewal funds, and thus its effect on segregation.

If urban renewal was used as a lever to increase segregation, we should find a positive relationship between participation in the program and later segregation levels. To provide evidence of this, I rely on a dataset gathered by Collins and Shester (2013). In their article, Collins and Shester show that slum clearance and urban development programs had quantifiable positive effects on city-level measures of income, property values, employment, and poverty rates. I seek to determine whether or not the program also increased race and class segregation. The data represent all funds disbursed under Title 1 of the 1949 Housing Act between 1950 and 1974. The data were gathered from the Department of Housing and Urban Development's Urban Renewal Directory. Cities applied for federal grants for particular urban renewal projects, and the directory listed the value of total approved and disbursed grants as of the date of publication. I add to these data each city's level of white/nonwhite and renter/owner segregation in 1980, measured using the H index described in Chapter 3.

---

[6] The Housing Acts were not the only mechanism cities used to engage in urban renewal, but patterns were similar with regard to other programs. For instance, Barrett and Rose (1999) provide evidence that local business, politicians, and real estate interests utilized highway construction to produce similar outcomes.

[7] Collins and Shester (2013) provide significant evidence that these measures accurately capture urban renewal activity undertaken by cities.

I analyze the effect of urban renewal spending on future levels of *segregation* (H index measured in 1980), conditional on preexisting segregation (H index measured in 1950)[8]. The independent variable in these analyses is *total disbursed urban renewal funding* (in hundreds of millions of dollars), as of 1974. I add a series of city characteristics also measured in 1950 to account for the many demographic and environmental conditions that might have both led cities to apply for and win urban renewal funding and be correlated with segregation. These controls include the proportion of housing units that were *owner* occupied, *median home value*, the share of housing units that were *dilapidated*, the share that were *built prior to 1920*, and the share that lacked *indoor plumbing*. I include *total population*, the share of the population that was *nonwhite*, median *educational attainment* of the population over age twenty-four, the log of *median family income*, the *employment rate*, the share employed in *manufacturing*, and the percentage of families with *income below $2,000* in 1949.[9] Table 6.1 presents the results for renter segregation and Table 6.2 shows racial segregation (summary statistics are in available in the appendix, in Table A6.1).

Tables 6.1 and 6.2 reveal that the vigorousness with which a city pursued urban renewal affected the level of segregation after the completion of the program.[10] Those places that received more urban renewal funding witnessed higher levels of segregation in 1980 – even accounting for preexisting levels of segregation, and all of the physical factors that would have generated such applications. Generally, segregation declined between 1950 and 1980, but it declined more rapidly in places that spent less on urban renewal. Williamsport, Pennsylvania, had a segregation index of 0.16 in 1950. By 1974, the city had spent nearly $7 million in urban renewal funds. As of 1980, segregation had dropped a modest amount to 0.11. Newton, Massachusetts, began with a slightly higher level of segregation in 1950 (0.17), spent just over $1 million on urban renewal, and ended with a much lower level of segregation, 0.02. Two of the most segregated cities in the dataset – Gary, Indiana (1950 H index of 0.77), and Chicago, Illinois (1950 H index

---

[8] I do not have data on renter segregation in 1950, so these analyses use the 1950 level of racial segregation as the control.

[9] These variables were all provided by Collins and Shester (2013). I add fixed effects for region, and report robust standard errors clustered by state. Collins and Shester provide data for all cities with more than 25,000 residents in 1950 and 1980 (482 in total), but I only have segregation measures for 172 observations.

[10] It is also the case that cities with higher levels of preexisting segregation applied for more urban renewal funds.

TABLE 6.1 *Relationship between dispersed urban renewal funds and future renter segregation, 1950–80*

	Model 1			Model 2		
	β	Std. Err.	P > |t|	β	Std. Err.	P > |t|
Urban renewal funds as of 1974 ($100 millions)	0.023	0.006	0.001	0.020	0.009	0.037
Segregation, 1950	0.005	0.032	0.889	0.016	0.041	0.700
% Owner occupied, 1950				0.000	0.001	0.703
Median home value, 1950 (log)				0.059	0.030	0.060
% Dilapidated, 1950				0.000	0.001	0.676
% Built pre-1920, 1950				0.000	0.000	0.464
% Units w/o plumbing, 1950				0.001	0.000	0.052
Population (millions), 1950				0.003	0.011	0.761
% Nonwhite, 1950				0.000	0.001	0.997
% Employed manufacturing, 1950				0.000	0.001	0.826
% Employed, 1950				-0.001	0.003	0.715
Median education, 1950				0.016	0.007	0.032
Family income, 1950 (log)				0.008	0.118	0.946
% Incomes below $2000, 1950				0.001	0.003	0.800
Constant	0.129	0.013	0	-0.591	1.130	0.604
N	172			171		
R²	0.229			0.334		

Note: OLS regression, including fixed effects for region, robust standard errors clustered by state presented. DV is racial segregation measured in 1980.

of 0.78), also spent vastly different amounts on urban renewal ($13.8 million compared with more than $200 million). Segregation declined to 0.32 in Gary, while only dropping to 0.56 in Chicago.

The tables reveal that the results are much more powerful for racial segregation than for renter segregation. Every additional $100 million in urban renewal funds is associated with a 7% increase in racial segregation, compared with a 2% increase in renter segregation.[11] As was the case for

---

[11] Collins and Shester (2013) use an instrumental variable approach in their analysis. They estimate urban renewal funds with the number of years the city had access to the program as a result of state enabling legislation. Even more powerful results are evident when I replicate their strategy.

TABLE 6.2 *Relationship between dispersed urban renewal funds and future racial segregation, 1950–80*

	Model 1			Model 2		
	β	Std. Err.	P > |t|	β	Std. Err.	P > |t|
Urban renewal funds as of 1974 ($100 millions)	0.073	0.021	0.001	0.073	0.029	0.014
Segregation, 1950	0.514	0.11	0.000	0.476	0.087	0.000
% Owner occupied, 1950				0.002	0.001	0.088
Median home value, 1950 (log)				0.118	0.043	0.010
% Dilapidated, 1950				−0.004	0.004	0.350
% Built pre-1920, 1950				0.002	0.001	0.152
% Units w/o plumbing, 1950				−0.001	0.001	0.165
Population (millions), 1950				−0.004	0.017	0.832
% Nonwhite, 1950				0.007	0.002	0.003
% Employed manufacturing, 1950				0.003	0.001	0.003
% Employed, 1950				0.006	0.006	0.329
Median education, 1950				0.007	0.014	0.642
Family income, 1950 (log)				−0.292	0.187	0.127
% Incomes below $2000, 1950				−0.001	0.004	0.726
Constant	0.017	0.032	0.609	0.469	1.578	0.768
N	172			171		
R²	0.639			0.711		

Note: OLS regression, including fixed effects for region, robust standard errors clustered by state presented. DV is renter segregation measured in 1980.

the effects of zoning shown in Chapter 4, local policy implementation is more tightly linked to racial housing patterns than class housing patterns.

The second important feature linking urban renewal to segregation was underfunding. Basil Stockbridge, executive assistant to the United States Building and Loan League, complained that "it can readily be seen that the Authority's activities will hardly scratch the surface of the real needs of the country in eliminating urban slums and blighted areas" (Stockbridge 1938, p. 329). The Act required that the development of any new housing be accompanied by the razing of unsafe or insanitary dwellings "substantially equal in number to the newly constructed dwellings provided by the project" (Wagner-Steagall Act 1937, p. 5). But the new housing did not need to be located where the old housing had stood.

Additionally, it was possible to raze more housing than was actually built. The lack of adequate funds meant that many slums remained, and the number of new, affordable units was generally lower than the number cleared. Because of this, overcrowding in existing poor and minority neighborhoods worsened.

Furthermore, the receipt of federal funds required the local community to contribute funds for construction, typically in the form of land donation and property tax exemption, as well as funds for ongoing operation of the project (Levine 1941). Many cities eagerly accepted the federal dollars, but budgeted vastly insufficient amounts for the maintenance of public housing. So, even though by the 1950s most housing authorities stopped the explicit segregation of public housing tenants and, in some cases, promoted peaceful race relations (Weaver 1946, 1956; Collins 2004), the degradation of the units meant that they had already become housing of last resort. Those who could avoid public housing did, and preexisting segregation meant that it was whites who could most easily find housing in the private market.

The sad history of the Pruitt Igoe complex in St. Louis is instructive. Built in 1954, in a poor northside neighborhood, the Wendell Pruitt Homes and William Igoe Apartments gleamed. The thirty-three, eleven-story buildings were segregated. Even still, the housing units were highly desirable among both white and black St. Louis residents. But St. Louis budgeted next to nothing for ongoing maintenance of the sprawling high-rise complex. Elevators broke down, windows cracked, the stairwells and corridors became havens for drug sellers and robbers. Unsurprisingly, those who had the resources to leave did so, ensuring that the remaining tenants of public housing were the city's poorest residents – and overwhelmingly black. This large concentration of poor, black residents in a single neighborhood of St. Louis contributed to the city's stubbornly high level of race and class segregation. In 1980, St. Louis's segregation was nearly exactly the same as it had been in 1950.

If St. Louis's experience is representative of other cities, we should see the same pattern across a range of cases. To investigate this possibility, I add, to the data described earlier, a measure of the share of total expenditures each city spent on *housing and community development operations*[12] in 1972. I interact this variable with the measure of *total*

---

[12] This variable was constructed using the finance data described in Chapter 3. It is calculated as the total dollar amount spent on housing and community development, minus housing and community development capital outlays, divided by total expenditure.

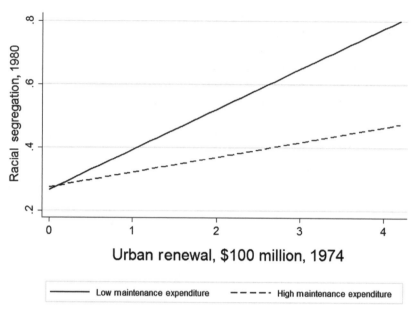

FIGURE 6.1 Urban renewal interacted with housing operations budget

urban renewal funding in Model 2 from Table 6.1 above.[13] I also add a control for the number of *public housing units per capita* built under the Housing Act to account for differences in the need for maintenance spending.[14] Figure 6.1 reveals how urban renewal funding operated differently when cities invested in ongoing maintenance and when they did not.

In cities that accepted urban renewal funds but budgeted nothing for operations in 1972, urban renewal had a steep positive effect on racial segregation. In places that provided municipal funds for the maintenance of renewal sites, increasingly vigorous renewal expenditures had a more modest effect on segregation. Of course, this analysis does not offer causal leverage. It is entirely plausible that cities that were inclined to invest in

[13] Adding the interaction to Model 2, Table 6.3 (analyzing renter segregation) produces a similar effect that is smaller in size than the effect on racial segregation.

[14] Interestingly, the coefficient on this variable is negative – meaning that cities that had more public housing overall were less segregated. However, interacting the number of public housing units with urban renewal funding results in a positive coefficient. This indicates that slum clearance and public housing were both factors in the increase in segregation that urban renewal produced.

maintenance had a social/political culture that led to a smaller increase in residential segregation for other reasons. Whatever the underlying cause was, cities that accepted federal funds without ongoing budget provision for housing operations saw higher levels of segregation in 1980.

This variation in maintenance funding aside, generally speaking, segregation levels remained higher than they would have without urban renewal policies where slums were cleared and public housing was built. Yet, even while urban renewal was largely carried out to the benefit of white homeowners and land-oriented businesses, their control over public policy was not absolute; the rising civil rights movement threatened it significantly. As of 1960, not a single large city in the United States had elected a black mayor. By 2010, more than a third had (Vogl 2014). Changes to voter eligibility brought by the Twenty-fourth Amendment and the 1965 Voting Rights Act increased turnout of racial minorities and the poor during this period as well (Filer, Kenny, and Morton 1991).

In 1942, only 36% of whites said that they would not be bothered if a black person with their same income and education moved into their block (Schuman and Bobo 1988); the majority of whites "expect[ed] a vigilant government to protect their segregated neighborhoods" (Sugrue 1996, p. 63). These beliefs were intimately intertwined with opposition to public housing, which was viewed as "Socialist housing" (CREA Plans Aid Against Public Housing Projects 1952, p. E1); specifically, public housing was viewed as "a taxpayer-subsidized handout for the feckless" (Sugrue 1996, p. 63). Although a majority of the poor in central cities were white, racial minorities were disproportionately poor and poorly housed.[15] Many whites opposed public housing because they feared "a change in the racial character of the neighborhood" (Report Cites Snag in Public Housing 1952, p. 28). Efforts to locate low-income housing in homeowner neighborhoods and/or integrate white areas were viewed as a government assault on owners' "right to protect one's own property" (Thomas 1949).

To prevent integration in housing, white homeowners organized neighborhood associations, encouraged vigilant city inspectors to fine overcrowded minority homes, sent hundreds of letters to city governments, turned out in droves at public hearings, and engaged in violent assaults on black residents (Sugrue 1996; Hirsch 1983). But defending white, homeowner neighborhoods was a zero-sum game. For every area that

---

[15] About 62% of persons below the poverty line in central cities were white in 1959. Approximately 14% of whites were poor compared with 41% of blacks (www2.census .gov/prod2/popscan/p60–068a.pdf, p. 7).

successfully halted integration or low-income housing, another had to absorb (or block) it. This led to a lack of unity among segregationist forces. At the same time, support for scientific racial categorization plummeted (Hayward 2013), and outright, public expressions of racism were "placed on the defensive" (Hirsch 1983, p. 175; Schuman et al. 1985).

Advocates of open housing began to win concessions from the government. By 1945, in more than 200 cities, municipal authorities dedicated to maintaining peaceful race relations established interracial commissions, committees, or agencies that advocated for civil rights reform (Hirsch 1983, p. 42). These often appeared in the wake of violent riots (Meyer 2000). The racial restrictive covenant, long used by real estate developers and homeowners' organizations to keep minorities out of white neighborhoods, became unenforceable with a Supreme Court decision in 1948 (*Shelley v. Kraemer* 1948). Even before this decision, some municipal judges were refusing to enforce covenants (Hirsch 1983).

Because the government owned and operated public housing, it was an obvious target for constitutional claims of unequal treatment. As early as 1944, New York City enacted an ordinance prohibiting tax-exempt status for housing projects that denied access to tenants on the basis of race. The ordinance had been spearheaded by the city's interracial relations commission. In other places, civil rights organizations pressured municipal housing authorities to integrate public housing (Meyer 2000; Sugrue 1996). Then, in 1951 the NAACP brought this matter before the San Francisco Superior Court. In 1953, the California Court of Appeals ruled in *Banks v. Housing Authority of San Francisco* that San Francisco's Housing Authority must assign residents to public housing without regard to race or color. When the Supreme Court declined to hear the appeal (thereby allowing California's ruling to stand), the case became precedent. By 1954, twenty-one cities had passed some form of antidiscrimination law (Meyer 2000), and in 1962, President Kennedy signed an executive order,

directing Federal departments and agencies to take every proper and legal action to prevent discrimination in the sale or lease of housing facilities owned or operated by the Federal Government; housing constructed or sold as a result of loans or grants to be made by the Federal Government; and housing to be available through the development or redevelopment of property under Federal slum clearance or urban renewal programs. (Kennedy 1963, p. 832)

Not only did cities and states pass antidiscrimination laws covering public housing, some also enacted open housing legislation that sought to prevent discrimination in the private housing market. The leader of the movement was again New York City, passing an ordinance prohibiting "race, creed or national origin" discrimination in rental housing in 1957 (Bennett 1957b, p. 9). The ordinance was "bitterly fought by property owners and real estate representatives" (Bennett 1957a, p. 7) and explicitly exempted room rentals in single-family homes or duplexes unless they were located in large housing developments (Bennett 1957b). Still, the passage of open housing laws represented clear policy change, largely emerging from the bottom up. By 1968, twenty-two states had enacted fair housing laws that covered nearly all sales and rentals (Collins 2006). Such laws were passed in response to vocal, mobilized advocates in black and liberal white communities (Collins 2006). The 1968 Federal Fair Housing Act extended this coverage nationwide.

Despite such policy progress, even as of 1973, the General Social Survey found 64% of white respondents believed that a homeowner should be able to "decide for himself whom to sell his house to, even if he prefers not to sell to Negroes," and a homeowners' rights movement arose in response to the open housing laws. In Detroit, a collection of neighborhood organizations gathered more than 44,000 signatures in support of a homeowners' right initiative (Detroit Homeowners Seek Rights Vote 1963). The ordinance passed but was declared unconstitutional by the Wayne County Circuit Court in a suit brought by the NAACP (Seek Repeal of City Ordinance 1964; Sugrue 1996).

In California, after the state legislature passed a fair housing law known as the Rumford Act in 1963, a statewide campaign for its repeal was led by the California Real Estate Association and the California Apartment Owners Association, who combined to form the Committee for Home Protection (Self 2003; Duscha 1964; Turner 1964). Proposition 14, confusingly referred to as the California Fair Housing Initiative, prohibited the state from "denying, limiting, or abridging the right of any person to decline to sell, lease, or rent residential real property to any person as he chooses."[16] In an analysis of the campaign for Proposition 14, Self (2003) and Brilliant (2010) show that supporters rarely invoked race in their arguments, focusing instead on freedom and property rights. Reporting on the initiative battle, the *Washington Post* quoted a pamphlet issued by the Committee for Home Protection that stated, "Those who stand for the preservation of individual property rights today are in direct line of descent from the patriots who endured the hardships of the long

---

[16] Sales and Rentals of Residential Real Property, California Proposition 14 (1964). repository.uchastings.edu/ca_ballot_props/672

winter at Valley Forge with George Washington" (Duscha 1964, p. A2). Prominent Democrats, including Governor Edmund Brown, opposed the initiative, and a number of "right-wing Republicans," including Ronald Reagan and Barry Goldwater, were "extremely active" in support of the initiative (Duscha 1964, p. A2). In the end, the initiative passed with more than 65% of the vote, even as Johnson won the presidential race decisively (Greenberg 1964, p. 1).

Scholars have identified varying patterns of opposition to open housing in different places. For instance, Sugrue (1996) shows that in Detroit, the staunchest integration resisters were working-class white ethnics who owned modest, single-family homes (see pp. 236–7). In Oakland, Self (2003) finds that it was not solely "an anti-liberal white working class engaged in direct struggle with African American," but rather middle- and upper-class whites who "understood property rights as sacrosanct expressions of their personal freedom" (p. 168). Collins (2004) shows that states with higher union membership rates were more likely to pass fair housing legislation, and Self (2003) provides evidence that the UAW campaigned against Proposition 14, although Brilliant (2010) argues that rank-and-file union members were staunch supporters.

To better understand the individual correlates of opposition to open housing, I gathered data from the 1964 Field Poll in California.[17] Carried out in seven waves between January and October, the poll asked respondents about their support for the Rumford Act and Proposition 14. I recoded these questions to a variable coded 1 if the respondent *opposed open housing*.[18] I use logistic regression to regress this variable on several

---

[17] Ideally, I would have analyzed the relationship between community segregation and public opinion on open housing. Unfortunately, the Field Poll recorded no geographic identifiers other than the very broad categories of Northern and Southern California.

[18] For waves 2, 3, and 5, I used the question about the Rumford Act. In waves 1 and 7, no Rumford Act question was asked, so I used a question about Proposition 14 instead. Waves 4 and 6 did not include open housing questions. Where possible, I use the question about the Rumford Act instead of Proposition 14, because the waves included different wording of the Proposition question (adding more and less detail about the content). The texts of the questions are as follows: (Rumford Act) "Well, as you know the Rumford Act is a Law which makes it illegal for apartment house owners, owners of publicly assisted housing, and real estate brokers to discriminate against anyone because of race, color, religion, national origin or ancestry in the renting or selling of housing accommodations. From what you know of it, do you approve or disapprove of the Rumford Act?" (Proposition 14) "If you were voting today, would you approve or disapprove of this addition to the state constitution? (the amendment reads as follows – prohibits state, subdivision, or agency thereof from denying, limiting, or abridging right of any person to decline to sell, lease, or rent residential real property to any person as he chooses).

TABLE 6.3 *Demographic characteristics of open housing opponents*

	β	Std. Err.	P > |t|
Homeowner	0.193	0.065	0.003
White	1.205	0.412	0.003
Education level	−0.177	0.035	0.000
Union member	0.284	0.111	0.011
Age	−0.004	0.053	0.934
Economic level	0.003	0.026	0.897
Democratic presidential voter	−0.896	0.386	0.020
Constant	0.33	0.334	0.323
N	4,860		
R²	0.0575		

Note: Logistic regression with errors clustered by poll wave. DV is opposition to open housing legislation.

demographics, including whether or not the respondent *owns* (vs. rents) her home, her *race* (coded 1 for white, and 0 for nonwhite or other), her *age*, her level of *education*, whether or not the respondent or her spouse belongs to a *union*, and her *economic level* (with higher values representing lower classes).[19] In addition, I include a measure indicating whether or not the respondent planned to vote for the *Democratic presidential* ticket (Johnson/Humphrey). I cluster the standard errors by poll wave. The results, presented in Table 6.3, paint a picture that both confirms and undermines various aspects of the historical accounts. Summary statistics are presented in the appendix, in Table A6.2.

White homeowners were clearly in opposition to open housing, as were less educated respondents, Republicans, and union members. After controlling for these characteristics, economic status and age played no role in the determination of political opinions on open housing. Since the earliest years of the century, the most consistent opponents of integration have been white homeowners who came to view the protection of their neighborhoods as a right to be protected by government. These residents

Prohibition not applicable to property owned by state or its subdivisions, property acquired by eminent domain, or transient lodging accommodations by hotels, motels, and similar public places."

[19] The coding of this variable is obscure. The codebook suggests that ten categories were used and lists the following labels: "upper," "upper middle," "upper middle," "middle," "middle," "middle," "lower middle," "lower middle," "lower," and "lower." One can only assume that the coders were instructed in some way to make distinctions across categories.

understood the "very essence" of Proposition 14 to be the avoidance of "state involvement in private decisions in the sale of rental of privately owned residential property" (Blake 1964, p. K1).[20]

RACIALLY CONTESTED MAYORAL ELECTIONS

Ensuring that the government adequately protected white neighborhoods required political control. Specifically, white homeowners needed to be assured of their influence in land-use decisions and public goods allocations through control of the local government – a situation that was no longer as certain as it once had been. While the open housing movement was advancing, local elections became increasingly contested by people of color, particularly in places where segregation had severely restricted their housing options. During the late 1960s, "black leaders turned their attention to bringing political and institutional power to African American communities. To remake opportunity was to tackle, and attempt to counter, the social and spatial arrangements of the ghetto and the legacies of both slavery and segregation embedded in it" (Self 2003, p. 179).

Nelson and Meranto (1977) explain that the black power movement included, among other goals, "the quest for a political organization that speaks directly for blacks and represents their needs and interests," as well as "black control for full participation in the decision-making processes of institutions that shape the lives of black people" (p. 14). Achieving these goals necessitated political power. The 1960s and 1970s witnessed increasing contestation for local office by people of color, particularly in segregated places.

To provide evidence of this pattern, I use data collected by Vogl (2014) to investigate the relationship between levels of segregation and interracial electoral competition. Vogl (2014) analyzes mayoral election returns between 1965 and 2010 for all cities that had 1960 populations that were at least 50,000 and 4% black (194 cities). His data record the race of the top two candidates (either black or not black) and their vote totals. I add segregation measures to Vogl's data, resulting in complete

---

[20] In 1966, the California Supreme Court declared Proposition 14 in violation of the Constitution, and the Rumford Act was allowed to stand. However, the lack of support for open housing among whites and property owners would prove to be a formidable barrier for integrationists. Collins (2004) reveals that fair housing policy had little effect on black housing market outcomes and did nothing to affect levels of segregation.

data for 122 cities.[21] During the 1960s, only thirteen black candidates sought the mayor's seat in Vogl's dataset; this number rose to fifty-seven in the 1970s, and eighty-four in the 1980s. Interracial electoral competition was much more likely in more segregated cities. To show this, I regress a variable coded 1 if the election was *interracial* (e.g., featured a black candidate running against a nonblack candidate) on the city's *H* index of *segregation* for the election year (interpolated between censuses). I add the share of the city's residents who were *white,* and the share *renting* their homes, as well as the natural log of total *population,* and a trend variable for the *year* as controls.[22] The regression includes 731 elections from 117 cities. Figure 6.2 shows the marginal effect of segregation on the probability of witnessing an interracial election, holding all other variables at their mean values.

Figure 6.2 makes clear that racially segregated cities were much more likely to experience interracial elections – even controlling for the share of the population that was white. As will be shown in Chapters 7 and 9, segregated cities are also more likely to have racially divisive politics. Although the dividing lines were in place long before the 1960s, they became much more visible in electoral politics during the postwar period. Elections featuring black candidates (and white contenders) were contentious – driving up turnout among both blacks and whites, and decreasing margins of victory (Vogl 2014; Lublin and Tate 1995; Washington 2006). However, the vast majority of elections were still won by whites. Blacks only won 13% of the 731 contests reflected in Figure 6.2; moreover, these wins were concentrated in places with majority black populations. Although whites maintained power in most cities throughout the 1960s and 1970s, their hold was tenuous.

FEDERAL DESEGREGATION OF SCHOOLS AND INCREASED RESIDENTIAL SEGREGATION

In previous decades, white control over neighborhoods and public goods could be completely assured by local political dominance. But in the postwar period, threats came also from the long arm of the federal

---

[21] I am missing pre-1970 segregation measures for twenty cities in Vogl's dataset. I use 1970 segregation for the thirty-six elections between 1965 and 1970 for these places. Results are robust to the exclusion of these observations.

[22] I use a random-effects logit model with errors clustered by city. I restrict the analysis to elections that occurred between 1965 and 1990 to focus on the postwar period.

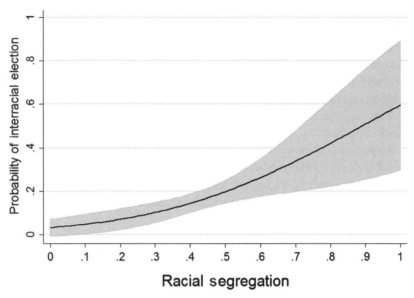

FIGURE 6.2 Segregated cities saw more interracial elections in the postwar period

government. In 1954, *Brown v. Board of Education of Topeka* declared that separate but equal schools were unconstitutional, and should be desegregated with all deliberate speed. But throughout the 1960s and 1970s, many urban school districts remained segregated. Between 1972 and 1996, the General Social Survey asked respondents whether they favored or opposed the busing of black and white children from one school district to another. On average across this time period, 78% of whites opposed busing. This is despite the fact that the same respondents overwhelmingly declared that black and white children should (in theory) attend the same schools. Resistance to integration in schools led many white homeowners to seek out segregated residential areas. In combination with neighborhood school assignment, segregated neighborhoods ensured that white children would be provided a homogenous educational environment. We can see this by analyzing the effect that desegregation orders had on the demographics of neighborhoods. In short, pressures for desegregation of schools increased residential segregation both within cities and, even more importantly, across city lines.

   To study this process, I created a measure of each census tract's demographic makeup, compared with the larger metropolitan area in each decade between 1970 and 2000.[23] I refer to neighborhoods that have a greater share of white residents than the metropolitan area as a whole as white-defended neighborhoods; conversely, neighborhoods that have a greater share of residents of color than the metro area are called minority-dominated neighborhoods. I use this relative conception because many residents are constrained to a particular metropolitan area by preferences or needs (Mummolo and Nall 2017), but the choice of neighborhood within that metro area may be more flexible. The variable *tract-metro difference in percent white residents* takes a positive value for neighborhoods that are whiter than the metro area,[24] and a negative value for neighborhoods with more people of color.[25]

To determine the effect that pressures for school desegregation had on neighborhood demographics, I take advantage of a dataset compiled by Nathaniel Baum-Snow and Byron Lutz (2011) that records the timing of federal court orders for desegregation of public schools in central cities.[26] Although *Brown v. Board of Education* determined the unconstitutionality of segregated schools, a specific court order was nearly always required for large, central city districts to pursue desegregation plans. The data include court orders implemented between 1960 and 1990 for ninety-two central school districts in metropolitan statistical areas. Of these ninety-two orders, forty-eight are in the South, nine are in the Northeast, twenty are in the Midwest, and fifteen are in the West.[27]

---

[23] These data rely on the Neighborhood Change Database described in Chapter 3.

[24] The census did not tabulate whites separately from Hispanics in 1970, but did in 1980, 1990, 2000, and 2011. Where possible, I use non-Hispanic whites.

[25] In 1970, the average neighborhood was very slightly whiter than the metro area (mean = 0.018), but the distribution has a long left tail, indicating many neighborhoods that were overwhelmingly populated by people of color. By 2000, the distribution was more normally distributed, with a mean just slightly less than zero. This difference in distributions reflects the diversification of the nation and the well-documented finding that neighborhood-level segregation between whites and people of color has declined substantially since the 1970s (Vigdor and Glaeser 2012; Frey 2014).

[26] The data are described completely in the statistical appendix to Baum-Snow and Lutz's 2011 paper. The appendix is available at: www.aeaweb.org/aer/data/dec2011/20080918_app.pdf.

[27] My examination does not include metropolitan areas that never faced a desegregation order. The factors that led some metro areas to receive court-ordered school desegregation plans while others did not are most certainly not random and are likely related to the outcome of interest here (the presence of white-defended and minority-dominated neighborhoods). Inclusion of the districts with no court order would thus be likely to violate the identifying assumption on the desegregation parameter. However, for those central cities in metropolitan areas that did receive an order, the timing of that order is plausibly exogenous to unobserved time-varying factors within metropolitan areas that

My analysis compares the presence of defended/minority neighborhoods before and after the implementation of the court order in each metro area, while accounting for variation across Metropolitan Statistical Areas (MSAs) by including fixed effects. For each metropolitan area, in each of the four census years (1970, 1980, 1990, and 2000), I calculated the mean *tract-metro difference in percent white,* and the standard deviation of this measure. I then generated a count of census tracts that were either greater than or less than one standard deviation away from the mean racial difference for each census year in each MSA. These counts form the numerator for the share of all neighborhoods that are *white defended* or *minority dominated.* These shares serve as dependent variables in my analyses.

The key independent variable in my analysis, *desegregation order,* is a dummy indicator coded from the Baum-Snow and Lutz (2011) data noting whether or not a desegregation order was in place in the MSA's central city for a given census year. The analysis compares the number of defended/minority neighborhoods before and after the implementation of desegregation by the federal government in each MSA.[28] As controls, I add the log of the *total population* in the MSA, the share of MSA households *renting* their homes, the *wealthy* share of households (households with incomes above the ninetieth percentile), and the population *density* of the MSA. While it is unlikely that these factors are related to desegregation order timing directly, it is possible that they reflect an underlying time trend that influenced implementation as well as the propensity for segregation. Figure 6.3 displays the marginal effects of desegregation orders, holding the control variables at their mean values.

The figure shows that desegregation orders significantly increased the share of neighborhoods that were both white defended and minority dominated. On average, desegregation orders generated about thirty new homogeneous neighborhoods in metropolitan areas. Homogeneity was achieved when whites moved within cities to new neighborhoods and

---

might affect segregation due to the vagaries of the judicial process. The precise date at which court orders took effect was related to differences in the length of the appeals process for otherwise similar metropolitan areas (Baum-Snow and Lutz 2011).

[28] Of the ninety-two metro areas in the dataset, sixty-four had orders implemented between 1970 and 1990. Because tract-level data were not available for most areas in 1960, I am unable to estimate change for twenty-eight metro areas. These MSAs are still included in the regressions – just with no change on the desegregation order variable.

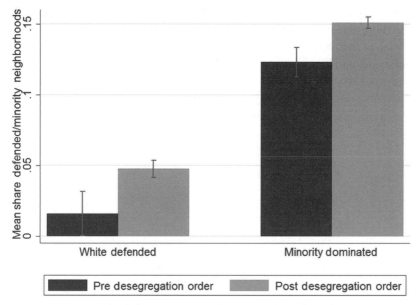

FIGURE 6.3 Federal desegregation orders increase residential segregation

to the suburbs.[29] Approximately two-thirds of the exclusive white neighborhoods are located in suburban places, and about three-fourths of the homogeneous neighborhoods of color are located in central cities. The growing isolation of suburban neighborhoods would become the dominant pattern of segregation into the 1980s.

CONCLUSION

In the postwar period, white homeowners' ability to manage segregation and public goods was uncertain. During the late 1930s and throughout the 1940s, white homeowners and land developers convinced local governments to use urban renewal as a tool to harden the lines of segregation. But in later decades, the rise of black candidacies, the advancements of the Black Power and civil rights movements, and the changes to public policy

[29] Baum-Snow and Lutz (2011) provide evidence that black families responded to desegregation orders by moving into newly integrated central school districts, which suggests that changes in homogeneity of neighborhoods would have been driven by white, not black, movers.

encompassed in *Brown v. Board of Education*, the Voting Rights Act, and Fair Housing Act all threatened white control over central cities. Meanwhile, as the next chapter reveals, central city politics became ever more polarized and dysfunctional – a direct result of the segregation white homeowners had created. In the postwar period, central city growth stagnated, while suburbs began to boom and segregation across city lines increased. The next two chapters lay out these transformations.

7

Segregation's Negative Consequences

As Chapter 6 revealed, the postwar period witnessed great tumult in the nation's central cities*. Immediately following the war, central cities continued to use the varied tools at their disposal to manage the lines of segregated neighborhoods on behalf of white homeowners and their developer allies. Cities cleared slums, built public housing projects, razed neighborhoods to lay highways, and used zoning to manage the placement and location of different types of housing. But the many decades of defending white neighborhoods came at a significant cost. The politics of segregated cities became polarized – pitting racially defined neighborhoods against each other. In turn, polarization made cooperation difficult. In segregated cities, local officials have trouble convincing residents to fund public goods. As a result, services were underprovided. Living in a segregated city means residents suffer worse sewers, worse parks, worse public safety, worse social support services, and worse roads. This chapter provides evidence of the negative consequences of racial residential segregation.[1]

---

* Significant portions of this chapter were published as an article entitled "Segregation and Inequality in Public Goods," in the *American Journal of Political Science*, Vol. 60, No. 3, pp. 709–25.

[1] I focus here on racial segregation alone. A series of tests revealed that renter and wealth division do not produce the same patterns. These findings are bolstered by the historical evidence, which indicates that it is race and not class division that generates the starkest conflicts in city politics. Throughout, I control for indicators of wealth and homeownership to ensure that the results are not conflating race and class.

HOW SEGREGATION CREATES POLARIZED POLITICS

As demonstrated throughout this book, local politics concerns battles over space. This is because local governments control the location of negative and positive externalities (like pollution-producing factories or public parks), and also because many of the functions that local governments provide are allocated (e.g., where police officers will be deployed and which roads will be repaved). One of the few powers reserved, nearly exclusively, by local government is that of zoning or planning. When a city is residentially segregated by race, issues cleave along racial and not just spatial lines (Massey and Denton 1998).

In segregated cities, divisions across racial groups are exacerbated because the political priorities and opinions of racial groups are likely to be more divergent than they are in integrated places. Neighborhood racial isolation is associated with a high degree of racial intolerance, resentment, and competition among all racial groups (Oliver 2010). This correlation is due to both self-selection and interpersonal interactions (Rodden 2010). When deciding where to live, people with racially intolerant attitudes often seek same-race neighbors (Charles 2003; Boustan 2012), either because they want to minimize contact with other race individuals (Massey and Denton 1998) or because they associate other race neighborhoods with poor neighborhood quality on dimensions such as schools, crime, and property values (Helper 1969; Ellen 2000; Bayer, Ferreira, and McMillian 2007; Krysan et al. 2008). However, living in different types of neighborhoods may also change individuals' perspectives. In integrated neighborhoods, regular, casual interaction may work to counteract dominant, negative stereotypes (Allport 1954; Oliver and Wong 2003). The result of both population sorting and neighborhood influence is that individuals who live in homogeneous neighborhoods are more likely to harbor negative stereotypes about other groups (Oliver 2010; Oliver and Wong 2003).

Yet, at higher levels of geography (e.g., in cities, counties, and metropolitan areas), it is integration or diversity that correlates with intolerance, prejudicial attitudes, increased racial tension, less cooperative behavior, and lower spending on public goods. As a result, racial competition, racial resentment, and racial conservatism are positively correlated with homogeneity at the neighborhood level, but negatively correlated with homogeneity at the city level (see Oliver 2010 for a detailed account of these conflicting patterns).[2] A severely segregated city is one that is diverse overall and has many homogeneous neighborhoods – both characteristics that point toward a high degree of racial conflict.

This higher degree of racial conflict in segregated cities has obvious political implications. Levine (2012) has found that racial segregation is strongly predictive of partisan political divisions in metropolitan areas and that these political divides result in an unwillingness to cooperate on metropolitan-wide policy solutions. The same pattern plays out at the city level. First, in segregated cities, racial groups are likely to be more divided with respect to political priorities than they are in integrated cities. Second, diverse-but-divided cities are likely to be less able to come to a consensus about the production of basic government services and, thus, will be less supportive of public goods provision. Some scholars have claimed that diversity drives down collective investment (Alesina et al. 1999). But not all diversity is equivalent. When whites and nonwhites live in the same city, the pattern of residential integration factors into expectations about public goods expenditures. White and nonwhites may live as next-door neighbors, but they also may not. Because segregation represents preferences or attitudes that are incompatible with collective investment, the uneven distribution of groups, not diversity per se, correlates with lower public goods spending.

SEGREGATION AND POLITICAL POLARIZATION

In municipal politics, vote patterns and policy priorities are shaped by racial cleavages more so than any other demographic division (Hajnal and Trounstine 2013a, 2013b, 2014). While ideology, partisanship, and class all play important roles in determining vote choice and support for municipal administrations, conflicts among racial groups are predominant. If segregated cities are more politically polarized, these racial divides should be most pronounced in places with a high degree of residential

---

[2] There are a few exceptions to this pattern. A handful of scholars have not found that diversity increases tolerance at the neighborhood level. Gay (2006) and Oliver and Mendelberg (2000) find no relationship between neighborhood racial context and racial attitudes. Enos (2016) shows that that homogeneity decreases voter turnout among whites, and also decreases support for conservative candidates. Cho, Gimpel, and Dyck (2006) find that homogeneity decreases turnout among Asian Americans in some cases, but increases it (or has no effect) in others. Leighley and Vedlitz (1999) find that homogeneity correlates positively with turnout for whites.

segregation. To determine whether this is the case, I analyze the relationship between residential segregation patterns and racial divisions in mayoral elections in the nation's largest cities between 1990 and 2010.

To estimate the effect of segregation on racial polarization, I use a dataset compiled by Hajnal and Trounstine (2014) that measures support for winning mayoral candidates across different racial groups in primary and general elections in large cities. The data include ninety-one separate contests from twenty-five cities. Votes by race data were compiled from a combination of exit polls, preelection surveys, homogenous precinct analyses, and ecological inference.[3] Summary statistics and a list of cities included in the analysis are provided in the online appendix, in Tables A7.1 and A7.2.

For each election, I calculated the difference in support for the winning candidate between black and white voters, Latino and white voters, and black and Latino voters. The dependent variable in this analysis is the absolute value of the largest difference in support for the winning candidate between any two racial groups. For instance, in Philadelphia in 2003, exit polls reported that 24% of white voters supported the winner, John Street, compared with 88% of black voters and 47% of Latino voters. In this election, the black-white divide was 0.64, the Latino-white divide was 0.23, and the black-Latino divide was 0.41. Therefore, the dependent variable takes the value of the black-white divide: 0.64. In sixty-two of the ninety-one contests, the largest divide was between black and white voters; in thirteen contests, it was the divide between Latino and white voters; and in sixteen contests, the largest divide was between black and Latino voters.[4] The distribution of racial divides across cases is listed in the online appendix, in Table A7.2.

As described in Chapter 3, my primary independent variable is a measure of segregation called Theil's H index. The H index measures the degree to which the diversity in each neighborhood differs from the diversity of the city as a whole, expressed as a fraction of the city's total diversity and weighted by the neighborhood's share of the total population. I calculated the H index for all United States cities using census tract-level demographic data from the 1980, 1990, and 2000 Censuses

---

[3] These data are described completely in Hajnal and Trounstine (2014).

[4] As an alternate measure of division, I took the difference in support between white voters and the average of support among black and Latino voters. The results are extremely similar.

of Population and Housing and from the 2011 American Community Survey.[5] To start, I use four groups in the calculation of entropy: white (non-Hispanic), black (non-Hispanic), other (non-Hispanic), and Hispanic/Latino.[6] I then combine blacks, Hispanics, and other races into a single nonwhite group for comparison. For reference, the mean *H* indices for each city in the analysis are shown in the online appendix, in Table A7.2.

I include a number of control variables in addition to the *H* index. One of the primary arguments in the literature is that racially and ethnically diverse populations will have heterogeneous political preferences, which then drives low spending on public goods. If this is the case, we should see more racial polarization in the vote as diversity rises. Thus, I include the proportion of *blacks*, *Latinos*, and *Asian Americans* in the city, and a measure of *diversity* known as the Herfindahl Index.[7]

I include control variables that are shown by Hajnal and Trounstine (2014) to affect racial polarization in voting, which may also be correlated with segregation. I account for the *median household income*, proportion of the population *renting* their homes, proportion of the population with a *college degree*, the race of the candidates in the election (a dummy variable coded 1 if the election featured *biracial* candidates), a measure noting whether or not the election was *nonpartisan*, an indicator for *primary* elections, and the size of the total *population* (logged). Finally, I include fixed effects for year and region, and random effects for cities.

In Model 3, I also add a measure of the average *ideology* among the city's white residents to determine whether or not segregation is merely a proxy for a conservative white population. This measure was constructed using General Social Survey (GSS) data from 1998, 2000, 2002, 2004, 2006, and 2008. Using restricted access data, I geo-coded each respondent in the GSS to his/her city of residence. I then took the mean ideology

---

[5] Tract-level data for 1980, 1990, and 2000 come from a proprietary product developed by GeoLytics called the Neighborhood Change Database (NCDB), which matches and normalizes census tracts over time. The data from the 2011 American Community Survey (ACS) are available for download through the census ftp server located at www2.census.gov.

[6] The 1980 tract-level data only disaggregate the non-Hispanic population into whites, blacks, and others, so I am unable to include Asians as a separate group.

[7] *Diversity* $= 1 - \sum_{r=1}^{R} \pi_r^2$. This calculation includes five racial groups: white (non-Hispanic), black (non-Hispanic), Asian (non-Hispanic), Hispanic, and other.

score for each city's white respondents for each year (higher values indicate more conservative respondents).[8] I interpolated ideology for odd years, and then merged these data to the racial polarization dataset. In order to preserve as many observations as possible, I matched GSS data from the most recent year for each election.

The results presented in Table 7.1 indicate that more segregated cities are also more politically polarized. The relationship between segregation and political polarization is powerful. A city in the tenth percentile of the segregation distribution can be expected to have a 35 percentage point divide between different racial groups' support for the winning candidate, while a city in the ninetieth percentile of segregation has a predicted racial divide of sixty-three percentage points.[9] These results hold even with the inclusion of racial demographics. Segregation, not just diversity, matters for polarization. The data also indicate (comparing columns 1 and 2) that there is no significant difference in accounting for segregation among multiple racial groups, as opposed to accounting for segregation of whites from nonwhites.[10] This makes sense given that whites are much more likely to live in homogenous neighborhoods than are other racial and ethnic groups, and that the most pronounced political division is typically between whites and one or more minority groups, rather than among minority groups. These results suggest that political polarization depends on the degree to which white residents live in exclusively white neighborhoods.

I have argued that segregation generates political divisions because the politics of space become intertwined with race. It is possible, though, that segregation is simply correlated with a more ideologically conservative white population that then generates divides in support for candidates. As the third column reveals, the relationship between segregation and polarization appears to be unaffected by the conservatism of the white population. In fact, the relationship between ideology and polarization is such that cities with more conservative white populations have smaller racial divides, underscoring the conclusion that racial polarization is not driven

---

[8] I dropped city/years from the GSS that only contained a single respondent.

[9] Estimates were generated from the regression presented in column 1 with all other variables held at their mean values. Predicted effects were generated using the "margin" command in Stata 12.

[10] The 95% confidence intervals for these coefficients are nearly completely overlapping. Additionally, adding both coefficients to the same equation and running a post-estimation Wald test of equality indicates no significant difference.

TABLE 7.1 *Racial polarization in segregated cities*

	Racial divide w/multigroup segregation index			Racial divide w/two-group segregation index			Racial divide w/ideology control		
	β	SE	P > |t|	β	SE	P > |t|	β	SE	P > |t|
Multigroup H index	0.932	0.39	0.02						
White/nonwhite H index				0.756	0.30	0.01	0.835	0.30	0.01
Diversity	0.385	0.36	0.29	0.518	0.32	0.11	0.584	0.32	0.07
% Asian	-0.115	0.53	0.83	0.120	0.56	0.83	-0.004	0.52	0.99
% Black	-0.432	0.27	0.11	-0.237	0.22	0.27	-0.133	0.21	0.53
% Latino	-0.191	0.26	0.46	-0.059	0.25	0.82	0.095	0.28	0.73
Median household income (1000s)	-0.004	0.00	0.52	-0.007	0.00	0.32	-0.002	0.00	0.81
% Renters	-0.580	0.42	0.17	-0.806	0.43	0.06	-0.419	0.45	0.36
% College educated	0.328	0.71	0.65	0.723	0.73	0.32	0.123	0.87	0.89
Biracial contest	0.210	0.04	0.00	0.208	0.04	0.00	0.192	0.04	0.00
Nonpartisan election	-0.090	0.07	0.18	-0.089	0.07	0.18	-0.034	0.06	0.60
Primary election	-0.092	0.03	0.00	-0.09	0.03	0.01	-0.071	0.03	0.02
Population (logged)	0.035	0.06	0.53	0.048	0.05	0.38	-0.011	0.06	0.86
White ideology							-0.051	0.03	0.11
Constant	-0.242	0.57	0.67	-0.393	0.56	0.49	0.236	0.61	0.70
Wald χ²	187.12		0.00	189.68		0.00	222.92		0.00
N	91			91			86		

Note: Multilevel mixed-effects linear regressions with fixed effects for region and year, and random effects for cities.

by ideological divisions. In the next section, I ask whether or not this polarization extends beyond support for candidates to a lack of consensus over policy. In short, I find that it does.

DIVERSITY AND SEGREGATION IN THE AGGREGATE

Scholars have provided evidence that racially diverse places, and those that are becoming increasingly diverse, spend fewer public dollars on productive public goods (Alesina et al. 1999; Hopkins 2009). I have asserted that segregation, not just diversity, should matter in municipal politics. In the first section of this chapter, I showed that segregation is related to political polarization, even after accounting for racial demographics. If it is the case that segregated populations are less able to come to a consensus over citywide policy decisions, we should also see less support for government spending in segregated cities after accounting for racial demographics.

In order to analyze this claim, I draw on the Census of Governments city and township expenditure data from 1982, 1987, 1992, 1997, 2002, 2007, and 2012.[11] To these data, I merged interpolated data from the 1980, 1990, 2000, and 2010 Census of Population and Housing, and from the 2007–11 American Community Survey (ACS). In the broadest sample, I have data for 3,113 cities, which range in size from about 750 residents to more than 8 million.[12] To capture overall spending on public goods, I analyze the effect of segregation on per capita *direct general expenditures*.[13] I follow this with analyses of operations expenditures on specific budgetary categories including *roads and highways, police, parks, sewers*, and a combined category of *welfare, health, and housing and community development*.[14] I also analyze per capita

---

[11] Available at www2.census.gov/pub/outgoing/govs/special60. Filename is "IndFin_ 1967–2012.zip."

[12] Data are available for many more cities in 2012 than in prior years (largely because I have census data for more places in 2011). I only use observations from 2012 that are also included in 2007 to create a consistent panel.

[13] All analyses are restricted to cities with nonzero expenditures in the category in question because the data do not distinguish between zero expenditures and missing data.

[14] Operations expenditure totals were generated by taking the total spending in each category, less any capital expenditures in that particular year. The category of welfare, health, and housing/community development represents the primary expenditures by cities used to directly support people in economic need.

revenues coming from the city's own residents (as opposed to intergovern-mental revenues) as an indication of the burden of funding the populace is willing to bear.[15] All spending data are in thousands of 2012 dollars. Summary statistics are shown in the online appendix, in Table A7.3. As above, the primary independent variable is the *H* index to measure segregation. In the tables and figures below, I present results using the two-group (white and nonwhite) index; results from the multigroup index are very similar.

To account for the alternative explanation that diversity drives down spending, the analyses include the proportion of the population that is *black, Asian,* and *Latino,* as well as a measure of overall *diversity.* Controlling for demographics also helps account for the fact that white and minority preferences for government spending differ. Racial and ethnic minorities support more government spending than whites on a large number of programs at all levels of government (Hutchings and Valentino 2004). In the aggregate, then, we might expect cities with larger populations of racial and ethnic minorities to support more per capita expenditure, just as Boustan et al. (2013) find. But if my theory is right, cities with more segregation and similar shares of minority residents ought to witness smaller budgets and lower spending on public goods, compared with cities with less segregation, because the likeli-hood of cooperation ought to be fundamentally different in these types of places.

The analyses below also control for the total *population* (logged), the proportion of the population *over age sixty-five,* the proportion of the population with a *college degree,* the proportion of each one hundred residents *employed as local government* workers, the proportion of households that *rent* their home, and the *median household income.* These controls are meant to capture demographic dimensions that affect both segregation and expenditures (through both preferences and need). For instance, we might expect cities with large populations of govern-ment workers to have higher levels of spending, while the reverse might be the case in cities with older populations. An important alternative explanation for a negative relationship between segregation and spend-ing could be city wealth. Segregated cities might be poorer cities for some reason, and may simply have fewer resources to spend on public

---

[15] In contrast, the categorical expenditure variables include all spending on a certain target, regardless of the source of the funds.

goods. Controlling for the proportion of the city that rents and the median household income is intended to account for this possibility.[16]

I begin, in Table 7.2, by regressing per capita *direct general expenditure* on *segregation* with the controls described here. Then, in the second column, I replace *diversity* with *five-year changes* in racial group shares (following Hopkins 2009) to determine whether or not changes in diversity could be the driving factor.[17] In the third column, I add the mean *ideology* of city residents (calculated from the GSS for all city residents as described in the previous section) to account for the possibility that segregated cities are more ideologically conservative. In alternate models (not shown), I add a control for renter segregation. The coefficient is insignificant and does not affect the results presented below.

Table 7.2 provides strong evidence that segregation and public goods spending are negatively related, even in the presence of changing demographics, diverse populations, and conservative residents. The effects of segregation are substantively meaningful and statistically significant. Increasing the segregation index from the twenty-fifth to seventy-fifth percentile (from .01 to .10) in the base model lowers per capita direct general expenditure from $1,413 to $1,299. A difference in total spending of more than $100 per resident could dramatically affect the quality of public goods that individuals experience, given that the average per capita operating expenditure on police is about $190 and about $51 on parks. As Figure 7.1 reveals, the depressive effect of segregation extends to individual categories of public goods spending as well.

Clearly, spending on public goods is lower in cities with greater segregation. Across all six categories displayed in Figure 7.1, segregation exerts a significant negative effect. Table 7.2 also reveals that while segregation is negatively related to public goods investment, more diverse communities are mostly associated with higher levels of spending as the positive coefficients on diversity and on percentage black and Latino indicate.

---

[16] In alternative analyses, I tested the inclusion of proportion of the city in poverty and median home values with no change to the pattern of results. In all analyses, I include fixed effects for cities. This allows me to analyze the effect of segregation within the same location over time, and controls for the many factors (such as age of the city, differentials in costs for service provision, taxation powers and limits, etc.) that might lead cities to differ in expenditure patterns cross-sectionally. I cluster standard errors by city. I exclude from the analyses cities with only a single census tract because the measure of evenness is constant (by definition).

[17] Hopkins (2009) uses ten-year changes in racial group shares. I chose five years in order to preserve more observations in the time-series. The results are similar with ten-year changes.

TABLE 7.2 *Effect of segregation on overall per capita city expenditures*

	Direct general expenditure per capita			Direct general expenditure w/changing demographics			Direct general expenditure w/ideology control		
	β	SE	P > |t|	β	SE	P > |t|	β	SE	P > |t|
Segregation	-1.266	0.218	0.000	-1.141	0.231	0.000	-1.731	0.45	0.000
Diversity	0.199	0.133	0.134				0.060	0.257	0.816
% Black	0.726	0.179	0.000	0.854	0.168	0.000	0.117	0.641	0.856
% Asian	-0.88	0.288	0.002	-1.212	0.307	0.000	-0.565	0.74	0.445
% Latino	1.634	0.171	0.000	1.721	0.19	0.000	1.560	0.394	0.000
5-yr Δ % black				-1.918	0.691	0.006			
5-yr Δ % Latino				-1.695	0.725	0.02			
5-yr Δ % Asian				-1.389	1.073	0.196			
Median income (1000s)	0.006	0.001	0.000	0.005	0.002	0.001	0.009	0.003	0.001
% Local gov. employees	-0.004	0.015	0.787	-0.007	0.017	0.683	-0.077	0.051	0.132
% Renters	0.387	0.318	0.223	0.181	0.311	0.560	-0.123	0.693	0.860
% Over sixty-five	0.458	0.597	0.443	0.639	0.453	0.158	-1.139	0.887	0.200
% College grad	5.114	0.434	0.000	5.806	0.433	0.000	6.66	1.23	0.000
Population (logged)	-0.36	0.045	0.000	-0.439	0.07	0.000	-0.551	0.097	0.000
City ideology							-0.001	0.037	0.972
Constant	3.379	0.441	0.000	4.268	0.675	0.000	6.358	1.317	0.000
N	16,831			14,284			2,524		
Number of cities	3,113			3,113			395		

Note: Linear regressions with fixed effects for cities, robust standard errors clustered by city presented.

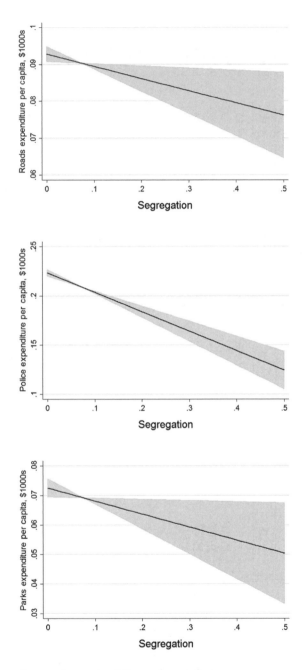

FIGURE 7.1 Segregation and public goods spending
Note: Panels show the predicted relationship between Theil's *H* segregation index and per capita spending on public goods in constant 2012 dollars. Gray shading represents 95% confidence intervals. Full regressions shown in the online appendix, in Table A7.4.

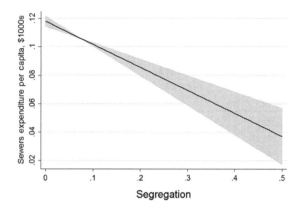

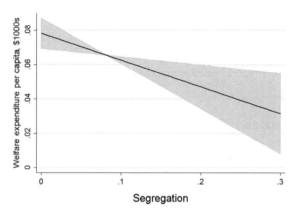

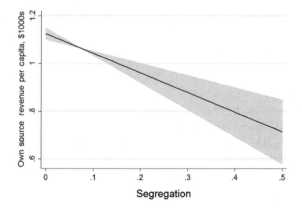

FIGURE 7.1 (*cont.*)

TABLE 7.3 *Change in direct general expenditure per capita by per cent nonwhite at minimum and maximum levels of segregation*

Quintile of % nonwhite	Average % nonwhite	Average segregation level	Change in predicted direct general expenditure per capita*	95% confidence interval
1	4%	0.030	–$490	(–$656, –$325)
2	10%	0.041	–$870	(–$1,163, –$576)
3	19%	0.066	–$970	(–$1,298, –$643)
4	33%	0.108	–$930	(–$1,244, –$616)
5	65%	0.125	–$846	(–$1,132, –$561)

* Predicted values generated from regression displayed in column 1, Table 7.2. Change is from the minimum to maximum level of segregation within a quintile of percentage nonwhite.

Given that racial and ethnic minorities are both more supportive of public goods spending and more likely to live in segregated places (which see less support for public goods), it is important to ask what the overall impact of these countervailing effects is. Table 7.3 shows how segregation affects public goods provision across the range of values of diversity. I divide the sample of cities into quintiles of percentage nonwhite (with 3,366 city-years in each quintile), and then, after estimating the model displayed in column 1 of Table 7.2, I predict *direct general expenditure* per capita at the minimum and maximum values of segregation for each quintile, holding all other variables at their mean values given the quintile. Table 7.3 shows the difference in these predicted values for each quintile of percentage nonwhite.

Table 7.3 reveals substantial declines in direct general expenditure as segregation increases, regardless of the size of the minority population. Segregation has the largest effect in cities with moderately sized minority populations (where minorities comprise 19–33% of the population), but even in majority-minority cities (where minorities make up more than 50% of the population) and cities that are overwhelmingly white, increasing segregation decreases investment in public spending. The fact that segregation has the most pronounced effect in the middle quintiles offers indirect evidence that it is white residents responding to significant

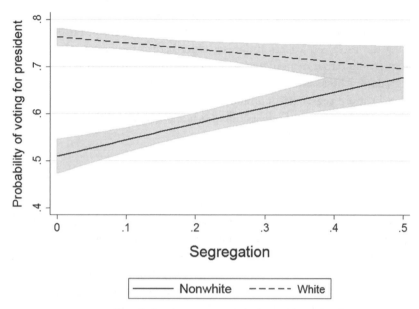

FIGURE 7.2 Correlation between segregation and turnout by race

minority concentrations driving the negative relationship between segregation and public goods spending. An alternative possibility is that low turnout among minority residents drives this pattern. As Figure 7.2 shows, this case is extremely unlikely, given that turnout among minority residents is actually higher in more segregated cities, while turnout among whites is lower.

To estimate this relationship, I draw on data from the General Social Surveys conducted between 1998 and 2008, years for which I was able to determine respondents' city of residence (see Chapter 9 for additional details on this dataset). I estimate the probability that a respondent *voted* in the most recent presidential election. Using logistic regression, I regress this variable on the level of *segregation* in the respondent's city. To understand how segregation operates differently for different groups, I interact the level of segregation with a dummy variable coded 1 if the respondent is *white and non-Hispanic*, and 0 otherwise. I control for the respondent's level of *education*, whether or not they have *kids at home*, their *gender*, whether or not they are *married*, their *income*, and whether or not they are a *government employee*.

At low levels of segregation, white turnout is much higher than minority turnout, but the lines converge as segregation increases. Furthermore, using the racial polarization dataset described in the first section of this chapter, I find that turnout and segregation are positively correlated in the aggregate. These patterns strongly suggest that politics is more contentious in more segregated communities. Thus, a lack of participation by residents who support high spending is not likely to be the cause of lower public goods investment.

EVIDENCE OF CAUSALITY

Even with controls, one might still worry about the causal relationship between segregation and spending. I have argued that segregation should suppress public goods spending. However, it is entirely possible, perhaps quite likely, that some unmeasured set of factors affects both spending and segregation (or that the reverse is true, and spending levels affect segregation patterns). Since we cannot randomly assign segregation to determine its effect on city spending, I use an instrumental variable approach to study the relationships.

A great many factors affect residential location and the distribution of different types of residents across neighborhoods. One set of factors that affects both property values and the ability for communities to maintain a preferred degree of homogeneity are natural and man-made barriers. For instance, freeways and railroad tracks frequently divide more desirable and less desirable parts of town (Ananat 2011). But railways and freeways are often built with the intent to segregate racial communities (Bayor 1996). Instead, I focus on waterways (including large streams and rivers), which vary in number across cities and are arguably exogenous to segregation and spending, given that they are not man-made. At the same time, the presence of natural barriers ought to make it easier for politicians to justify land-use restrictions that define particular neighborhoods.

The use of waterways as an instrumental variable was introduced by Hoxby (2000), who used streams to estimate the governmental fragmentation of metropolitan areas. Cutler and Glaeser (1997) rely on Hoxby's waterways data as an instrument for metropolitan area racial segregation. My instrument differs in two ways. First, and most importantly, my data capture waterway counts and segregation patterns at the city level, rather than at the metropolitan-area level. Second, I use a different source file for the waterways data and a different method for determining whether a waterway ought to be counted within the boundaries of a community.[18] In order to use waterways as an instrument for segregation, I gathered the "rivers and streams" geographic information system map file from the National Hydrologic Remote Sensing Center, which is part of the National Oceanic and Atmospheric Administration (an agency in the US Department of Commerce).[19] I added Census TIGER Line boundary files for all places in the United States as of 2000.[20] I then generated counts of waterways for each place and added these counts to the finance data described previously. Overall, the correlation between the number of waterways and the H index is a powerful 0.37, and the F-statistic on the excluded instrument is 3,999 – which is considerably higher than the typical target of 10.[21]

The current analyses use the same dependent variables as were presented in Table 7.2 and Figure 7.1 (per capita spending on various public goods). The number of waterways is used as an instrument for the H index. Waterways are also correlated with other characteristics that are important to both segregation and spending patterns. The most important of these characteristics is the size of the population, which is correlated with both the number of waterways and the level of segregation. People have settled near waterways since antiquity, and larger cities are also much more likely to be segregated than smaller cities (perhaps because there are more neighborhoods from which to choose). To account for this, I include logged population as an instrument in the first stage.[22] In both the first and second stage regressions, I include the same control variables as presented in Table 7.2, with two changes. Because the number of waterways is constant in my dataset, I do not add fixed effects

---

[18] Hoxby (2000) uses a hand count of streams that are 3.5 miles in length and "of a certain width" supplemented with data from the Geographic Names Information System, which lists the latitude and longitude of smaller streams. Instead, I use geographic information system maps as described in the main text and include all large streams and rivers regardless of length and width. Hoxby (2000) attributes a stream to a Metropolitan Statistical Area (MSA) if it terminates in the MSA (Rothstein 2007), whereas my analysis attributes a waterway to a community if it flows through the community at all (not just at its origin or destination).

[19] The "rivers and streams" shape file is available at: www.nohrsc.noaa.gov/gisdatasets/. It was most recently updated in 2008.

[20] Boundary files are available for download by state here: www2.census.gov/geo/tiger/TIGER2010/PLACE/2000/.

[21] This F-statistic is drawn from a simple two-stage regression, instrumenting segregation with waterways and including no additional controls.

[22] In alternative specifications, I use the number of waterways per capita as the instrument. The pattern of the results is exactly the same.

at the city level.[23] Instead, I include fixed effects for region and year. Second, I add a lagged version of the dependent variable to account for the high correlation between observations over time for the same city and the fact that local budgets are typically changed incrementally from prior years. The results from this instrumental variable approach are displayed in Table 7.4.[24] For presentation purposes, the first stage results are relegated to the online appendix, in Table A7.5.

Regardless of the statistical approach used, segregation appears to have a powerful, depressive effect on public goods provision in cities. The pattern of results in Table 7.4 reflects the OLS regression findings presented in Table 7.2 and Figure 7.1. After accounting for demographic differences, cities with more segregation tend to have smaller budgets, extract fewer resources from their residents, and spend less on roads, policing, parks, sewers, and support for the poor.

But perhaps lower spending is what residents prefer. After all, many elections have been won on platforms promising austerity and frugality. In the final section of this chapter, I explore what the consequences of low spending might be by analyzing a universally disliked event: sewer overflows.

SEGREGATION AND SEWER OVERFLOWS

The federal Environmental Protection Agency (EPA) monitors municipal sewer systems for overflow events. According to a 2004 EPA report to Congress, approximately 860 billion gallons of untreated wastewater were released into communities between 2001 and 2003 when sewer systems' capacities were exceeded. Any single overflow might occur for many reasons: excessive wet weather, pipe blockages, equipment failure, or insufficient capacity. However, generally, as Tessin (2009) explains:

The performance of a sewer system is strongly related to capital fund-raising ... Without adequate investment, excessive groundwater can enter sewers through

---

[23] The omission of fixed effects allows for the inclusion of all cities, regardless of the number of census tracts.

[24] Readers may worry that the exclusion restriction is not met. That is, the presence of waterways may directly affect spending. This is unlikely to be the case for all of the categories of spending that I examine. Additionally, any direct effect is likely to be positive if the presence of waterways is an important driver of development. Finally, although we might expect the presence of one waterway to increase spending, there is no reason to believe that a count of the number of waterways should increase spending linearly.

TABLE 7.4 *Effect of segregation on city expenditures, instrumental approach*

	Direct general expenditure			Roads			Law enforcement			Parks		
	β	SE	P > |t|	β	SE	P > |t|	β	SE	P > |t|	β	SE	P > |t|
Segregation instrumented	-3.806	1.09	0.00	-0.385	0.05	0.00	-0.353	0.10	0.00	-0.025	0.02	0.18
Lagged DV	0.858	0.00	0.00	0.490	0.00	0.00	0.966	0.00	0.00	0.822	0.00	0.00
Diversity	-0.418	0.38	0.27	-0.027	0.02	0.15	-0.001	0.04	0.97	0.004	0.01	0.57
% Black	0.798	0.36	0.03	0.080	0.02	0.00	0.080	0.03	0.02	0.000	0.01	0.98
% Asian	-0.848	0.99	0.39	-0.088	0.05	0.07	-0.082	0.09	0.38	-0.029	0.02	0.08
% Latino	1.121	0.31	0.00	0.086	0.02	0.00	0.078	0.03	0.01	0.007	0.01	0.18
Median income (1000s)	0.012	0.00	0.00	0.001	0.00	0.00	0.001	0.00	0.00	0.000	0.00	0.00
% Local gov. employees	0.276	0.03	0.00	0.017	0.00	0.00	0.020	0.00	0.00	0.002	0.00	0.00
% Renters	2.627	0.39	0.00	0.159	0.02	0.00	0.159	0.04	0.00	0.033	0.01	0.00
% Over sixty-five	2.260	0.81	0.01	0.270	0.04	0.00	0.233	0.08	0.00	0.089	0.01	0.00
% College grad	-0.495	0.62	0.42	-0.013	0.03	0.68	-0.051	0.06	0.39	0.045	0.01	0.00
Constant	-2.034	0.31	0.00	-0.105	0.02	0.00	-0.149	0.03	0.00	-0.026	0.01	0.00
N	25,669			25,121			25,034			23,197		

	Sewers			Welfare			Own Source Revenue		
	β	SE	P > |t|	β	SE	P > |t|	β	SE	P > |t|
Segregation instrumented	-0.393	0.06	0.00	-0.194	0.06	0.00	-3.344	0.95	0.00
Lagged DV	0.082	0.01	0.00	0.936	0.00	0.00	0.712	0.00	0.00
Diversity	0.075	0.02	0.00	0.000	0.02	1.00	-0.373	0.33	0.26
% Black	0.054	0.02	0.02	0.065	0.02	0.01	0.686	0.31	0.03

(continued)

TABLE 7.4 (*continued*)

	Sewers			Welfare			Own Source Revenue		
	β	SE	P > |t|	β	SE	P > |t|	β	SE	P > |t|
% Asian	−0.229	0.06	0.00	−0.008	0.05	0.87	−0.909	0.86	0.29
% Latino	−0.048	0.02	0.01	0.045	0.02	0.01	1.01	0.27	0.00
Median income (1000s)	0.000	0.00	0.89	0.000	0.00	0.57	0.013	0.00	0.00
% Local gov. employees	0.000	0.00	0.88	0.007	0.00	0.00	0.294	0.03	0.00
% Renters	0.082	0.02	0.00	0.090	0.02	0.00	2.573	0.34	0.00
% Over sixty-five	0.344	0.05	0.00	0.109	0.05	0.03	2.435	0.71	0.00
% College grad	0.057	0.04	0.11	0.009	0.04	0.81	−0.433	0.54	0.42
Constant	0.007	0.02	0.69	−0.057	0.02	0.00	−2.025	0.27	0.00
N	20,258			17,827			25,671		

Note: Two-stage least squares regressions with fixed effects for regions and year (not shown); instrumented: two-group *H* index of segregation; excluded instruments: # of waterways, population logged.

cracked pipes and ingrown tree roots. Aging pipes can break and send sewage to the surface. Growing populations can cause wastewater flow to exceed the system's design capacity . . . For these reasons, local governments that do not invest enough capital typically experience more sewer overflows and other system failures. (p. 168)

Some federal and state grants are available for sewer system mainten-ance, but the vast majority of funding to reduce overflows comes from local sources (Environmental Protection Agency 2004). According to my data, the most segregated cities spend about $200 less per capita each year on their sewer systems. In the aggregate, this translates to an average of about $60,000 less per year spent on sewers (after controlling for all of the other demographic variables included in the regressions above). When city engineers plan, build, extend, and repair sewer systems, they take into account variables like population growth and average precipitation, as well as potential deviations from those estimates.

Analyses of effective or responsive governmental policy typically need to take into account variation in constituent preferences. For instance, a community that spends very little on protection of open space or on recycling may be accurately representing the views of its residents. Sewer overflows are different. No one wants a river of fecal matter running down their street or flooding their basement. Thus, it seems reasonable to assume that more frequent overflows are, without qualification, worse than fewer overflows. That said, voters and sewer engineers may not agree on the level of resources needed to prevent overflows, and, therefore, raising funds for capital improvements may be challen-ging. If it is the case, as I have asserted, that more segregated cities will have more trouble coming to political consensus about public goods provision, then we ought to expect more segregated cities to witness more sewer overflows – all else equal. In order to determine whether or not this is the case, I utilize data collected by the Environmental Protec-tion Agency in 2004.

In this data collection, the EPA gathered information on overflows from twenty-five state environmental agencies between 2001 and 2003.[25] In total, the EPA reported about 35,000 different overflow events from several thousand sewer agencies. The EPA data do not include any geographic identifiers other than the name of the sewer agency, so I matched these names to cities by hand. After dropping cases in which

---

[25] The data were generously provided to me by Jeff Tessin, who had secured the data from an EPA staff member for his PhD dissertation.

the sewer operator was not a municipal government (e.g., metropolitan water districts or county governments), and cases in which the EPA data provided insufficient detail to identify the municipality, I determined the location of 19,817 overflow events. I aggregated these events to the city level and was able to match these data to segregation measures and census data for 1,417 cities.

The median number of overflows during this period was 2, while the mode was 1. A few cities with enormously high numbers of overflow events pull the mean to 50. For this reason, I take the natural log of the number of overflow events for each city, and standardize it by the city's population. This *logged overflows per 1,000 persons* measure serves as my dependent variable. My main independent variable is the city's *H* index of racial segregation, measured in 2000, if available, and 2010 if not. I control for the natural log of the *total population* to account for the possibility that cities serving more people are likely to have more advanced engineering for their sewer systems by necessity.[26] In a second regression, I add controls for other city demographics. I add the share that *rents* their homes to account for the possibility that homeowners may be more likely to act politically to prevent overflows. I include the share of the population that is *urban* to capture the difficulties rural areas may face in providing sewer systems to a dispersed population. I include the share of the population that is *black, Asian*, and *Latino* to determine whether or not diversity alone can account for poor performance. I add the city's *median household income* and *per capita subventions* to measure the city's capacity to raise funds for sewer maintenance and expansion. The results of these OLS regressions with robust standard errors are shown in Table 7.5 (summary statistics are in the online appendix, in Table A7.6).

The data reveal a significant correlation between segregation and sewer overflows. Living in a city with very little segregation, one can expect about 1.5 overflows per year on average. This increases to nearly 2.5 overflows in cities at the ninety-fifth percentile of the segregation distribution. Not only do segregated cities see lower spending on public goods, but they also witness worse performance as well.

---

[26] I add fixed effects for states for two reasons. The first is that the EPA data collection gathered statistics from state agencies that may have had different reporting standards. The second reason is to account for the different environmental, regulatory, and funding environments cities in different states face.

TABLE 7.5 *Correlation between segregation and sewer overflows*

	β	SE	P > |t|	β	SE	P > |t|
Segregation	2.166	0.53	0.00	2.398	0.78	0.00
Population (logged)	−0.347	0.05	0.00	−0.325	0.07	0.00
% Renters				−0.424	0.40	0.29
% Urban				−0.129	0.09	0.16
% Black				−0.524	0.37	0.16
% Asian				3.813	1.01	0.00
% Latino				−0.080	0.28	0.77
Median income (1000s)				−0.001	0.00	0.66
Subventions per capita (1000s)				−0.031	0.01	0.00
Constant	3.678	0.53	0.00	3.554	0.59	0.00
N	1,417			1,417		
R²	0.199			0.207		

Note: Linear regressions with fixed effects for states, robust standard errors presented. DV is sewer overflows per 1,000 residents, logged.

CONCLUSION

The evidence presented here indicates that racial segregation plays a significant role in access to public goods. Segregated cities are comprised of homogeneous neighborhoods embedded in larger diverse communities. While African Americans, Latinos, and Asians are fairly likely, today, to live as neighbors, whites remain in isolated enclaves. Because local governmental decisions often concern spatial allocation, neighborhoods are important municipal actors in local politics. In more segregated places, neighborhood interests become overlaid with racial division. Segregated cities have more racially polarized elections and may be less likely to generate policy consensus. The result is that cities with more segregation have smaller public goods budgets. Segregated cities raise fewer dollars from their residents and spend less money on roads, law enforcement, parks, sewers, welfare, housing, and community development. This low spending has significant consequences. For example, segregated cities see more sewer overflows.

Political polarization and underfunding of public goods in segregated cities may also affect their attractiveness to prospective homebuyers. In combination with the many factors discussed in Chapter 6 (e.g., rising minority political competition and open housing pressures) and newly available federally backed mortgages, suburban living would come to be a more desirable option – one that offered white homeowners more complete control over the political arena. In moving to the suburbs and then preventing diversification through restrictive land-use policies (as will be shown in the next chapter), white homeowners created a much larger and more protected set of white enclaves throughout the nation.

8

Locking in Segregation through Suburban Control

In 2012, the Manhattan Institute issued a report entitled "The End of the Segregated Century," declaring that "all-white neighborhoods are effectively extinct" (Glaeser and Vigdor 2012). Though not all demographers shared the optimism of Glaeser and Vigdor, many trumpeted the decline of neighborhood segregation in America following the release of the 2010 census (Frey 2014). While segregation between neighborhoods has declined, another type of segregation has remained remarkably stable – even rising in the postwar period. Segregation between cities is persistent along both race and economic lines (Fischer et al. 2004; Massey and Hajnal 1995). This means that while integration within cities has increased, cities as a whole have become less racially and economically diverse over time. As a result, a greater share of total segregation in metropolitan areas is now accounted for across cities, rather than within them (see Chapter 3). This is what is commonly understood as the process of suburbanization.

While we have substantial evidence on the role federal policies have played in generating suburbanization (Jackson 1987; Massey and Denton 1998; Hayward 2013), our understanding of the ways in which local politics affects suburbanization has been limited. In previous chapters, I argued that segregation was pursued by local governments to enhance property values and target local public goods toward white homeowners and land-oriented businesses. Such strategies, combined with political control of city councils and mayors' offices, ensured that local governments operated to protect the homogeneity of white homeowner neighborhoods, and provide them with disproportionate benefits. As Chapter 6 revealed, in the postwar period, this control was threatened by increasing minority electoral participation and policy achievements. Chapter 7 showed that segregated cities also struggle with racial polarization and underfunding of public goods. Here, I demonstrate that these factors contributed to suburbanization.

The analyses in this chapter rely on a measure of segregation that incorporates patterns of sorting both within cities, and between cities and suburbs. This strategy allows for a consideration of residential sorting at multiple geographic levels at the same time. Most scholars focus either on metropolitan-level segregation (e.g., Dreier et al. 2004; Jackson 1987) or neighborhood segregation (e.g., Massey and Denton 1998) – but these types of sorting are intricately linked. In this chapter, I am interested in identifying the factors that encouraged suburbanization – not those that generated segregation within cities. But because white homeowners may choose either suburbanization or segregation within a city, analyzing suburbanization requires controlling for the level of segregation in the inner city. By drawing on this nested measure of segregation for all metropolitan areas over a long time span (1980–2011), I am able to show that residents traded one type of homogeneity for another in response to political outcomes.

I utilize time lags and metro area fixed effects to handle the problem of endogeneity, as race and class sorting can, in turn, generate different political outcomes (Massey and Hajnal 1995; Friesema 1969; Nelson 1990). In this chapter, I analyze the relationships between cities within metropolitan areas. I concentrate on the ways in which the politics of the central city (the city with the largest population in the metro area) and the pull of suburban opportunities affect demographic residential patterns in the metro area. When central cities elect minority mayors and when central city expenditures are higher and favor policing, a greater share of metropolitan area segregation is accounted for between cities rather than within them. Consistent with the desire to protect homogeneity in schools, metro areas with larger numbers of school districts and strict land-use controls also witness more segregation across cities. In short, when central city politics does not favor their interests (and suburbs do), white and upper-class residents are more likely to reside in different cities, rather than in different neighborhoods, and they lock in these sorting patterns through public policy. In the final section of the chapter, I show that communities with more whites and homeowners receive a disproportionate share of municipal spending.

UNDERSTANDING THE LINK BETWEEN SEGREGATION AND SUBURBANIZATION

People choose where they live based, in part, on the types and quality of public goods and services provided in a community, as well as the taxes required to provide those goods and services (Tiebout 1956; Ely and Teske 2015; Banzhaf and Walsh 2008). However, not all residents are equally able to match these preferences with housing location. Low-income households have less choice than do high-income households because amenities (including schools, parks, and public safety) are capitalized into housing prices and rents. Racial and ethnic minority households have been severely limited in their ability to live where they choose. In part, this is the due to the fact that minorities have lower average levels of income and wealth. But, as previous chapters have shown, it is also the result of concerted efforts by white homeowners to segregate them through public policy.

In an effort to protect property values, white homeowners and their allies utilized a variety of mechanisms to bar minorities and renters from moving to their communities. Organizing collectively through home-owners' associations, white homeowners controlled government decision-making on matters such as the implementation of zoning and land-use regulation, the razing of slums, the rebuilding of downtowns, the placement of public housing, and zoning decisions that concentrated negative externalities in poor and minority neighborhoods.

However, as Chapter 6 revealed, starting slowly during the 1940s and then more rapidly during the 1950s and 1960s, white homeowners began to see their exclusive political control chipped away. The massive influx of wartime workers dramatically changed the racial and socioeconomic makeup of many large cities. Among cities that had populations of at least 50,000 in 1940, the white population share declined about eight percentage points between 1940 and 1970 (from ninety to eighty-two). By 2011, the white share of these cities decreased dramatically to 52%. However, the share of renters also declined during this period, as home-ownership rates expanded.[1] Meanwhile black and Latino Americans'

---

[1] I only have time series data on homeownership rates for sixty cities. In these places, the share of homeowners rose from 35% in 1940 to 48% in 1970. Nationwide, the home-ownership rate expanded from 43.6% to 63% during this period (Bureau of the Census, Historical Statistics of the United States, Colonial Times to 1970). www.census.gov/library/publications/1975/compendia/hist_stats_colonial-1970.html

sustained battle for civil, economic, and political rights gained ground. As racial minorities began to contest, and even win, political representation, the open housing movement brought the possibility of neighborhood integration, and the federal court ordered desegregation of public schools. This period became fraught with uncertainty and fear. Many whites placed an increasingly high value on segregation as they joined the ranks of homeowners.

The rapid increase in the population of the suburbs during the postwar period was mostly not the result of white flight. Rather, rising incomes, low-cost, federally backed mortgages, the lucrative federal mortgage deduction, new housing construction in suburban tracts, and an extensive highway system all worked to bring residents to the periphery (Gotham 2000; Nall 2018). Yet, in the early decades of the postwar period, suburban living was nearly exclusively accessible to whites and home-owners, compared with people of color and renters (Kruse and Sugrue 2006; Jackson 1987). This pattern eventually changed. Many racial minorities and renters live in suburban communities today (Frasure-Yokely 2015). However, as Briffault (1990) explains, "[T]he increased heterogeneity of suburbia as a whole is usually not matched by a greater diversification *within* particular suburbs. There are now more poor and working-class people, more minorities and more industrial and commer-cial sites in suburbia. But poorer, working-class or black suburbanites are likely to live in different jurisdictions separate from those inhabited by affluent or white suburbanites" (p. 353). These trends have converged to increase divisions along race and class lines across city lines (Fischer et al. 2004; Fischer 2008).

In previous decades, processes of consolidation and annexation made city boundaries malleable so that those moving away from the center of the city would have resided within city limits (Teaford 1979). However, in the postwar period, state annexation laws changed and political bound-aries ceased to keep pace with residential spread (Briffault 1990). As a result, the number of incorporated municipalities in metropolitan areas grew, and suburbs gained population, economic activity, and political power (Danielson 1976; Miller 1981; Burns 1994).

Since the 1990s, white homebuyers' willingness to pay a premium for homogenous neighborhoods has been the central factor perpetuating seg-regation (Cutler, Glaeser, and Vigdor 1999). Overt racism has decreased dramatically over the last several decades (Schuman et al. 1997), but whites continue to express a preference for same-race neighbors (Charles 2003) and minority neighborhoods continue to be perceived as having poor-quality amenities (Bobo, Kluegel, and Smith 1997; Ellen 2000; Emerson, Chai, and Yancey 2001; Krysan 2002; Bayer, Ferreira, and McMillian 2007). A growing black population leads whites to leave neighborhoods and/or be unwilling to enter others. The size of the minority population that affects white population flows (the tipping point) ranges from about 5% to 20% (Card, Mas, and Rothstein 2008). Once a neighborhood reaches the tipping point, it quickly becomes predominantly inhabited by racial and ethnic minorities. White preferences for homogeneity are undoubtedly enhanced by persistent discrimination in the real estate and mortgage industries, which limit minority access to some neighborhoods (Pager and Shepherd 2008; Galster and Godfrey 2005; Bobo 2001; Farley et al. 1994; Bobo and Zubrinski 1996).

However, while white preferences for white neighbors help to make sense of the fact that whites live in different *neighborhoods* than nonwhites, they do not help to clarify why whites live in different *cities*. Why, even as neighborhoods have grown more integrated, have cities become less so? The answer is politics and political control.

A sophisticated literature on public opinion and political behavior reveals that whites' perceptions of racial and ethnic minorities are strongly predictive of their views toward government spending and government policies that have become racially coded, like crime and policing.[2] If an individual holds negative stereotypes of racial minorities, she is likely to oppose government expenditures, especially when she believes that there is a racial disparity in who shoulders the tax burden and in who benefits from public services (Sears and Citrin 1982; Kruse 2005). After spending nearly one hundred years creating segregated neighborhoods, many white homeowners living in diverse central cities subscribed to such beliefs and, so, opposed rising government spending in central cities.

We know that white residents are willing to pay a 7% premium on housing in order to live in a higher-income suburb, in part, to gain access to higher school quality and lower property tax rates (Boustan 2010). We also know that court-ordered integration of city schools led some white parents to seek out homogenous, suburban school districts (Baum-Snow and Lutz 2011; Lassiter 2006), and that in particular cities, like Atlanta,

---

[2] The literature is voluminous. But some representative studies include Bobo and Kluegel 1997; Sears 1988; Kinder and Sanders 1996; Rabinowitz et al. 2009; Federico 2005; Gilens 1999; Quadagno 1994; Luttmer 2001; Winter 2006; Valentino et al. 2002; Mendelberg 2001; Hurwitz and Peffley 1997.

losing segregation battles led many whites to choose suburban homes (Kruse 2005). What we don't yet know is how political patterns in central cities and opportunities in the suburbs shaped segregation patterns. This chapter shows that suburban sorting along race and class lines is linked to central city elections of minority mayors, larger city budgets, and a greater share of spending on police. It is also linked to greater use of land-use regulations in the suburbs and availability of suburban school districts. In the next sections, I provide evidence of these local political contributors to suburban segregation.

MEASURING SUBURBANIZATION: A NEW APPROACH

To show that political outcomes affect segregation across city lines, I use a segregation measure that can be decomposed into within-city and across-city components. This measure allows me to take advantage of different predictions, depending on the level at which segregation occurs, and to control for aggregate preferences for homogeneity. In some metropolitan areas, whites and homeowners tend to be segregated from nonwhites and renters in different neighborhoods (indicating segregation at a low level of geography). In other metro areas, race and class sorting is more prevalent across city lines (indicating segregation at a higher level of geography). If a city increases its budget, there is no reason to believe that this would induce residents to sort into different neighborhoods, but, I argue, it could lead to sorting into a different city.

While households may choose residential locations that result in more homogenous neighborhoods for a variety of reasons, only cross-city segregation ought to be affected by the total bundle of public goods provided by the city and the election of city officials. Because different racial and economic groups have different preferences for local representatives and policies, when budgets or election outcomes are less favorable to white and homeowner preferences, these residents should be more likely to sort into residential locations outside of city boundaries.[3]

---

[3] There is no evidence that the inverse is true. When budgets favor white/wealthy preferences, poor and minority residents have not been found to move to communities that prioritize their demands and needs. For instance, Levine and Zimmerman (1999) investigate the potential for states' welfare programs to act as magnets for the poor. They find little support for this hypothesis. The process of gentrification – where affluent residents return to the central city – is another scenario that could lead to movement among poor residents. Here, too, scholars have found no evidence that gentrification leads poor households to leave their housing units (Vigdor, Massey, and Rivlin 2002). The most

We most commonly think of segregation across city lines as a process of suburbanization, but sorting between suburbs is another version of the same pattern. The result should be an increase in the share of metropolitan segregation across cities, as opposed to within them.

To determine whether city political patterns favoring nonwhite and renter interests affect metropolitan segregation, I use the census data described in Chapter 3 to generate a panel dataset measuring segregation at the census-tract level for each metropolitan area. To measure segregation, I use the H index, which allows for decomposition of within-city and across-city components.[4] It measures the evenness of dispersal of groups across geographic units (in this case, census tracts, cities, and metropolitan areas).

The groups I use to calculate the H index here are white/nonwhite, renter/homeowner, and wealthy/non-wealthy.[5] As explained in Chapter 3, the H index measures the degree to which the diversity of subunits differs from the diversity of the larger unit, expressed as a fraction of the larger unit's total diversity and weighted by the subunit's share of the total population. For each census year, I calculate an H index for all cities within a metropolitan area, denoted H_{m_c}, and all tracts within each city, and denoted H_{c_t}.[6] These H indices reveal how diverse each census tract is

---

likely explanation, of course, is that it is whites and the wealthy have had a greater ability to choose where they live. Beyond this, political outcomes are typically much more responsive to the preferences of whites and the wealthy (Hajnal 2009; Gilens 2014).

[4] The approach is similar to the one taken by Fischer et al. (2004), who analyze trends over time in the level at which segregation occurs. In contrast to Fischer et al. (2004), I seek to determine whether such patterns are related to city policy choices, not just time.

[5] Since 1980, the census has tabulated the number of residents in each census tract that self-identify as racially white and ethnically not-Latino; these individuals are classified as whites in my analysis. All other racial/ethnic combinations are classified as nonwhites. The census gathers tenure information on all occupied housing units, noting whether they are rented or owned. The share of units rented versus owned comprises my measure of segregation. Finally, the census reports income categorically, not continuously, so wealthy refers to the share of families in each census tract with incomes above particular thresholds for each census year. These thresholds were determined by calculating the average family income for all census tracts in the United States for each census year. The wealthy threshold represents the income bin with its starting point closest to the ninetieth percentile of the distribution. The thresholds for each census year are: $35,000 for 1980, $75,000 for 1990, $100,000 for 2000, and $150,000 for 2011. All families with this amount of income or more are included as wealthy. Census tracts range from 0 to 100% wealthy, with a mean of 18%, a median of 13%, and a standard deviation of 16%.

[6] Census tracts are perfectly nested within states and counties. However, in some cases, tracts cross city lines. In these cases, GeoLytics assigned the tract to the city containing the largest share of the tract population. In 2011, tracts are weighted by the share of population contained in each city. Observations are unique when defined by year, tract, city,

given the diversity of the city, and how diverse each city is given the diversity of the metropolitan area:

$$H_{m\_c} = \sum_{c=1}^{C} \frac{P_c}{P_m} \left(\frac{E_m - E_c}{E_m} \right)$$

$$H_{c\_t} = \sum_{t=1}^{T} \frac{P_t}{P_c} \left(\frac{E_c - E_t}{E_c} \right),$$

where P represents total population of the geography t, c, or m.

These two indices can be combined produce a total H index for the metropolitan area, which is equal to the H index calculated for the metropolitan area at the tract level, H_{m_t}:

$$H_{m\_t} = \sum_{t=1}^{T} \frac{P_t}{P_m} \left(\frac{E_m - E_t}{E_m} \right) = H_{m\_c} + \sum_{c=1}^{C} \left(\frac{P_c}{P_m} \right) \left(\frac{E_c}{E_m} \right) H_{c\_t}.$$

I analyze the percentage of total metropolitan area segregation that can be attributed to cross-city segregation as opposed to within-city segregation. I have one observation per metropolitan area in 1980, 1990, 2000, and 2011. The dependent variable in my analyses is the share of total segregation in a metropolitan area that is determined by segregation across cities versus within them:

$$share\_across = \frac{H_{m\_c}}{H_{m\_t}}.$$

My argument is that city politics affects segregation patterns. Because I only have one measure of segregation for each metropolitan area, I analyze the effect on segregation of city politics in the city with the largest population in the metropolitan area. For example, in the Detroit-Warren-Livonia metropolitan area, I estimate the relationship between Detroit's city expenditures and the share of metropolitan segregation that is attributed to whites living in different cities than nonwhites (which happens to rise from 51% to 88% between 1970 and 2011). Table 8.1

county, and metropolitan area. Tracts located in unincorporated areas within a metropolitan area are combined as a single unincorporated unit. Tracts outside of metropolitan areas are not included in the analysis. I use Metropolitan Statistical Areas and, where possible, Primary Metropolitan Statistical Areas as the highest level of aggregation (not Consolidated Metropolitan Statistical Areas, which are much larger).

TABLE 8.1 *Central vs. non-central cities, 2011*

	Central cities	Suburbs
% White	58%	73%
% Black	19%	9%
% Latino	16%	12%
% Asian	4%	4%
% In poverty	21%	12%
% Renters	47%	32%
Median household income	$42,796	$61,670
% Wealthy	9%	13%
N	323	4,145

provides aggregate descriptive statistics for the central cities versus non-central cities in my analysis as of 2011. The table reveals that suburbs are whiter, wealthier, and filled with more homeowners than central cities.

In Chapter 6, I argued that in the postwar period, white homeowner neighborhoods felt threatened by increasing electoral contestation by minority candidates and the successes of the open housing movement. Public opinion surveys reveal that racial and income groups are divided over the proper size of government. Further, studies have shown that white opinion on government spending is powerfully shaped by attitudes toward the group perceived to be the beneficiaries of the spending (Nelson and Kinder 1996). During the 1960s and 1970s, many central cities became associated with rising crime rates (Wilson 1987). Today, whites link crime and criminality with blackness (Peffley, Shields, and Williams 2010; Gilliam and Iyengar 2000; Gilliam et al. 1996). For wealthy, white homeowners with the ability to choose suburban living, the election of minority mayors, increases in the municipal budget, and shares of the budget going toward policing in central cities all played a role in encouraging segregation across city lines. Residents were pulled to the suburbs by the promise of homogenous schools and strict land-use controls.

To analyze these relationships, I begin by regressing the share of metropolitan area segregation determined across cities on independent variables capturing political and policy control in the central city. The first is a variable noting whether or not the central city had a *minority mayor* (African American, Hispanic, or Asian) at any point in the decade prior to the year in which segregation is measured.[7] Next, I add two spending measures: inflation-adjusted *direct general expenditure per capita* and the proportion of the city budget spent on *policing*.[8] These variables come from the Census of Governments State and Local Government Finance files from 1977 to 2012.[9] I add the natural log of the *population* as a control because large cities have different spending patterns than small cities, and size may affect segregation patterns by offering residents greater ability to sort themselves into like neighborhoods. Finally, I add a measure of the *violent crime rate* in the central city to capture local conditions to which both policy and movers might have reacted.[10] These data represent 209 metropolitan areas, and include a total of 618 observations. Summary statistics are included in the online appendix, in Table A8.1.

There is an obvious endogeneity problem with the assertion that city elections and budgets can affect residential locations. That is, we know that as homeowning whites choose to locate in the suburbs as opposed to central cities, the remaining central city population will have different policy and candidate preferences. The success of black mayoral candidates in this scenario is what Friesema (1969) called the "Hollow Prize," winning election in a city with profound governance challenges. To attempt to mitigate problems this pattern might cause for the analysis, the mayoral data are measured in the decade prior to the segregation data and all of the remaining measures are lagged ten years. Additionally, my analyses include fixed effects for metropolitan area, so that the estimated effects of politics are within, rather than across, areas.

Is it the case that politics favoring nonwhite and poor preferences in central cities is associated with additional cross-city segregation? In short, yes. Table 8.2 presents the results.

---

[7] These data are from a number of different sources, including Vogl (2014), Hopkins and McCabe (2012), and my own research using websites and newspaper accounts of elections. The variable is a dummy variable coded 1 if the central city had a minority mayor, and coded 0 if the mayor was white in all years of the prior decade.

[8] Police protection expenditures include "expenditures for general police, sheriff, state police, and other governmental departments that preserve law and order, protect persons and property from illegal acts, and work to prevent, control, investigate, and reduce crime." Pages 5–58 in the U.S. Bureau of the Census Government Finance and Employment Classification Manual, available at: www2.census.gov/govs/pubs/classification/2006_classification_manual.pdf

[9] The data are collected in years that end with 2 and 7, and I used linear interpolation to generate estimates of city expenditures in 1980, 1990, 2000, and 2011 to match the census population data. Available at www2.census.gov/pub/outgoing/govs/special60/. Filename is "IndFin_1967–2012.zip."

[10] These data are from the Department of Justice Uniform Crime Reporting Program: Offenses Known and Clearances by Arrest reports for 1980, 1990, 2000, and 2011.

TABLE 8.2 *Effect of city spending patterns on share of metropolitan segregation attributed to cross-city segregation*

	Racial segregation			Renter segregation			Wealth segregation		
	β	SE	P > |t|	β	SE	P > |t|	β	SE	P > |t|
Politics favoring minorities and renters									
Minority mayor	0.032	0.01	0.01	0.019	0.01	0.08	0.027	0.01	0.01
Direct general expenditure per capita	0.052	0.01	0.00	-0.004	0.01	0.58	0.013	0.01	0.07
% Policing	0.723	0.14	0.00	-0.223	0.12	0.06	0.458	0.12	0.00
Controls									
Population (logged)	0.046	0.03	0.12	-0.057	0.03	0.03	-0.013	0.03	0.60
Crime rate	0.566	0.13	0.00	0.134	0.11	0.24	0.159	0.11	0.15
Constant	-0.380	0.35	0.28	1.051	0.31	0.00	0.341	0.30	0.25
Number of observations	618			618			618		
Number of MSAs	209			209			209		
R^2 (within)	0.211			0.035			0.078		

Note: OLS regressions, fixed effects for metro area included in all models; *minority mayor* refers to previous decade, all other measures lagged ten years; DVs are share of segregation attributed across rather than within cities in metro areas.

Table 8.2 tells a consistent story particularly for race and wealth segregation. When central cities elect minority mayors, when they spend more money, and when a larger proportion of their budget is spent on policing, a larger proportion of the metropolitan area's total segregation along race and class lines is accounted for across cities rather than within them. In short, more liberal policy in the central city is associated with more segregation across city lines, while more conservative spending patterns in center cities are associated with less. As Table 8.1 makes clear, non-central cities are whiter, wealthier, and more heavily populated with homeowners than central cities. This suggests that it is wealthy whites who make the choice to reside outside of the central city when policies favoring poor and minority interests are enacted. Conversely, wealthy white residents choose to remain in the central city when budgets are more austere. Overall, the results are strongest and most consistent for racial segregation. As has been true throughout this book, race – not class – is the clearer dividing line.

With regard to racial segregation in particular, the results are powerful. If we compare, on the one hand, a city with a white mayor in the twenty-fifth percentile of the distribution on per capita spending and police expenditure with one with a minority mayor and in the seventy-fifth percentile on the spending measures, the metro-area racial segregation accounted for across cities increases from 35% to 46%. This is equivalent to the difference between the patterns of segregation in the Wichita, Kansas, area (*share_across_race* = 0.355) and the Waco, Texas, area (*share_across_race* = 0.468), as well as the Charlotte, North Carolina, area (*share_across_race* = 0.358) and the Portland, Oregon, area (*share_across_race* = 0.465).[11]

SCHOOLS, LAND-USE REGULATION, AND SUBURBAN SEGREGATION

The previous section analyzed what we might call the push factors contributing to segregation between cities. There are also pull factors. Here, I analyze the contribution of school choice and stringent land-use regulations on suburbanization. Metro areas with larger numbers of school districts allow residents more opportunity to jurisdiction shop, thereby increasing the potential for segregation across city lines.

---

[11] These statistics are for the year 2011.

Land-use regulation is instrumental in the maintenance of segregation. Scholars have often argued (although not demonstrated) that this tendency has generated a shift from the predominance of racial segregation toward class segregation (Mieszkowski and Mills 1993; Fischel 2004). The work that empirically investigates the relationship between land-use regulation and segregation (e.g., Rothwell and Massey 2009; Glaeser and Ward 2006; Berry 2001) has not made a distinction between segregation within cities and segregation across them. This is an important omission, because homogenous suburban municipalities ought to be able to utilize land-use regulation much more effectively than homogenous neighborhoods within cities, as municipalities wield more political power. If it is the case that whites and homeowners seek to use local policy to protect home values and control the distribution of public goods, then metropolitan areas with more intense land-use regulation in the suburbs should also have greater race and class segregation across cities. This is exactly what I find.

To provide evidence of these links, I use the Wharton Residential Land Use Regulatory Index (WRLURI) developed by Gyourko, Saiz, and Summers (2008). This index is built from a 2006 survey of local governments regarding the characteristics of the regulatory process, rules of local residential land-use regulation, and regulatory outcomes. These data were combined to measure the "stringency of the local regulatory environment in each community" (Gyourko et al. 2008, p. 3). The survey contains data for more than 2,700 municipalities. For each metropolitan area, I determined the average WRLURI for all suburban communities. I then calculated the difference between the center city WRLURI and suburban WRLURI. This difference measure provides an estimate of the degree to which suburban municipalities have more stringent land-use regulations than the central city for each metro area. I combined these data with the segregation measures described in the previous analyses – the share of the metropolitan area segregation accounted for across cities rather than within them. The WRLURI data are only available at one point in time, so I analyze the correlation between each region's *share across* and the *WRLURI difference* in 2011 using OLS regression. The regression also includes the *number of elementary school districts* in each metro area to capture the lure of homogenous, suburban schools.

Figure 8.1 displays the marginal effect of suburban land-use regulation stringency and school choice on race, renter, and wealth segregation across cities (regressions are presented in the online appendix, in Table A8.2).

Suburban land-use controls and availability of school districts are significantly related to the degree to which segregation is accounted for

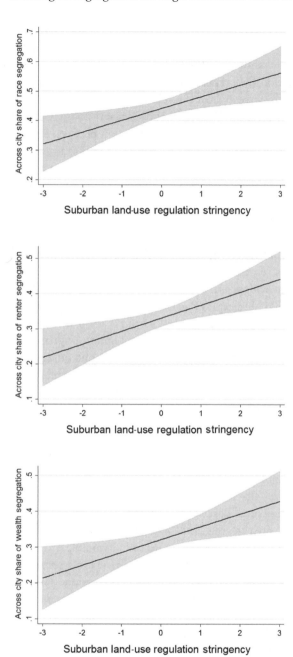

FIGURE 8.1 Correlation between suburban land-use regulation and segregation across cities

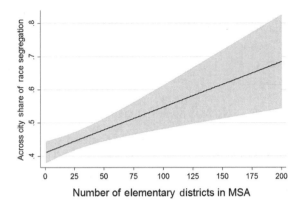

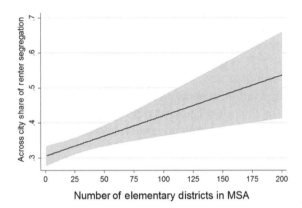

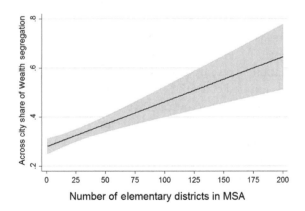

FIGURE 8.1 (*cont.*)

across, rather than within, cities in metropolitan areas. The graphs also make clear that there is no difference between the effects of land-use regulation and school choice on race versus class segregation. They are equally affected.

SUBURBAN INEQUALITY

I've argued that white homeowners institutionalized segregation in order to protect their public goods and property values. The result of these policies in the postwar period has been to increase the disparity in service provision across cities. To show this, I draw on the same spending and segregation data described in the previous section. First, I aggregate all inflation-adjusted expenditures per capita by metropolitan area, for each year. This total expenditures per capita variable represents the collective dollars spent by municipal governments in a metropolitan area. I divide each municipality's expenditure by this total to generate the share of metropolitan spending accounted for by each city. I calculate a similar measure for population, generating the share of metropolitan population accounted for by each city. The ratio of these two quantities, the *spending equity ratio*, is my first dependent variable:

$$Spending\ Equity\ Ratio_j = \frac{E_j/E}{P_j},$$

where E_j is the per capita expenditure by city j, E is the total expenditures in the metropolitan area, and P_j is the share of the metropolitan population represented by city j.

This ratio measures the disparity between the percentage of the population represented by a city and the percentage of total resources received by that population. If resources are distributed exactly equally across the population, the ratio takes a value of 1; values less than 1 indicate that the community receives fewer resources than its population size would predict, and values greater than 1 indicate an abundance of resources. Between 1972 and 2012, this measure averaged 0.4 for central cities and 2.5 for suburbs.[12] Suburban residents receive two-and-a-half times the resources that their population share justifies, while central city residents receive less than half of the amount of resources that their

---

[12] Calculated for all cities with more than 1,000 residents and all metropolitan areas for which I have data on more than one city.

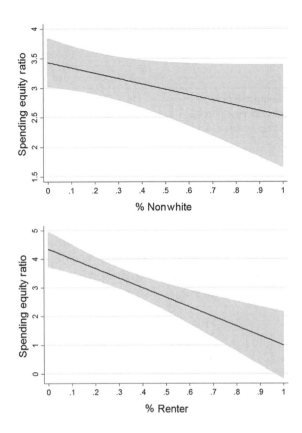

FIGURE 8.2 Effect of cityrace and class on spending equity

population share justifies. This is the case in the aggregate, despite the fact that central cities spend more, on average, per resident than do suburbs. Unsurprisingly, communities with larger populations of racial and ethnic minorities and more renters have a lower *spending equity ratio*. Regressing the *spending equity ratio* on the share of the city that is *nonwhite* and the share that *rents* their homes, including fixed effects for years and errors clustered by metropolitan area, yields Figure 8.2.

Given that cities with more homeowners and white residents are more likely to garner a larger share of total resources spent in metropolitan areas, we should also expect that metropolitan areas with more segregation along race and class lines will witness more variation in spending from city to city. This is exactly what I find. My dependent variable in this analysis is

TABLE 8.3 *Correlation between spending heterogeneity and segregation*

	Column 1		
	β	Std. Err.	P > |t|
Racial segregation across cities	1.02	0.321	0.001
Renter segregation across cities	1.83	0.661	0.006
Wealth segregation across cities	−0.086	0.917	0.925
Constant	1.295	0.066	0.000
N	3,149		
R²	0.031		

Note: Fixed effects for year included but not presented.

a measure developed by Rhode and Strumpf (2003) called the coefficient of variation (CV). The CV captures the degree of heterogeneity in spending for a metropolitan area. It is calculated as the ratio of the standard deviation of spending to the mean of spending:

$$CV_{msa} = \frac{\sqrt{\sum_j P_j (E_j - M)^2}}{M},$$

where E_j is the per capita expenditure of city j, M is the mean per capita expenditure for all cities in the metropolitan area, and P_j is the share of the total metro area population in city j. Rhode and Strumpf (2003) use this measure (calculated for the entire nation, not by metropolitan area) to show that over time, governments across the United States have grown more alike in their spending. I find the same: the mean CV declined about 17.5% between 1972 and 2012, from 1.32 to 1.09. However, more segregated metropolitan areas changed slower than less segregated areas. To see this, I regress the CV on racial, renter, and wealth segregation across cities (H_{m_c}). I add fixed effects for year to account for the declining time trend. Table 8.3 presents the results.

The data reveal that in metropolitan areas with more racial and renter segregation across cities – that is, where whites/nonwhites, renters, and owners tend to live in different municipalities – we see more heterogeneity in municipal budgets. In a separate analysis, I find that a similar pattern exists for school spending – but only for racial segregation, not renter segregation. Metro areas with higher racial segregation across cities witness more variation in school district expenditures. Combined with the results presented in Figure 8.2, we can see that communities with large populations of renters and racial minorities in segregated metropolitan areas have access to a much smaller share of the total dollars spent by local governments. They have worse service, worse schools, and worse opportunities. Segregation is correlated with inequality – exactly as its architects intended. White homeowners are the beneficiaries of this design.

CONCLUSION

Even after decades of progressive change in racial attitudes and growing concern over income inequality, America remains a segregated nation. Increasingly, segregation along race and class lines has occurred between cities rather than within them. City politics has played a role in this change. When city policy does not favor the interests of white homeowners, these residents are more likely to trade homogenous neighborhoods within cities for new homogenous cities instead. When central cities in metropolitan areas have minority mayors, more active policy agendas, and spend more on policing, we see greater segregation across city lines. Segregation across city lines is also related to the pull of homogenous school districts in the suburbs. Whether this is because white homeowners leave central cities or never move in, the result is a higher degree of separation between cities in metropolitan areas. These patterns become fixed by local politics. The result is dramatic inequalities across places. Suburban communities garner a vastly disproportionate share of resources and guard their advantage using land-use regulations to shape the character and structure of their communities.

9

The Polarized Nation That Segregation Built

Between the late 1940s and mid-1960s, America's cities were embroiled in fights over racial desegregation. Residents battled over the integration of many different types of public places (e.g., pools, parks, golf courses, and schools). In this chapter, I show that battles over the control of public space and public goods in postwar urban America contributed to the transformation of public opinion. As explained in Chapter 2, white resistance to desegregation in urban centers across the country gave rise to a new rhetoric that emphasized the protection of private property and homeowners' rights (Kruse 2005; Lassiter 2006; Self 2003; Sugrue 1996). The conservatism and Republican allegiance associated with suburban America today was actually rooted in the conflict of racial politics of central cities. The drive to protect property values and maintain exclusive access to public goods, like schools, led white homeowners and their allies to generate segregation. Neighborhoods that successfully defended their white homeowner turf, despite the massive demographic and policy transformations of the postwar period, became the locus of modern conservatism. The heart of the Republican community lives in these spaces, designed and built for certain types of people – white home-owners. The reverse is also true: white voters who reside in neighbor-hoods that were filled with people of color in the postwar period are more liberal and more Democratic today. People who live in neighborhoods that were segregated by 1970 – by choice, compulsion, or happenstance – have political attitudes and loyalties that differ significantly from similarly situated residents in more integrated places. Segregation and political polarization are deeply intertwined.

In this chapter, I begin by linking white residential spaces in 1970 to three important neighborhood characteristics: property values, single-family homeownership, and the whiteness of public schools. Then, I provide evidence that the relative whiteness of a neighborhood in 1970 is a powerful predictor of political attitudes and loyalties today. People who live in places that were whiter than their metropolitan area was in 1970 were more likely to vote for the Republican presidential candidate in 2008 and are more conservative than their individual attributes (e.g., race, gender, marital status, age, education, income, presence of children) would otherwise predict. Conversely, those who live in places that were populated by people of color in 1970 are more liberal today. I argue that neighborhoods develop particular political orientations that magnify the aggregated individual attributes of the people who inhabit them. The consequences of segregation on individuals' life chances are well known, and as Thomas Sugrue (2015) writes, "[T]he effects ... are devastating."[1] Segregation increases inequality on many different socio-economic dimensions. The results presented here indicate that segregation also has powerful political consequences: increasing divisions in both public opinion and voting behavior.

THE EFFECT OF CONTEXT

Why would living in a neighborhood that was identifiably white in 1970 affect political views in 2008? The whiteness of a neighborhood could produce individual-level conservatism through two different mechanisms: the nonrandom migration of individuals into or out of whiter neighborhoods (i.e., sorting/selection) or by directly affecting the ideology of residents (i.e., treatment). We know from past research that both mechanisms occur. Some whites did flee central cities in response to black in-migration (Boustan 2010), and today residents choose their neighborhood, in part, based on who else lives there (Mummolo and Nall 2017; Cho, Gimpel and Hui 2013; Bishop and Cushing 2008; Card, Mas, and Rothstein 2008; Charles 2006). By this reasoning, 1970s white neighborhoods produce conservatism today because conservative people move to white neighborhoods. If we picked up and moved these people around to different places, they'd still be just as conservative. If this is the case, the importance of aggregating conservatives in particular places is in the political

---

[1] www.washingtonpost.com/opinions/its-not-dixies-fault/2015/07/17/7bf77a2e-2bd6-11e5-bd33-395c05608059_story.html

representation it produces. Such clustering increases political polarization as elected officials can be responsive to a politically homogeneous base.

But perhaps the experience of living in a 1970s white neighborhood actually makes residents conservative. Particular types of places can generate distinctive preferences as a result of features of the place, like population density or community size (Rodden 2011; Gainsborough 2001; Ogorzalek 2018; Oliver 2001). That is, if your neighborhood is very dense, you may be more inclined to see the need for rodent control or sewage treatment. Places can also magnify the individual attributes of inhabitants – such as when minority neighborhoods lack elite networks (Wilson 1987; Widestrom 2015). Neighborhood homogeneity might breed racial hostility and intolerance due to a lack of exposure to or contact with neighbors of different backgrounds (Oliver and Mendelberg 2000; Oliver and Wong 2003). Additionally, past political experiences can shape current views. Acharya, Blackwell, and Sen (2016) refer to this as the "historical persistence of political attitudes" (p. 2). Patterns of race relations developed during early periods of American history can generate opinions and behaviors that are transmitted over time and remain detectable in modern politics (Hersh and Nall 2016). Such distinctive political attitudes are communicated through processes like neighborhood social interaction (Huckfeldt and Sprague 1995) and/or "low-intensity cues" – such as the casual observation of ones' neighbors (Cho and Rudolph 2008). More straightforwardly, it seems reasonable to suspect that moving to a neighborhood with high property values and good schools leads homeowners to become obsessively concerned with keeping those values high and the schools good.

Very likely, both selection and treatment processes are at work here. Some residents of defended white neighborhoods brought their conservatism with them; others adopted it after arriving. Today, defended neighborhoods are also likely to continue to attract movers with conservative preferences. Without detailed panel survey data, I cannot discern which is the more powerful factor – but it makes no difference to the conclusions. What I demonstrate is that neighborhood traits from the 1970s are associated with conservatism at aggregate, and individual levels are above and beyond the mobility of the population and the demographic makeup of the neighborhood today.

LINKING SEGREGATION AND CONSERVATISM

For the first half of the twentieth century, white homeowners who wanted city governments to protect their property values and their public goods could make a straightforward racial case. They argued, simply, that certain types of buildings and certain types of people were incompatible with the values of their community (Freund 2007). Government agencies at every level of government agreed with them and worked to defend white homeowner neighborhoods. Federal loans were refused in diverse neighborhoods because these properties were seen as bad investments. As David Freund (2007) explains, the government "invoke[d] a theory of market behavior and housing economics that assumed the necessity of racial segregation." Segregation had a market imperative.

Today, many homeowners also argue that the character of their community is endangered when they are confronted with increased densification, multifamily developments, or affordable housing (Monkkonen 2016). But these arguments are typically not couched in explicitly racial terms. Homeowners will talk about increased traffic, limited open space, or a change in the feel of the neighborhood as reasons for their opposition to development. They'll talk about their right to protect their neighborhoods and their schools from increased crime, property degradation, or poor academic performance. But they do not, usually, say that they want to limit the presence of black, Latino, or poor neighbors. This turn in language represents, at once, the dramatic success of governmental policy in creating a market for segregation (it is no longer necessary to invoke race to achieve racial segregation) and the successes of the civil rights movement (which demanded changes to racially restrictive policies). Midcentury, to generate government support for segregation, neighborhood defenders turned to a set of arguments that highlighted their meritocratic success. Because the Republican Party protected defenders' rights to choose their neighbors, it won their allegiance. Today, these same views resonate with residents of segregated neighborhoods

EMPIRICAL EVIDENCE

To provide evidence that homogenous neighborhoods of the 1970s produce identifiably different politics today, I draw on the same measure of neighborhood whiteness that I used in Chapter 6. This measure takes the difference between the share of the census tract that is white and the share of the larger metro area that is white. The variable *tract-metro difference in percent white residents* takes a positive value for neighborhoods that are whiter than the metro area and a negative value for neighborhoods with more people of color. I begin by offering evidence of the correlates of neighborhood whiteness. Then, I analyze the effect of neighborhood homogeneity on the aggregate 2008 presidential vote. Finally, I turn to individual-level data. I find that homogeneity in 1970 is associated with conservatism today.

CORRELATES OF SEGREGATION

In an ideal analysis, I would identify neighborhoods that, in earlier decades, had been granted some form of regulatory protection with regard to land use. Such a measure would allow me to identify places that had truly been defended by local government. Such data are not available. What I can identify are neighborhoods that had a constellation of properties as of 1970 – white schools, single-family homes, high homeownership rates, a long way from the city center, and good property values – that would have been very likely to benefit from restrictive local governmental policy.[2] In this section, I show that these properties map neatly onto the relative whiteness of a neighborhood: the *tract-metro difference in percent white residents* described earlier. The relative conception is helpful here: in diverse metro areas, how is it that some neighborhoods remain white? The power of local politics. Unsurprisingly these variables are extremely highly correlated with each other. So, rather than add them to a regression, I present a simple correlation matrix in Table 9.1.

These places far from the city center, with white schools, lots of single-family homes, many homeowners, and high property values are generally whiter than the metro area as a whole. Neighborhoods in the top quintile of relative whiteness featured an average of 70% homeowners, 70% single-family homes, and a mean housing value of $15,239. Public school children would have been 97% white, and the neighborhood would have been eleven miles from the nearest city center. Neighborhoods in the first quartiles of the distribution had an average of 52% homeowners, 56% single-family homes, and a mean housing value of $6,948. Only 47% of public

---

[2] These variables are drawn from the 1970 census. They are the share of the census tract households that *owns* their homes, the share of the housing units that are *single family*, the share of children enrolled in *public school* who are *white*, the mean *housing value* for the tract, and the log of the *distance* to the nearest central city.

To measure distance from the nearest central city, I used 2010 place boundaries available from the National Historic Geographic Information System. Using data from the 2011 American Community Survey, I determined the largest population center in each metropolitan area. I converted these central cities and 2000 census tracts to centroids in ArcGIS. I measured the Euclidean distance between the closest central city and each census tract (using a near table with only one match). To generate a normal distribution, I took the natural log of this distance.

TABLE 9.1 *Correlates of neighborhood whiteness, 1970*

	Relative whiteness, 1970	% Homeowners, 1970	% Single-family homes, 1970	Mean housing value, 1970	% White public school, 1970
% Homeowners, 1970	0.3068				
% Single-family homes, 1970	0.2179	0.7557			
Mean housing value, 1970	0.3052	0.6556	0.5673		
% White public school, 1970	0.8912	0.3613	0.2751	0.3171	
Distance to city center (logged)	0.1732	0.2167	0.2558	0.2187	0.1715

Note: All entries are significant at the 0.0001 level.

school children would have been white, and the neighborhoods would have been about seven miles from the nearest city center. In the next two sections, I show that the whiter the neighborhood in 1970 (relative to the whiteness of the MSA), the more conservative are its modern-day politics.

HISTORICAL PERSISTENCE OF SEGREGATED NEIGHBORHOODS

To establish the modern-day conservatism of 1970 defended neighborhoods, I begin with an analysis of the 2008 presidential election. The dependent variable is the 2008 *democratic share* of the two-party presidential vote aggregated to the census tract level for the forty-nine states that collect vote data by precinct.[3] Precinct-level vote returns are available from the Harvard Elections Database Archive.[4] Using ArcGIS, I combined the precinct vote data with 2000 census tract boundaries available from the National Historic Geographic Information System archive.[5] I aggregated precinct-level votes to the census tract level.

[3] Oregon conducts all elections by mail, so geographically allocated votes are not available.

[4] A combined projected polygon shapefile was very generously provided to me by Clayton Nall.

[5] Because precinct boundaries sometimes cross tract boundaries, I calculated the land-area share of each precinct falling within each census tract. I used this geographic share as a weight on the total votes for the Democratic and Republican candidates before aggregating precinct vote totals to the tract level.

My independent variable is the *tract-metro difference in percent white, 1970*. I also test for the *tract-metro difference in percent renters, 1970* and the *tract-metro difference in percent wealthy, 1970*. Demographic patterns are persistent: whiter homeowner tracts in 1970 may simply be populated by more whites and homeowners today, and be more conservative as a result of their current demographics, not their history. So in a second estimation, I control for the tract-level *percent white*, the share of the tract that *rents* their home, and the share of the tract's households that are *wealthy* (incomes above the ninetieth percentile) as of the year 2000. I also add the *density* of the census tract (total population divided by total area) to account for Rodden's (2011) argument that the source of modern liberalism is housing density. To investigate the role of selection more directly, I add a measure of the share of the tract's residents who lived in the same house in 1995.[6] Table 9.2 presents the results of these regressions. Summary statistics are shown in the online appendix, in Table A9.1.

A neighborhood mostly populated with people of color in 1970 (*tract-metro difference = −0.5*) delivered about 84% of its votes to Barack Obama in 2008. A neighborhood that was white defended in 1970 (*tract-metro difference = 0.5*) offered Obama only 42% of its votes in 2008.[7] This is the combined selection and treatment effect of 1970 neighborhood segregation on modern political outcomes. Figure 9.1 presents the results graphically.

In the second column of Table 9.2, I add the controls described earlier. Even accounting for contemporary demographics, neighborhoods that were relatively whiter in 1970 were less likely to support Obama, relative to McCain. We see a similar effect of neighborhoods that were filled with homeowners in the 1970s. They were about 4.5 percentage points less likely to support Obama on average. However, there is no similar effect of relative wealth. The coefficient on this variable is not statistically significant. The effects of relative whiteness and homeownership hold, even when accounting for differences in mean levels of Democratic support across regions. We might take the coefficient in the second model to represent the effect of neighborhood treatment net of selection - about 7 percentage points. Contrary to a pure selection story, census tracts with more stable populations were no more or less likely to support Obama,

---

[6] I add fixed effects for region. I use ordinary least squares regression and cluster errors by MSA.

[7] Estimates generated using the margins command in Stata 14.

TABLE 9.2 *Effect of 1970 relative whiteness on 2008 Democratic vote share*

	β	SE	P > |z|	β	SE	P > |z|
Tract-metro difference in % white, 1970	-0.421	0.016	0.000	-0.070	0.019	0.000
Tract-metro difference in % renters, 1970				0.045	0.011	0.000
Tract-metro difference in % wealthy, 1970				0.000	0.024	0.994
% White 2000				-0.411	0.021	0.000
% Renters 2000				0.162	0.027	0.000
% Wealthy 2000				0.124	0.049	0.013
% Same house 1995				0.047	0.041	0.263
Density				-0.122	0.679	0.858
Midwest				0.019	0.012	0.126
South				-0.108	0.018	0.000
West				-0.073	0.020	0.000
Constant	0.631	0.013	0.000	0.825	0.042	0.000
R^2	0.206			0.645		
N	45,156			44,887		

Note: OLS regression, robust standard errors clustered by MSA presented. DV is % Democratic vote in 2008 presidential election.

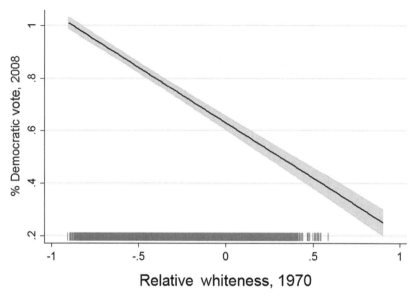

FIGURE 9.1 Uncontrolled effect of 1970 neighborhood characteristics on 2008 presidential election votes

and there is no interaction effect between stability of the population in 1995 and the whiteness of the neighborhood in 1970.

INDIVIDUAL-LEVEL CONSERVATISM

Obtaining individual-level survey data that is representative of city populations is notoriously difficult (Tausanovitch and Warshaw 2014). The costs of sampling across many localities, in addition to the complexity of designing specific surveys for each community, are typically prohibitive for scholars. Instead, I take advantage of the long time series and consistent battery of questions asked by the General Social Survey (GSS). The GSS administers a survey to an average of 2,000 respondents representing adults living in noninstitutional arrangements in the United States on a biennial basis. I create a new dataset built from restricted access GSS data from the 1998, 2000, 2002, 2004, 2006, and 2008 surveys.[8] To the GSS

---

[8] These are the years for which the GSS was able to provide census tract-level information for every respondent, which is essential to my analysis. The tract-level information was

dataset, I merge tract-and MSA-level census data from 1970. To measure contemporary neighborhood demographics, I add linearly interpolated data from the 1990 and 2000 Census of Population and Housing and the 2007–11 American Community Survey. For tracts not included in the American Community Survey, I use 2000 census data for all years of the GSS. The combined dataset includes tract-level data for 12,188 respondents from 117 metropolitan areas with an average of about one hundred respondents per metro area.[9] Although the GSS asks an enormous range of questions each year, only a subset of the survey questions is repeated. This repetition is crucial for my ability to estimate neighborhood effects because I rely on pooling across years to gain a large enough sample size. As a result, I restrict my analyses to questions that include at least 5,000 usable responses. At this threshold, the analyses include an average of fifty responses from each MSA. For the most part, my analyses only include white respondents, as this is the relevant population for my theory.[10]

I begin by determining the demographic characteristics of individuals who live in neighborhoods that were defended/segregated in 1970. In this analysis, my dependent variable is the 1970 *tract-metro difference in percent white,* described earlier. My independent variables include several demographic traits that are known to correlate with vote choice and ideology (Miller and Shanks 1996; Carmines and Stimson 1989; Green, Palmquist and Schickler 2002): the respondent's race (a dummy variable coded 1 for *white, non-Hispanic*),[11] *age, education* (where 0 is less than high school and 4 is a graduate degree), sex (coded 1 for *female*), the total number of *kids* under the age of 18 living at home, marital status (coded 1 for *married*), and inflation-adjusted *income.*[12] I also add the variable *mover,* that is coded 1 if the respondent lived in a different city or state

provided in response to a sensitive data request submitted to the National Opinion Research Center at the University of Chicago.

[9] Respondents who live outside of metro areas are excluded from these analyses.

[10] It is interesting to note that the results hold for nonwhite respondents as well. This adds further evidence to my claim that neighborhood context is associated with political conservatism above and beyond the aggregation of residents' demographic traits.

[11] The GSS has a relatively small sample of nonblack racial and ethnic minorities, so I combine all nonwhite racial/ethnic categories.

[12] Approximately 10% of the observations are missing income data. I imputed observations by regressing income on age, education, gender, race, work status, marital status, the number of people in the household, the size of the city, the presence of children at home, and dummy indicators for years with the non-missing observations, generating predicted values and replacing the missing observations with the predictions.

TABLE 9.3 *Modern demographic characteristics of 1970 neighborhoods*

	β	SE	P > |z|
White, non-Hispanic	0.104	0.004	0.000
Age	−0.001	0.000	0.000
Education	0.003	0.001	0.018
Female	−0.008	0.003	0.013
Kids at home	−0.003	0.002	0.082
Married	0.019	0.004	0.000
Income	0.000	0.000	0.000
Mover	0.031	0.003	0.000
Constant	−0.057	0.009	0.000
Random effects parameter	0.069	0.005	
N	10,701		
Number of MSAs	117		

Note: Mixed-effects maximum likelihood regression with random effects for MSA; DV is 1970 tract-metro difference in percentage white.

when she was sixteen years old, and 0 otherwise.[13] To account for the hierarchical structure of the data, I estimate a multilevel mixed-effects linear regression via maximum restricted likelihood, with random effects at the MSA level. This strategy adjusts the estimates and their errors for place-based correlations in attitudes. Table 9.3 presents the results (summary statistics are shown in the online appendix, in Table A9.2).

The estimation reveals few surprises. For example, holding all other variables at their mean values, white respondents live in neighborhoods that were whiter than the metro area in 1970 (0.06), while respondents of color live in neighborhoods that were less white (−0.04). More educated respondents live in neighborhoods that were whiter, as do married and higher-income respondents. Respondents who had moved cities or states since they were sixteen years old chose neighborhoods that were about four percentage points whiter than the metro area. Those with children living at home tend to live in neighborhoods that were less white in 1970, but among middle- and high-income respondents, this effect reverses; that is, middle- and high-income families with kids at home live in significantly whiter neighborhoods. A similar interactive effect occurs with age. Among the poor, older residents live in neighborhoods that

---

[13] Ideally, we would like to know whether or not the respondent moved neighborhoods as well, but the GSS does not ask this question.

were significantly less white in 1970, but among middle- and high-income residents, there is no relationship between age and neighborhood characteristics. These results point to several interesting conclusions: first, they indicate that neighborhoods that were whiter than the metro area in 1970 are more expensive and more desirable. They also suggest that sorting is likely to have played a role in the development of ideology and partisanship of particular places. Finally, these results indicate that it is necessary to control for all of these individual demographic characteristics in any estimation seeking to identify neighborhood associations. I turn to this task next.

I begin with an overview of individual-level partisan affiliation and ideology. I use the 1970 *tract-metro difference in percent white* as my independent variable in all analyses. My first dependent variable is the respondent's *partisan identification*. Respondents were asked, "[G]enerally speaking, do you usually think of yourself as a Republican, Democrat, Independent, or what?" Follow-up questions asked for the strength of partisanship and pushed independents to identify as "leaners." The resulting measure is a seven-point scale running from strong Democrat to strong Republican. Next, I analyze *ideology* (where 1 is extremely liberal, and 7 is extremely conservative), and finally *Republican presidential vote*, coded 1 if the respondent voted for the Republican candidate in the most recent election, and 0 otherwise.[14] I control for all of the demographic traits included in Table 9.3 except one: *mover*. I omit this variable because it is missing for a large share of the total observations. Its inclusion does not affect the results presented (and the coefficient is not significant in any of the estimations). In a second set of analyses, I add controls for current neighborhood attributes to provide additional evidence that the political character of neighborhoods was developed historically. These neighborhood variables are the *percent white* and *percent homeowners* in the tract, linearly interpolated for each year of the survey. Both sets of analyses are presented in Table 9.4.

As was true in the aggregate, at the individual level, the historical persistence of neighborhoods is clear. Places that had defended their exclusive white character as of 1970 are home to significantly more Republican and conservative residents today. This is the case even when we account for both individual and aggregate demographic traits that predict partisanship and ideology.

---

[14] For this last analysis, I use a multilevel mixed-effects logistic regression to account for the binary dependent variable.

TABLE 9.4 *Effect of 1970 neighborhood whiteness on modern partisanship and conservatism*

	Partisan identification			Political ideology			Republican pres. vote		
	β	SE	P > |z|	β	SE	P > |z|	β	SE	P > |z|
Tract-metro difference in % white, 1970	1.003	0.241	0.000	0.963	0.190	0.000	1.259	0.318	0.000
Age	-0.001	0.001	0.555	0.010	0.001	0.000	0.011	0.002	0.000
Education	-0.051	0.019	0.008	-0.113	0.015	0.000	-0.005	0.022	0.831
Female	-0.310	0.043	0.000	-0.194	0.034	0.000	-0.150	0.050	0.003
Kids at home	0.107	0.025	0.000	0.080	0.020	0.000	0.140	0.028	0.000
Married	0.326	0.049	0.000	0.342	0.039	0.000	0.303	0.056	0.000
Income ($100k)	0.417	0.058	0.000	0.177	0.046	0.000	0.477	0.066	0.000
Constant	2.845	0.091	0.000	3.590	0.071	0.000	-1.446	0.112	0.000
	β	SE	P>|z|	β	SE	P>|z|	β	SE	P>|z|
Tract-metro difference in % white, 1970	0.899	0.254	0.000	0.898	0.197	0.000	1.131	0.332	0.001
Age	-0.002	0.001	0.168	0.009	0.001	0.000	0.010	0.002	0.000
Education	-0.045	0.019	0.018	-0.106	0.015	0.000	0.000	0.022	1.000
Female	-0.315	0.043	0.000	-0.198	0.034	0.000	-0.155	0.050	0.002
Kids at home	0.096	0.025	0.000	0.068	0.020	0.000	0.130	0.029	0.000
Married	0.298	0.049	0.000	0.317	0.039	0.000	0.276	0.056	0.000
Income ($100k)	0.355	0.059	0.000	0.118	0.047	0.012	0.420	0.068	0.000
% White tract	-0.153	0.146	0.294	-0.232	0.113	0.040	-0.052	0.175	0.768
% Homeowners tract	0.635	0.122	0.000	0.633	0.096	0.000	0.595	0.144	0.000
Constant	2.646	0.125	0.000	3.446	0.097	0.000	-1.703	0.153	0.000
Random effects parameter	0.130	0.026		0.052	0.012		0.247	0.046	
N	8,049			6,558			7,563		
Number of MSAs	116			116			116		

Note: Mixed-effects maximum likelihood regression with random effects for MSA; white non-Hispanic respondents only.

The same pattern holds when I replace the dependent variable with particular policy items.[15] Respondents who live in neighborhoods that were whiter in 1970 are more likely to view government spending as adequate or too high in categories like social security, parks, and mass transit, and they are more likely to believe that individuals, not the government, should be responsible for their health, wealth, and the standard of living.[16] For instance, respondents were asked to place themselves on a five-point scale where at one end the government should do more to solve our country's problems, and at the other end the government should leave things to individuals and private businesses. Comparing whites who live in neighborhoods that were minority dominated in the 1970s with those who live in neighborhoods that were white defended, responses moved in a conservative direction by about half of a standard deviation on this scale (from an average of 2.8 to 3.3).

PREJUDICE AND POLICY

If integration battles are linked to the ideology of defended neighborhoods, then we would expect residents of these places to have particularly conservative views when it comes to race. I find strong support for this contention. There are many different questions that tap racial views included in the GSS. I use several as dependent variables that are both common in the literature and have a long enough time span to generate sufficient respondents. I begin with an analysis of racial affect and prejudice. The first question asks respondents whether or not they would be in favor of having a family member marry a black person. The second question asks about the respondents' preferred neighborhood composition. Respondents were presented with a picture of several houses, and asked which racial group they'd like have as neighbors. I analyze the effect of 1970 neighborhood demographics on a preference for all-white,

[15] These questions were not asked of all respondents in all years. As a result, in some of the specific policy areas discussed below the total number of respondents falls below 5,000. However, it never falls below 3,000.

[16] One question on which 1970 neighborhood whiteness was not associated with support for lower spending was education. When asked whether or not the government was spending the right amount "improving the nation's education system," there was no difference in the responses of individuals who live in neighborhoods that were whiter in 1970. Although this is obviously circumstantial evidence, it is plausible that the defended neighborhoods have higher quality schools, and this is a feature that attracts certain residents who are supportive of higher educational expenditures.

close neighbors. Next, I use a question that probes views on inequality. It states, "On the average (Negroes/Blacks/African-Americans) have worse jobs, income, and housing than white people." Then it asks: "Do you think these differences are mainly due to discrimination?" and/or "Because most (Negroes/Blacks/African-Americans) don't have the chance for education that it takes to rise out of poverty?" Finally, I analyze responses to the question, "Do you agree strongly, agree somewhat, neither agree nor disagree, disagree somewhat, or disagree strongly with the following statement: Irish, Italians, Jewish, and many other minorities overcame prejudice and worked their way up. Blacks should do the same without special favors."

All dependent variables are coded so that higher values equate to a more conservative position. The structure of these analyses is the same as those included in the top panel of Table 9.4 (mixed-effects maximum likelihood estimation with random effects for MSAs and controls for individual demographic characteristics). Rather than present regression tables, Figure 9.2 graphically displays the marginal effects on *tract-metro difference in percent white, 1970,* holding all other variables at their mean values.

The results presented in Figure 9.2 offer a consistent picture of white residents who live in neighborhoods that were whiter than the metro area in 1970. They are more strongly opposed to having a relative marry a black person; more likely to prefer white neighbors; less likely to see persistent racial inequality as the result of discrimination or a lack of educational opportunities; and more likely to agree that blacks should have to work their way up like white ethnic groups. In sum, residents of whiter neighborhoods are more likely to want to avoid close contact with blacks, to blame blacks for conditions of inequality, and put the onus on individuals to advance their position.

These attitudes translate into conservative views on race-targeted policies. To show this, I analyze three questions. The first question reads, "Some people think that (Blacks/Negroes/African Americans) have been discriminated against for so long that the government has a special obligation to help improve their living standards. Others believe that the government should not be giving special treatment to (Blacks/Negroes/African Americans). Where would you place yourself on this scale?" Responses were coded on a five-point scale ranging from strong obligation to no special treatment. The second question focuses on affirmative action and asks whether or not respondents are "for or against preferential hiring and promotion of blacks." Finally, I analyze a question asking

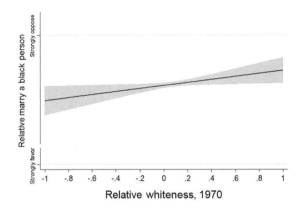

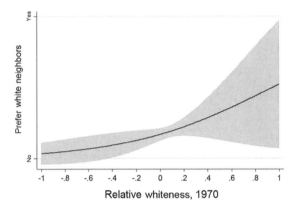

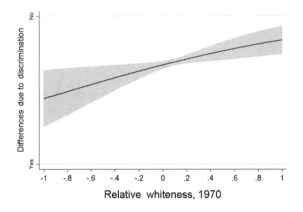

FIGURE 9.2 Effect of 1970 whiteness of neighborhood on white racial prejudice

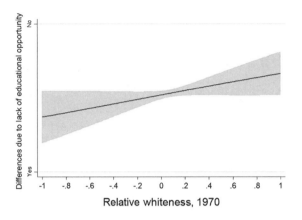

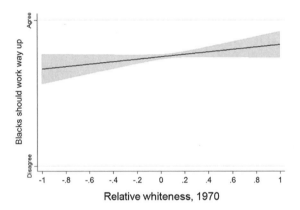

FIGURE 9.2 (*cont.*)

whether homeowners should have the right to decide to whom to sell their house without government interference, "even if he prefers not to sell to African Americans." Figure 9.3 presents the marginal effects of the regression of these policy responses on *tract-metro difference in percent white, 1970*, holding all other variables at their mean values.

Figure 9.3 reveals that residents who live in neighborhoods that were whiter in 1970 are more likely to hold conservative views on race-targeted policy. They are less likely to feel that the government has an obligation to reduce discrimination against blacks, less likely to support affirmative action, and more likely to oppose open housing laws.

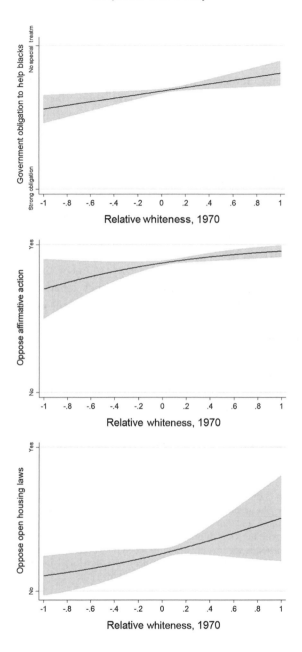

FIGURE 9.3 Effect of 1970 whiteness of neighborhood on support for
race-targeted policy

CONCLUSION

In summary, there is powerful evidence that the language and ideology developed around integration battles in postwar urban America persists. During the tumultuous 1940s, 1950s, and 1960s, faced with changing legal and rhetorical regimes, white homeowners seeking to keep minorities out of their neighborhoods began to shed the language of racial exclusivity. They understood the defense of their homes and spaces as a defense of their rights as homeowners and freedoms as individuals. Hayward (2013) describes this as the development of an "identity story," a story about "who 'we Americans' are: about what we value, what we want and deserve, and what it is that serves our good" (p. 119). Hayward is clear though: the Americans included in this vision were not all Americans, but rather all *white* Americans.[17] Yet, the privileged residents of defended neighborhoods promulgated the argument that "race doesn't matter" (Hayward 2013, p. 176). Instead, they relied on a frame that emphasized their hard work, frugality, and investment in their children's education. This perspective persists in these places. This chapter links 1970s neighborhood demographics to feelings of distance from African Americans, a belief that racial inequality is the result of lack of individual motivation, opposition to policies that redress disparities in outcomes across racial groups, and commitment to conservatism more generally. Residents who live in defended neighborhoods today are more likely to identify as Republicans and more likely to vote for Republican presidential candidates. The local roots of modern conservatism are deep.

---

[17] Hayward (2013) situates the genesis of this identity story earlier in the twentieth century than I do here. She argues that it was borne of economic need among developers seeking land-use planning and financial support from the government. My narrative is not incompatible with her view. It makes sense that the language adopted by rights-oriented white neighborhoods was readily available when they needed to use it. Hayward argues that the narrative of Americans as a homeowners developed by real estate interests functioned as a "frame to many ordinary stories" (p. 167).

10

Concluding Thoughts and New Designs

From the earliest days of America's urban development, local governments have shaped the environment to influence property values and strategically allocate public goods for the benefit of white property owners. As Peterson (1981), explained, local politics is "above all the politics of land use" (p. 25). This is a politics that is dominated by white property owners who seek to enhance their wealth and control the allocation of local benefits like public education. As a result, through the regulation of land use, planning, zoning, and redevelopment, local governments create and recreate segregation along race and class lines. When white property owners have had their preferred land-use design or their control over public goods threatened by demographic change, higher-level government policy, or shifts in political power, they have changed the scale of segregation by moving from isolated blocks to isolated neighborhoods, and then to isolated cities where today segregation remains stubbornly persistent. The consequence of these local policies and political battles has been unequal access to public benefits and polarization in local and national politics.

Contrary to prominent scholarship on segregation, neither economic inequality across racial groups nor racial antipathy among whites is sufficient to explain variation in the level of segregation across time and place. And contrary to prominent scholarship on local politics, these processes have not been pluralistic nor universally beneficial. They have again and again favored some residents at the great expense of others. For more than one hundred years, the winners in this process have been white property owners and their allies; the losers have been people of color and those at the margins of economic stability. After having designed this self-perpetuating landscape, white property owners became free to claim that segregation was simply the result of differences in individual effort, and that governmental attempts to desegregate neighborhoods and public goods were an infringement upon their rights – dismissing claims of inequality by people of color as identity politics or reverse racism. *Segregation by Design* has offered a theoretical structure for understanding these processes, and empirical evidence to support the conclusions.

Using new data on municipal expenditures and demographic trends, Chapter 3 revealed that cities became modern service providers in the early 1900s. They built sewage systems and water treatment plants. They began to collect garbage and light their streets. And, as Chapter 4 explains, for the first time, they began to manipulate and direct the uses of land. They engaged in planning and zoning to define where certain types of housing and buildings would be located (or not), and decided where public amenities and nuisances would be placed. From the beginning, city governments sought to protect white homeowner neighborhoods and business properties from integration, concentrating delivery of public goods to politically powerful constituents. Chapter 5 shows that these strategies resulted in neighborhood-level residential segregation and inequalities in the provision of municipal services. Later, as Chapter 6 reveals, when the federal government offered funds for urban renewal and public housing, cities utilized these processes to deepen earlier patterns.

Where and when people of color had political voice, segregation and inequality were lessened. In the decades following World War II, the political voices of the marginalized grew louder. As people of color contested municipal elections, as they demanded an end to Jim Crow, and as the federal government began to assert an intolerance of *de jure* and *de facto* segregation, white property owners' control became increasingly uncertain.

At the same time, several factors drew white property owners to the suburbs where they could maintain political power and police the borders of their communities more easily. As a result, Chapter 8 explains, segregation changed form: moving first from block to neighborhood, then from neighborhood to cities, where it has remained, inching upward, for the last thirty years. For every attempt that city, state, and the federal governments have made to desegregate neighborhoods and public goods, white homeowners have insulated their communities in new ways. Chapters 7 and 9 detail the profound political consequences of segregation. In cities, segregation drives down collective expenditure and results in the underfunding of public goods. Segregation between cities means that excluded residents have no access to or ability to influence the distribution of public goods. As a result, segregation generates inequalities in local public goods like schools, safe streets, and clean water. Segregation also produces political polarization, leading to deep racial divisions in support for candidates and partisan divisions in national elections.

By focusing on the political power of white property owners, *Segregation by Design* departs from existing work. Generally, people of color earn less income, have lower levels of education, and have less wealth than whites. This is not in dispute. If individuals convert higher socioeconomic status into higher housing quality, some scholars argue that segregation can largely be explained by these differences (see, for example, Clark 1986). Furthermore, other scholars find that whites are willing to pay higher housing prices for more exclusive neighborhoods (Cutler et al. 1999). So, it would be easy to conclude that the cause of segregation is economic inequality. But individual choices are fundamentally constrained by the type and value of housing available – factors that are dictated by local government policy. It is this policy that must be explained in order to understand segregation.

Other scholarship pins segregation and the inequality it produces on prejudicial attitudes among whites. If white attitudes regarding the inferiority of people of color were the primary explanation for the policies that generate segregation, we would expect the presence of people of color or degree of intolerance among whites to predict the adoption of such policies. I do not find this. For instance, the presence of African Americans and foreign-born people of color actually decreased the adoption of restrictive zoning. Additionally, I offer evidence of segregation-inducing policy in every region of the nation; the South holds no special place in this story. Finally, simple prejudice cannot explain why neighborhood-level segregation was exchanged for city-level segregation in the postwar period. Only when we account for the varying political power of white property owners and understand their goals for the formation of the built environment can we explain the genesis of these policies.

I argue that the policies that generate segregation and racial inequality are driven fundamentally by whites' economic and political self-interest, which both interact with and produce racist beliefs. Whiteness – particularly among the working class – is defined in opposition to blackness (Roediger 1991). DuBois (1935) explains that white laborers, instead of joining the black working class to oppose low wages and class subjugation, work instead to perpetuate segregation, to maintain their "racial prerogatives," and deny opportunities to black Americans (p. 701). White property owners have drawn on this identity to build political coalitions and implement policies that generate segregation. As Ibram Kendi (2016) explains, "the common conception that ignorance and hate lead to racist ideas, and that racist ideas initiate racist policies, is largely ahistorical. It has actually been the inverse relationship – racial discrimination has led to racist ideas which has led to ignorance and hate." "Racist ideas," Kendi explains, are used to justify "racist policies ... in order to redirect the blame for racial disparities away from those policies and onto Black people" (p. 9).

Once racist policies are in place, individual beliefs (e.g., racism) among the beneficiaries of the system become largely irrelevant. Obviously, the level of racism among whites is both variable and impactful for political and economic outcomes. Some (perhaps many) whites, explicitly or implicitly, harbor anti-black affect, racial resentment, and negative stereotypes of people of color, particularly blacks. Others less so. But, in the end, because government policy generates segregation through land use, the consequences of this variation are reduced. The choices of the racially resentful and those less racially resentful can become indistinguishable. Whites tend to make decisions that reinforce their privilege without thinking too deeply about it because they want stable property values, good schools, nice parks, and low-crime neighborhoods, and they have the financial opportunity to pursue these goals.

The argument and findings in this book suggest a reconceptualization of the fundamental drivers of local politics. Despite a great deal of scholarship studying cities, generalized frameworks for understanding the fundamental role of race and class in determining local political phenomena are not common. To be sure, scholars have developed specific theories to explain, for instance, the effects of mass incarceration on political participation (Burch 2014), or the conditions under which we expect multiracial coalitions to form (Browning, Marshall, and Tabb 1986). But we lack broader perspective. How do race and class play a role in who governs in city politics? What determines the policy choices that are made? How do we explain patterns of urban development?

Theories of urban politics have largely answered these questions within three broad frames: pluralism, structural forces, or regimes. Simply put, none of these theories can make sense of patterns of residential segregation, and so cannot adequately explain fundamental drivers of inequality. Pluralists assert that power is fragmented and decentralized; varied interests participate in the political process and outcomes are democratically determined. While many scholars have examined the empirical failures of pluralist predictions (see e.g., Pinderhughes 1987), *Segregation by Design* asserts that across time and place, white property owners have achieved power, access, and policy that is unrepresentative of their share of the population. They turn out to vote at higher rates and dominate decision-making bodies. As a result, political outcomes at the local level are not pluralistic. If they were, we would not have entire neighborhoods of color without access to sewers, or have witnessed the clustering of public housing in black neighborhoods, or see land-use policies that restrict housing development to the upper end of the income distribution. In the future, scholars can build on these insights to analyze more precisely how white property owners have achieved their local policy goals. Who are members of their political coalitions during different time periods? What drives divisions among white property owners? What are the policy consequences of these variations? We also need more detail regarding the ways in which property owners achieve their policy goals. For instance, exactly what kinds of zoning board decisions do they pursue?

Structuralists, on the other hand, argue that city policy is determined by a quest to enhance the local economy. Some argue that this pursuit is for the benefit of local elites (Logan and Molotch 1987), others claim it is a consensual approach benefiting the entire community (Peterson 1981). Scholars in this tradition view external economic conditions as the driving force behind city politics; negotiation among political actors is irrelevant to the bigger picture. *Segregation by Design* offers several challenges to this thinking. First, structural conditions that are taken as preexisting, such as the number of municipalities competing for population and businesses in a metro area, are endogenous. Incorporating new municipalities is a mechanism to institutionalize segregation. So, competition among municipalities is an outcome generated by white property owners' quest for property wealth and public goods exclusivity – not an independent driver of local policy-making. Second, we know that segregation negatively impacts economic growth. If economic growth is the underlying goal of city policy, structural theories cannot account for patterns of local land-use policies that intentionally generate segregation. As Mollenkopf (1994) asserts, structural theories "have a hard time explaining real and important variation over time and across places" (p. 35).

Regime theories have similar difficulty predicting variation. Scholars using this approach propose to explain local policy outcomes as the result of negotiation and coalition building among elected officials who need votes to remain in power and actors with private resources whose support is needed for the city to thrive (see, e.g., Stone 1989). But regime theory fails to account for the power of white property owners, and to understand how their quest to enhance property values and exclusive access to public goods guides policy. As a result, regime theory is unable to adequately predict who is likely to be members of the governing and electoral coalitions, and what policy goals are likely to be served.

At a minimum, if we are to understand what animates local political battles, what drives urban development, and what structures political regimes, we must contend with the politically institutionalized power of the white property-owning community. Through the political process white property owners have advantaged themselves in residential life, in property values, in neighborhood amenities, and in the allocation of public goods through local land-use control. They used the government to build their wealth, grant themselves exclusive access to good schools, paved roads, and nice parks, while shifting the burdens of urban life to the poor and communities of color. But we must also understand the limits to this power. Higher levels of government have disrupted white property owners' power. Mobilization among people of color has limited their power too. *Segregation by Design* tells this story. Of course, there are still many unanswered questions. To start, this book has neglected to interrogate how property owners differ from one another across time and place, and has completely ignored the role and agency of property owners of color. What happens when neighborhood property owners conflict with residential developers? What determines who wins? We need to know how variation in goals and perspectives may affect land-use policy, segregation, and inequality.

LOOKING AHEAD

What can we expect going forward? The United States has continued to diversify. The census predicts that by 2044 the nation will become a "plurality of racial and ethnic groups,"[1] in which no group will have a majority share of the population. And scholars have shown that many suburbs have been subject to the same trends (Frasure-Yokely 2015). At the same time, the research in this book has revealed that the most privileged communities have remained overwhelmingly white and continue to garner an outsized share of public benefits. Figure 10.1 offers a

---

[1] www.census.gov/content/dam/Census/library/publications/2015/demo/p25-1143.pdf

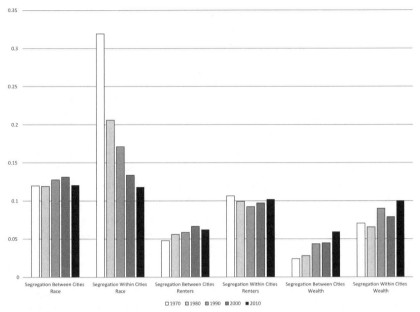

FIGURE 10.1 Trends in segregation over time

visualization of the trends in segregation between 1970 and 2010 that were presented in Chapter 2.

The graph reveals remarkable decline in neighborhood-level (within-city) racial segregation, but little cause for optimism in other measures. Without concerted effort, we are unlikely to see significant changes, even as our nation diversifies. Indeed, as inequality worsens, the increase in wealth segregation is likely to intensify (Bischoff and Reardon 2013). We can see this in the process of gentrification. Since the 1990s, some cities have seen a resurgence of interest among white residents for living in the central business district, tracts that were once among the most segregated in the nation. The sustained power of white property owners means that while these tracts are likely to become more racially integrated, they are also likely to push poorer, renting residents to the political periphery.

Where white property owners do not exert such influence, privatization of public services is a common response. Trounstine (2015) finds that a greater share of communities' security and educational needs is met through private provision in more diverse communities. Similarly, Betts and Fairlie (2003) show that native-born American families is more likely to send their children to private high school in response to increased immigration. Privatization then serves as just one more step in the increasing scale of segregation. When public goods become club goods (i.e., only accessible to those who pay), inequality in access to high-quality services increases.

We can also expect political polarization to continue to be fostered by segregation. Political segregation maps onto the patterns of race and class segregation that are driven by white property owners. This is partially due to the strong correlations between race, class, and partisanship. If land-use policy restricts poor people of color from residing in a particular community, that community is likely to have lower levels of support for the Democratic Party. Further research might determine whether we see public officials motivated by shaping their electorate in this way. But, additionally, a great deal of evidence also reveals that who we interact with on a regular basis influences our partisan affiliations, our ideologies, our policy views, our vote choices, and even our understanding of information (e.g., Sinclair 2012; Nicholson 2012; Klar 2014; Oliver 2010; Huckfeldt and Sprague 1995; Berelson et al. 1954). Simply put, segregation affects our social networks. And segregation affects tax rates, wealth acquisition, and educational opportunities, which in turn affects political preferences. Increasingly, people feel hostile toward those on the other side of the political aisle (Iyengar and Westwood 2014). People who live in different kinds of places have different political orientations. So, metropolitan areas that are extremely segregated are ideologically heterogeneous in the aggregate. McCarty et al. (2018) show that this kind of electoral heterogeneity drives polarization in legislatures, making compromise difficult and legislative gridlock likely. Local land-use policy underlies these divisions.

POLICY SOLUTIONS

As the prologue to the book indicated, it is not likely that the devil of segregation will be undone by individual choices. Individual white homebuyers will predominantly tend to reinforce the patterns that are embedded in the real estate market, the provision of city/school services, and local land-use decisions. So, then, what policy solutions are available?

State and federal governments can compel desegregation on various fronts. In his excellent comparative historical study of Atlanta and Charlotte, Matthew Lassiter (2006) finds that the large geographic footprint of Charlotte's school district meant that white families could not escape desegregation by moving to the suburbs, as they could in the fragmented metro region of Atlanta. As a result, the forced busing of white and black children in the Charlotte-Mecklenburg School District successfully produced integrated schools in the postwar period. Even today, Charlotte has much lower levels of segregation both within and across cities than does Atlanta. The lesson here is clear: desegregation policies from higher levels of government *can* be effective – but they must interact with local institutions like school district boundaries and local land-use policy. Thus, desegregating neighborhoods and schools is likely to require stripping, to some degree, local control. At a minimum, going forward, states could analyze school district and municipality incorporation with an eye toward integration, limiting fragmentation and opportunities for segregation. Importantly, states can also require the building of multifamily housing, although this latter solution may only serve to increase segregation within cities if exclusive suburbs shove multifamily housing into concentrated neighborhoods. New Jersey's experience with the Mt. Laurel decision has taught us that decisions by state courts ordering the building of multi-family units will remain toothless without legislative backing. At the end of the day, many states will lack a powerful enough political coalition to engage these solutions.

Alternatively, we might try to address individual choices by giving lower-income residents massive housing subsidies – allowing them access to segregated neighborhoods. But, given the lack of support for even extremely small welfare programs, housing subsidies are likely to be a political nonstarter. A recent grassroots movement in the Bay Area of California has sought to change the dialogue surrounding densification. The Yes-in-My-Backyard (YIMBY) campaign encourages governments to zone for higher density and encourages residents to support such changes. Although this movement is relatively new, it has made some headway – particularly in extremely expensive housing markets that have priced out middle-income residents (McCormick 2017).

Given that property owners' anxiety about protecting their investment is the driver of the many patterns I reveal in this text, another solution would be to address this concern directly. William Fischel (2015) has argued that reducing federal tax subsidies for owner-occupied housing would curtail homeowner demands for exclusivity. Elsewhere, Fischel suggests creating a market for home-value insurance, thereby protecting owners from declines in their property values and (potentially) making them more open to land uses that do not maintain exclusivity.

If tackling segregation itself proves politically unworkable, another approach would be to focus on reducing the public goods inequalities that segregation generates. Scholars have proposed regional solutions like tax-base sharing or regional governments (e.g., Orfield 2002; Katz 1998), yet experience indicates that these strategies are also likely politically infeasible or at least unsustainable. But state governments could make significant progress on this dimension. There are lessons to be learned from the history of public school provision and finance. Lafortune, Rothstein, and Schanzenbach (2016) show that recent school finance equalization policies have focused not on the gap in funding between advantaged and disadvantaged districts, but rather on ensuring a minimum adequate level of funding for all districts. They find that these reforms significantly reduce inequalities in student achievement outcomes between districts.

School finance reform has been possible because state constitutions guarantee the provision of public schooling, and lawsuits (and threats of lawsuits) have forced the hand of state legislatures. Education is not the only public good guaranteed in state constitutions though. In fact, state constitutions are the locus of many positive rights. As Zackin (2013) details, they also obligate state governments to "care for the poor, aged, and mentally ill, preserve the natural environment ... and protect debtors' homes and dignity" (p. 3). Bridges (2015) demonstrates that state constitutions provide state governments substantial authority in the regulation of water provision and the protection of labor. Leonard (2010) outlines state constitutional requirements mandating provision of health care and public health. Thus, the centralization of public goods financing, or at least the provision of a minimum level of public goods support through state governments, is possible, though obviously politically contentious.

Garnering state support for desegregation and/or the equalization of public goods will require tremendous political pressure from marginalized groups and their allies – an admittedly daunting task. However, these groups may also find support from both businesses and residents who have been priced out of unaffordable markets. California may be uniquely situated to lead such a change, given its substantial race and class diversity *and* extremely expensive housing.

The book began with a quote by Ta-Nehisi Coates (2015), a brilliant, lyrical theorist of race and racism. The quote describes the intimacy of the linkage between the punishing fear, violence, and failing schools that Coates experienced as a black child growing up in west Baltimore, and the tangible successes of white Americans. Coates explains that the "violence that undergirded the country so flagrantly on display during Black

History Month [commemorating the civil rights movement] and the intimate violence of [the street] were not unrelated. And this violence was not magical, but was of a piece and by design" (p. 33). What is clear is that if we do nothing about this design, politics will continue to polarize, and inequality in wealth, education, safety, and well-being will continue to worsen. Much is at stake.

References

ARTICLES, BOOKS, AND OTHER MATERIAL

Abrams, Charles. 1950. Housing. *The American Jewish Year Book* 51: 82–8.
   1955. *Forbidden neighbors: A study in housing prejudice*. New York: Harper and Brothers.
Acharya, Avidit, Matthew Blackwell, and Maya Sen. 2016. The legacy of American slavery. *Journal of Politics* 78 (3): 621–41.
Alesina, Alberto, Reza Baqir, and William Easterly. 1999. Public goods and ethnic divisions. *The Quarterly Journal of Economics* 114 (4): 1243–84.
Alesina, Alberto, Reza Baqir, and Caroline Hoxby. 2004. Political jurisdictions in heterogeneous communities. *Journal of Political Economy* 112 (2): 348–96.
Alesina, Alberto, and Edward Glaeser. 2004. *Fighting poverty in the US and Europe: A world of difference*. Oxford: Oxford University Press.
Alesina, Alberto, Roberto Perotti, and Jose Tavares. 1998. The political economy of fiscal adjustments. *Brooking Papers on Economic Activity* 1 (1): 197–266.
Alesina, Alberto, and Enrico Spolaore. 1997. On the number and size of nations. *The Quarterly Journal of Economics* 112 (4): 1027–56.
Algan, Yann, Camille Hemet, and David Laitin. 2011. Diversity and public goods: A natural experiment with exogenous residential allocation. *IZA Discussion Paper Series no. 6053*.
Allen, Robert. 1942. Housing in Camden. Housing Authority of the City of Camden. The Writers Program of the Works Projects Administration in New Jersey. www.dvrbs.com/hacc/CamdenNJ-HousingAuthority.htm
Allport, Gordon W. 1954. *The nature of prejudice*. Cambridge: Addison-Wesley.
Ananat, Elizabeth Oltmans. 2011. The wrong side(s) of the tracks: The causal effects of racial segregation on urban poverty and inequality. *American Economic Journal: Applied Economics* 3: 34–66.
Anderson, Alan. 1977. *The origin and resolution of an urban crisis: Baltimore, 1890–1930*. Baltimore: Johns Hopkins University Press.

Anderson, Martin. 1964. *The federal bulldozer: A critical analysis of urban renewal, 1949–1962.* Cambridge, MA: MIT Press.

Aoki, Keith. 1992. Race, space, and place: The relation between architectural modernism, post-modernism, urban planning, and gentrification. *Fordham Urban Law Journal* 20 (4): 699–829.

Arceneaux, Kevin. 2012. Cognitive biases and the strength of political arguments. *American Journal of Political Science* 56 (2): 271–85.

Armstrong, Gregory L., Laura A. Conn, and Robert W. Pinner. 1999. Trends in infectious disease mortality in the United States during the 20th century. *Journal of American Medical Association* 281: 61–6.

Avila, Eric, and Mark H. Rose. 2009. Race, culture, politics, and urban renewal: An introduction. *Journal of Urban History* 35 (3): 335–47.

Axelrod, Robert. 1973. Schema theory: An information processing model of perception and cognition. *The American Political Science Review* 67 (4): 1248–66.

Baar, Kenneth K. 1996. The anti-apartment movement in the U.S. and the role of land use regulations in creating housing segregation. *Netherlands Journal of Housing and the Built Environment* 11 (4): 359–79.

Bacote, Clarence A. 1955. The negro in Atlanta politics. *Phylon (1940–1956)* 16 (4): 333–50.

Banfield, Edward, and James Wilson. 1963. *City politics.* Cambridge, MA: Harvard University Press.

Banzhaf, Spencer, and Randall P. Walsh. 2008. Do people vote with their feet? An empirical test of Tiebout's mechanism. *American Economic Review* 98 (3): 843–63.

Barnes, P. H. 1936. *Delaware Township, Camden County, N.J.* Camden, NJ: County Historical Society.

Barrett, Paul, and Mark Rose 1999. Street smarts: The politics of transportation statistics in the American city, 1900–1990. *Journal of Urban History* 25 (3): 405–33.

Bartels, Larry M. 2008. *Unequal democracy: The political economy of the new gilded age.* Princeton: Princeton University Press.

Baum-Snow, Nathaniel, and Byron F. Lutz. 2011. School desegregation, school choice, and changes in residential location patterns by race. *American Economic Review* 101 (7): 3019–46.

Baybeck, Brady. 2006. Sorting out the competing effects of racial context. *Journal of Politics* 68(2): 386–96.

Bayer, Patrick, Fernando Ferreira, and Robert McMillan. 2007. A unified framework for measuring preferences for schools and neighborhoods. *Journal of Political Economy* 115 (4): 588–638.

Bayer, Patrick, Robert McMillan, and Kim S. Rueben. 2004. What drives racial segregation? New evidence using census microdata. *Journal of Urban Economics* 56 (3): 514–35.

Bayor, Ronald. 1996. *Race and the shaping of twentieth-century Atlanta.* Chapel Hill, NC: University of North Carolina Press.

Bennett, Charles G. 1957a. Ban on housing bias voted by city board: Housing bias bill wins final vote. *New York Times*, December 24.

1957b. Housing bias bill signed by mayor: Realty, commerce groups oppose action, but other organizations praise it. *New York Times*, December 31.

Benson, Charles S., and Kevin O'Halloran. 1987. The economic history of school finance in the United States. *Journal of Education Finance* 12 (4): 495–515.

Benson, Earl D., Julia Hansen, Arthur Schwartz, and Greg Smersh. 1998. Pricing residential amenities: The value of a view. *The Journal of Real Estate Finance and Economics* 16 (55): 55–73.

Berelson, Bernard, Paul Lazarsfeld, and William McPhee. 1954. *Voting: A study of opinion formation in a presidential campaign*. Chicago: University of Chicago Press.

Berry, Christopher. 2001. Land use regulation and residential segregation: Does zoning matter? *American Law and Economics Review* 3(2): 251–74.

Betts, Julian, and Robert Fairlie. 2003. Does immigration induce "native flight" from public schools into private schools? *Journal of Public Economics* 87: 987–1012.

Bicentennial edition: Historical statistics of the United States, colonial times to 1970. 1975. United States Census Bureau.

Bin, Okmyung, and Stephen Polasky. 2004. Effects of flood hazards on property values: Evidence before and after hurricane Floyd. *Land Economics* 80 (4): 490–500.

Bischoff, Kendra, and Sean F. Reardon. 2013. Residential segregation by income, 1970–2009. Russell Sage Foundation.

Bishop, Bill, and Robert G. Cushing. 2008. *The big sort: Why the clustering of like-minded America is tearing us apart*. Boston: Houghton Mifflin.

Blake, Gene. 1964. Proposition 14: The case for and against. *Los Angeles Times*, September 20.

Blalock, Hubert M. 1967. *Toward a theory of minority-group relations*. New York: Wiley.

Blumer, Herbert. 1958. Race prejudice as a sense of group position. *The Pacific Sociological Review* 1 (1): 3–7.

Bobo, Lawrence. 2001. Racial attitudes and relations at the close of the twentieth century. In *America becoming: Racial trends and their consequences*, Volume 1, eds. Neil J. Smelser, William J. Wilson, and Faith Mitchell. Washington, DC: National Academy Press.

1983. Whites' opposition to busing: Symbolic racism or realistic group conflict? *Journal of Personality and Social Psychology* 45 (6): 1196–210.

Bobo, Lawrence, and Vincent L. Hutchings. 1996. Perceptions of racial group competition: Extending Blumer's theory of group position to a multiracial social context. *American Sociological Review* 61 (6): 951–72.

Bobo, Lawrence, and James R. Kluegel. 1997. Status, ideology, and dimensions of whites' racial beliefs and attitudes: Progress and stagnation. In *Racial attitudes in the 1990s: Continuity and change*, eds. Steven Tuch and Jack Martin: 93–120. Westport, CT: Praeger.

Bobo, Lawrence, James R. Kluegel, and Ryan A. Smith. 1997. Laissez-faire racism: The crystallization of a kinder, gentler, anti-black ideology. In *Racial attitudes in the 1990s: Continuity and change*, eds. Steven Tuch and Jack Martin: 15–42. Westport, CT: Praeger.

Bobo, Lawrence, and Camille L. Zubrinsky. 1996. Attitudes on residential integration: Perceived status differences, mere in-group preference, or racial prejudice. *Social Forces* 74 (3): 883–909.

Bogue, Donald. 1975. *Census tract data, 1940: Elizabeth Mullen Bogue file. ICPSR02930-v1.* Ann Arbor, MI: Inter-university Consortium for Political and Social Research distributor, 2000.

Bolsen, Toby, James N. Druckman, and Fay Lomax Cook. 2014. The influence of partisan motivated reasoning on public opinion. *Political Behavior* 36 (2): 235–62.

Bonilla-Silva, Eduardo. 1997. "Rethinking racism: Toward a structural interpretation," *American Sociological Review* 62(3): 465–80.

 2009. *Racism without racists: Color-blind racism and the persistence of racial inequality in America*, 3rd ed. Lanham, MD: Rowman and Littlefield Publishers.

Books, John, and Charles Prysby. 1991. *Political behavior and the local context.* New York: Praeger.

Boustan, Leah. 2010. Was postwar suburbanization "white flight"? Evidence from the black migration. *The Quarterly Journal of Economics* 125 (1): 417–43.

 2012. Racial residential segregation in American cities. In *The Oxford handbook of urban economics and planning*, eds. Nancy Brooks, Kieran Donaghy, and Gerrit Knaap. New York: Oxford University Press.

Boustan, Leah, Fernando Ferreira, Hernan Winkler, and Eric Zolt. 2013. The effect of rising income inequality on taxation and public expenditures: Evidence from US municipalities and school districts, 1970–2000. *The Review of Economics and Statistics* 95 (4): 1291–302.

Bowler, Shawn, and Gary Segura. 2011. *The future is ours: Minority politics, political behavior, and the multiracial era of American politics.* Washington, DC: CQ Press.

Brabner-Smith, John. 1937. The Wagner Act: A definite housing program. *American Bar Association Journal* 23 (9): 681–2.

Bradford, David, R. A. Malt, and Wallace Oates. 1969. The rising cost of local public services: Some evidence and reflections. *National Tax Journal* 22: 185–202.

Brady, Henry E., and Paul M. Sniderman. 1985. Attitude attribution: A group basis for political reasoning. *The American Political Science Review* 79 (4): 1061–78.

Braman, Eileen, and Thomas E. Nelson. 2007. Mechanism of motivated reasoning? Analogical perception in discrimination disputes. *American Journal of Political Science* 51 (4): 940–56.

Branton, Regina, and Bradford Jones. 2005. Reexamining racial attitudes: The conditional relationship between diversity and socioeconomic environment. *American Journal of Political Science* 49 (2): 359–72.

Bridges, Amy. 1984. *A city in the republic: Antebellum New York and the origins of machine politics.* Cambridge: Cambridge University Press.

 1997. *Morning glories: Municipal reform in the southwest.* Princeton, NJ: Princeton University Press.

2015. *Democratic Beginnings: Founding the Western States.* Lawrence, KS: University Press of Kansas.

Briffault, Richard. 1990. Our localism: Part II – Localism and legal theory. *Columbia Law Review* 90 (2): 346–454.

Brilliant, Mark. 2010. *The color of America has changed: How racial diversity shaped civil rights reform in California, 1941–1978.* Oxford University Press.

Brooks, Richard R. W. 2002. Covenants and conventions. *Law and Economics Research Paper Series, Northwestern University School of Law.* Research Paper No. 02–8.

Brown, M. Craig, and Charles N. Halaby. 1984. Bosses, reform, and the socio-economic bases of urban expenditure, 1890–1940. In *The Politics of Urban Fiscal Policy*, eds. Terrence J. McDonald and Sally K. Ward: 60–99. Beverly Hills, CA: SAGE Publications, Inc.

Brownell, Blaine A. 1975. The commercial-civic elite and city planning in Atlanta, Memphis, and New Orleans in the 1920s. *Southern Historical Association* 41 (3): 339–68.

Browning, Rufus, Dale Rogers Marshall, and David Tabb. 1986. *Protest is not enough: The struggle of blacks and Hispanics for equality in urban politics.* University of California Press.

Brownwell, Blaine. 1975. The commercial-civic elite and city planning in Atlanta, Memphis, and New Orleans in the 1920s. *The Journal of Southern History* 41 (3): 339–68.

Burch, Traci. 2014. The old Jim Crow: Racial residential segregation and imprisonment. *Law and Policy* 36 (3): 223–55.

Burgess, Ernest. 1925. The growth of the city: An introduction to a research project. In *The city*, eds. Robert Park, Ernest Burgess, and Roderick McKenzie: 47–62. Chicago: University of Chicago Press.

Burgess, Patricia. 1994. *Planning for the private interest: Land use controls and residential patterns in Columbus, Ohio, 1900–1970.* Columbus: Ohio State University Press.

Burke Marshall Papers. 1962. *Equal opportunity in housing executive order.* Statement by the president, Office of the White House Press Secretary.

Burnham, Daniel H., and Edward H. Bennet. 1909. Plan of Chicago. *Ciudades* 7: 187–92.

Burns, Nancy. 1994. *The formation of American local governments: Private values in public institutions.* New York: Oxford University Press.

Cammarota, Ann Marie. 2001. *Pavements in the garden: The suburbanization of southern New Jersey.* Madison, NJ: Fairleigh Dickinson University Press.

Campbell, Andrea, Cara Wong, and Jack Citrin. 2006. Racial threat, partisan climate, and direct democracy: Contextual effects in three California initiatives. *Political Behavior* 28: 129–50.

Card, David, Alexandre Mas, and Jesse Rothstein. 2008. Tipping and the dynamics of segregation. *The Quarterly Journal of Economics* 123 (1): 177–218.

Carmines, Edward, and James Stimson. 1980. The two faces of issue voting. *American Political Science Review* 74 (1): 78–91.

1989. *Issue evolution: Race and the transformation of American politics.* Princeton, NJ: Princeton University Press.

Ceaser, James, and Daniel DiSalvo. 2006. Midterm elections, partisan context, and political leadership: The 2006 elections and party alignment. *The Forum* 4(3).

Centers for Disease Control and Prevention. 1999. Achievements in public health, 1900–1999: Control of infectious diseases. *Morbidity and Mortality Weekly Report* 48 (29): 621–9.

Chaiken, Shelly. 1980. Heuristic versus systematic information processing and the use of source versus message cues in persuasion. *Journal of Personality and Social Psychology* 39 (5): 752–66.

Charles, Camille Zubrinsky. 2003. The dynamics of racial residential segregation. *Annual Review of Sociology* 29 (1): 167–207.

2006. *Won't you be my neighbor? Race, class, and residence in Los Angeles.* New York: Russell Sage Foundation.

Chen, Yong. 2000. *Chinese San Francisco: 1850–1943.* Stanford, CA: Stanford University Press.

Cho, Wendy, James Gimpel, and Joshua Dyck. 2006. Residential concentration, political socialization, and voter turnout. *The Journal of Politics* 68 (1): 156–67.

Cho, Wendy Tam, James Gimpel, and Iris Hui. 2013. Voter migration and the geographic sorting of the American electorate. *Annals of the Association of American Geographers* 103 (4): 856–70.

Cho, Wendy Tam, and Thomas J. Rudolph. 2008. Emanating political participation: Untangling the spatial structure behind participation. *British Journal of Political Science* 38 (2): 273–89.

Chudacoff, Howard P. 1975. *Evolution of American urban society.* Englewood Cliffs, NJ: Prentice Hall.

Clark, William A. V. 1986. Residential segregation in American cities: A review and interpretation. *Population Research and Policy Review* 5: 95–127.

Coates, Ta-Nehisi. 2015. *Between the World and Me.* New York: Spiegel and Grau.

Cobb, Michael D., and James H. Kuklinski. 1997. Changing minds: Political arguments and political persuasion. *American Journal of Political Science* 41 (1): 88–121.

Cohen, Cathy, and Michael Dawson. 1993. Neighborhood poverty and African American politics. *The American Political Science Review* 87 (2): 286–302.

Collins, William J. 2004. The housing market impact of state-level anti-discrimination laws, 1960–1970. *Journal of Urban Economics* 55 (3): 534–64.

2006. The political economy of state fair housing laws before 1968. *Social Science History* 30 (1): 15–49.

Collins, William J., and Robert Margo. 1999. Race and home ownership 1900 to 1990. *National Bureau of Economic Research,* Working Paper 7277.

2011. Race and home ownership from the end of the Civil War to the present. *American Economic Review, Papers and Proceedings* 101 (2).

Collins, William J., and Katharine L. Shester. 2013. Slum clearance and urban renewal in the United States. *American Economic Journal: Applied Economics* 5 (1): 239–73.

Condran, Gretchen A., and Rose A. Cheney. 1982. Mortality trends in Philadelphia: Age- and cause-specific death rates 1870–1930. *Demography* 19 (1): 97–123.

Conley, Dalton. 1999. *Being black, living in the red: Race, wealth, and public policy*. Berkeley and Los Angeles: University of California Press.

Connerly, Charles E. 2005. *The most segregated city in America: City planning and civil rights in Birmingham, 1920–1980*. Charlottesville: University Press of Virginia.

Connolly, James. 2009. *The triumph of ethnic progressivism: Urban political culture in Boston, 1900–1925*. Cambridge: Harvard University Press.

Connolly, Nathan. 2014. *A world made more concrete: Real estate and the remaking of Jim Crow south Florida*. Chicago: University of Chicago Press.

Corn, David. 2013. Mitt Romney's incredible 47-percent denial: "Actually, I didn't say that." *Mother Jones*, July 29.

Costa, Dora L., and Robert W. Fogel. 2015. *Historical urban ecological data, 1830–1930*. ICPSR35617-v1. Ann Arbor, MI: Inter-university Consortium for Political and Social Research.

CREA plans aid against public housing projects. *Los Angeles Times*, March 23. 1952.

Cunningham, Roger. 1965. Zoning law in Michigan and New Jersey: A comparative study. *Michigan Law Review* 63 (7): 1171–202.

Current Population Reports. 1969. *Consumer Income: Poverty in the United States: 1959–1968*. Washington, DC, Series P-60 No. 68, December 31, 1969. www.census.gov/content/dam/Census/library/publications/1969/demo/p60-68a.pdf.

Cutler, David, Douglas Elmendorf, and Richard Zeckhauser. 1993. Demographic Characteristics and the Public Bundle, NBER Working Paper no. 4283.

Cutler, David M., and Edward L. Glaeser. 1997. Are ghettos good or bad? *The Quarterly Journal of Economics* 112 (3): 827–72.

Cutler, David M., Edward L. Glaeser, and Jacob L. Vigdor. 1999. The rise and decline of the American ghetto. *Journal of Political Economy* 107 (3): 455–506.

Cutler, David M., and Grant Miller. 2006. Water, water everywhere: Municipal finance and water supply in American cities. *In Corruption and reform: Lessons from America's economic history*, eds., Edward Glaeser and Claudia Goldin. Chicago: University of Chicago Press.

2005. The role of public health improvements in health advances: The twentieth-century United States. *Demography* 42 (1): 1–22.

Dahl, Robert. 1961. *Who governs: Democracy and power in an American city*. New Haven: Yale University Press.

Dancey, Logan, and Geoffrey Sheagley. 2013. Heuristics behaving badly: Party cues and voter knowledge. *American Journal of Political Science* 57 (2): 312–25.

Danielson, Michael. 1976. *The politics of exclusion*. New York: Columbia University Press.

Dawson, Michael. 1994. *Behind the mule: Race, class and African American politics*. Princeton: Princeton University Press.

Dean, John P. 1949. The myths of housing reform. *American Sociological Review* 14 (2): 281–8.

Debates in the Convention for the Revision and Amendment of the Constitution of the State of Louisiana. Assembled at Liberty Hall, New Orleans, April 6 1864: W. R. Fish Printer to the Convention.

Denton, Nancy A., and Douglas S. Massey. 1991. Patterns of neighborhood transition in a multiethnic world: U.S. metropolitan areas, 1970–1980. *Demography* 28 (1): 41–63.

Denzau, Arthur T., and Barry R. Weingast. 1982. The political economy of land use regulation. *Urban Law Annual; Journal of Urban and Contemporary Law* 23 (1): 385–405.

Deporting the Negroes. 1906. *The New York Times*, September 30.

Detroit homeowners seek rights vote. 1963. *Chicago Tribune*, July 13.

Dilworth, Richardson. 2005. *The urban origins of suburban autonomy.* Cambridge, MA: Harvard University Press.

Dreier, Peter, John Mollenkopf, and Todd Swanstrom. 2004. *Place matters: Metropolitics for the twenty-first century,* 2nd ed. Lawrence, KS: University Press of Kansas.

Druckman, James N., and Toby Bolsen. 2011. Framing, motivated reasoning, and opinions about emergent technologies. *Journal of Communication* 61 (4): 659–88.

Druckman, James N., Cari Lynn Hennessy, Kristi St. Charles, and Jonathan Webber. 2010. Competing rhetoric over time: Frames versus cues. *The Journal of Politics* 72 (01): 136–48.

DuBois, William Edward Burghardt. 1899. *The Philadelphia Negro.* Philadelphia: University of Pennsylvania Press.

   1935. *Black reconstruction in America: An essay toward a history of the part which black folk played in the attempt to reconstruct democracy in America, 1860–1880.* Rahway, NJ: Harcourt, Brace and Company, Inc.

DuBois, William Edward Burghardt, and Augustus Granville Dill. 1911. *The common school and the negro American.* Atlanta: The Atlanta University Press.

Durand, Roger. 1976. Some dynamics of urban service evaluations among blacks and whites. *Social Science Quarterly* 56 (4): 698–706.

Duscha, Julius. 1964. Fair housing issue on California ballot: Amendment explained. *The Washington Post*, September 7.

Easterly, William, and Ross Levine. 1997. Africa's growth tragedy: Policies and ethnic divisions. *The Quarterly Journal of Economics* 112 (4): 1203–50.

Einhorn, Robin. 1991. *Property rules: Political economy in Chicago, 1833–1987.* Chicago: University of Chicago Press.

Einstein, Katherine, David Glick, and Maxwell Palmer. 2017. The politics of delay in local politics: How institutions empower individuals. Paper presented at the Annual Meeting of the Midwest Political Science Association Meeting. Chicago, IL.

Ellen, Ingrid Gould. 2000. *Sharing America's neighborhoods: The prospects for stable racial integration.* Cambridge: Harvard University Press.

Ellickson, Robert. 1973. Alternatives to zoning: Covenants, nuisance rules, and fines as land use ontrols. *University of Chicago Law Review* 40(4): 681–781.

Ely, Richard. 1920. Land speculation. *Journal of Farm Economics* 2(3): 121–35.

Ely, Todd, and Paul Teske. 2015. Implications for public school choice for residential location decisions. *Urban Affairs Review* 51 (2): 175–204.

Emerson, Michael O., Karen J. Chai, and George Yancey. 2001. Does race matter in residential segregation? Exploring the preferences of white Americans. *American Sociological Review* 66 (6): 922–35.

Enos, Ryan D. 2011. A world apart. *Boston Review.* bostonreview.net/ryan-d-enos-race-demographics.

2016. What the demolition of public housing teaches us about the impact of racial threat on political behavior. *American Journal of Political Science* 60 (1): 123–42.

Environmental Protection Agency. 2004. *Report to Congress: Impacts and Control of CSOs and SSOs.* EPA 833-R-04-001.

Erbe, Brigitte Mach. 1975. Race and socioeconomic segregation. *American Sociological Review* 40(6): 801–12.

Erie, Steven P. 1988. *Rainbow's end: Irish-Americans and the dilemmas of urban machine politics, 1840–1985.* Berkeley: University of California Press.

Ethington, Philip, William Frey, and Dowell Myers. 2001. The racial resegregation of Los Angeles County, 1940–2000. Race Contours 2000 Study, University of Southern California and University of Michigan, Public Research Report No. 2001-04. www-bcf.usc.edu/~philipje/Segregation/Haynes_Reports/Contours_PRR_2001-04e.pdf.

Eulau, Heinz, and Lawrence Rothenberg. 1986. Life space and social networks as political contexts. *Political Behavior* 8 (2): 130–57.

Fair Housing Act, Title VIII of the Civil Rights Act of 1968 (1968): 42 U.S.C. 3601–3619.

Fairbanks, Robert B. 2000. Public housing for the city as a whole: The Texas experience, 1934–1955. *The Southwestern Historical Quarterly* 103 (4): 403–24.

Farley, Reynolds, Charlotte Steeh, Maria Krysan, Tara Jackson, and Keith Reeves. 1994. Stereotypes and segregation: Neighborhoods in the Detroit area. *American Journal of Sociology* 100 (3): 750–80.

Farrell, Chad. 2008. Bifurcation, fragmentation, or integration? The racial and geographical structure of US metropolitan segregation, 1990–2000. *Urban Studies* 45 (3): 467–99.

Fearon, James D., and David D. Laitin. 1996. Explaining interethnic cooperation. *The American Political Science Review* 90 (4): 715–35.

Federal Housing Administration. 1936. *Underwriting manual: Underwriting and valuation procedure under title II of the National Housing Act.* Washington DC.

Federal Housing Bill. 1936. *The Compass* 17 (8): 3.

Federico, Christopher. 2005. Racial perceptions and evaluative responses to welfare: Does education attenuate race-of-target effects? *Political Psychology* 26 (5): 683–97.

Federico, Christopher, and Samantha Luks. 2005. The political psychology of race. *Political Psychology* 26 (5): 661–6.

Feldman, Stanley. 1988. Structure and consistency in public opinion: The role of core beliefs and values. *American Journal of Political Science* 32 (2): 416–40.

Field Research Corporation. 1964. *The California Poll.* Vol. Waves 1, 2, 3, 5, 7.

Filer, John E., Lawrence W. Kenny, and Rebecca B. Morton. 1991. Voting laws, educational policies, and minority turnout. *The Journal of Law & Economics* 34 (2): 371–93.

Financial statistics of cities having a population of over 30,000. 1912. Department of Commerce, Bureau of the Census.

Fischel, William. 1992. Property taxation and the Tiebout model: Evidence for the benefit view from zoning and voting. *Journal of Economic Literature* 30 (1): 171–7.

    2001. *The homevoter hypothesis: How home values influence local government taxation, school finance, and land-use policies*. Cambridge, MA: Harvard University Press.

    2004. An economic history of zoning and a cure for its exclusionary effects. *Urban Studies* 41 (2): 317–40.

    2010. The congruence of American school districts with other local government boundaries: A Google-earth exploration. Available at SSRN: ssrn.com/abstract=967399.

    2015. *Zoning rules! The economics of land use regulation*. Lincoln Institute of Land Policy.

Fischer, Claude S., Gretchen Stockmayer, Jon Stiles, and Michael Hout. 2004. Distinguishing the geographic levels and social dimensions of U.S. metropolitan segregation, 1960–2000. *Demography* 41 (1): 37–59.

Fischer, Mary J. 2008. Shifting geographies: Examining the role of suburbanization in blacks' declining segregation. *Urban Affairs Review* 43 (4): 475–96.

Fiske, Susan T. 1980. Attention and weight in person perception: The impact of negative and extreme behavior. *Journal of Personality and Social Psychology* 38 (6): 889–906.

Flint, Herb. 1924. What a zoning law is and what it does. *Tampa Tribune*, January 6.

Florida, Richard, and Charlotta Mellander. 2015. *Segregated city: The geography of economic segregation in America's metros*. Toronto: Martin Property Institute, University of Toronto Rotman School of Management.

Fogelson, Robert M. 2005. *Bourgeois nightmares: Suburbia, 1870–1930*. New Haven, CT: Yale University Press.

Forsyth, Timothy. 2003. *Critical political ecology: political ecology and the politics of environmental science*. New York, NY: Routledge.

Fossett, Mark. 2006. Ethnic preferences, social distance dynamics, and residential segregation: Theoretical explorations using simulation analysis. *The Journal of Mathematical Sociology* 30 (3–4): 185–273.

Fox, Carroll. 1914. Public health administration in Baltimore: A study of the organization and administration of the city health department. *Public Health Reports (1896–1970)* 29 (24): 1488–564.

Fox, Cybelle. 2010. Three worlds of relief: Race, immigration, and public and private social welfare spending in American cities, 1929. *American Journal of Sociology* 116 (2): 453–502.

    2012. *Three worlds of relief: Race, immigration, and the American welfare state from the progressive era to the New Deal*. Princeton, NJ: Princeton University Press.

Frasure-Yokley, Lorrie. 2015. *Racial and ethnic politics in American suburbs.* Cambridge: Cambridge University Press.

Freedenberg, Oscar. 1941. Constitutional law: Eminent domain: Power of state to condemn land for low-cost housing and transfer to the United States. *Michigan Law Review* 39 (3): 457–62.

Freund, David. 2007. *Colored property: State policy and white racial politics in suburban America.* Chicago: University of Chicago Press.

Frey, William H. 2014. Glimpses of a ghetto-free future. *New Republic*, November 25.

Frey, William. 2014. *Diversity explosion: How new racial demographics are remaking America.* Washington, DC: Brookings Institution Press.

Friesema, H. Paul. 1969. Black control of central cities: The hollow prize. *Journal of the American Institute of Planners* 35 (2): 75–9.

Frymer, Paul. 1999. *Uneasy alliances: Race and party competition in America.* Princeton, NJ: Princeton University Press.

Gaines, Brian J., James H. Kuklinski, Paul J. Quirk, Buddy Peyton, and Jay Verkuilen. 2007. Same facts, different interpretations: Partisan motivation and opinion on Iraq. *Journal of Politics* 69 (4): 957–74.

Gainsborough, Juliet F. 2001. *Fenced off: The suburbanization of American politics.* Washington, DC: Georgetown University Press.

Galster, George, and Erin Godfrey. 2005. By words and deeds: Racial steering by real estate agents in the U.S. in 2000. *Journal of the American Planning Association* 71 (3): 251–68.

Garrett, Franklin M. 1969. *Atlanta and environs: A chronicle of its people and events*, Vol. II. Athens, GA: University of Georgia Press.

Garwood, Allison Marena. 1999. The evolution of Fettersville and the role of its sacred places: A Camden, New Jersey neighborhood. Master's Thesis. University of Pennsylvania.

Gay, Claudine. 2006. Seeing difference: The effect of economic disparity on black attitudes toward Latinos. *American Journal of Political Science* 50 (4): 982–97.

Gelfand, Mark I. 1975. *A nation of cities: The federal government and urban America, 1933–1965.* New York: Oxford University Press.

GeoLytics, Inc. 2008. *Neighborhood change database.* East Brunswick, NJ.

Ghetto, the. 1912. *The Crisis.* Volume 4, Number 6.

Gigerenzer, Gerd. 2008. Why heuristics work. *Perspectives on Psychological Science* 3 (1): 20–9.

Gilens, Martin. 1999. *Why Americans hate welfare: Race, media, and the politics of antipoverty policy.* Chicago: University of Chicago Press.

2005. Inequality and democratic responsiveness. *Public Opinion Quarterly* 69 (5): 778–96.

2009. Preference gaps and inequality in representation. *PS: Political Science and Politics* 42 (2): 335–41.

2014. *Affluence and influence: Economic inequality and political power in America.* Princeton, NJ: Princeton University Press.

Gilliam, Franklin, and Shanto Iyengar. 2000. Prime suspects: The influence of local television news on the viewing public. *American Journal of Political Science* 44 (3): 560–73.

Gilliam, Franklin, Shanto Iyengar, Adam Simon, and Oliver Wrights. 1996. The violent scary world of local news. *The International Journal of Press/Politics* 1 (3): 6–23.

Glaab, Charles N., and A. Theodore Brown. 1967. *History of urban America.* New York: Macmillan.

Glaeser, Edward. 2013. A nation of gamblers: Real estate speculation and American history. Richard Ely Lecture, American Economics Association, San Diego, CA.

Glaeser, Edward L., Matthew E. Kahn, and Jordan Rappaport. 2008. Why do the poor live in cities? The role of public transportation. *Journal of Urban Economics* 63 (1): 1–24.

Glaeser, Edward L., and Jacob L. Vigdor. 2012. *The end of the segregated century: Racial separation in America's neighborhoods, 1890–2010.* Manhattan Institute Report, No. 66.

Glaeser, Edward L., and Bryce A. Ward. 2006. Myths and realities of American political geography. *Journal of Economic Perspectives* 20 (2): 119–44.

Glaser, James M. 1994. Back to the black belt: Racial environment and white racial attitudes in the south. *The Journal of Politics* 56 (1): 21–41.

2002. White voters, black schools: Structuring racial choices with a checklist ballot. *American Journal of Political Science* 46 (1): 35–46.

Godsil, Rachel D. 2006. Race nuisance: The politics of law in the Jim Crow era. *Michigan Law Review* 105: 505–56.

Goldin, Claudia, and Lawrence F. Katz. 1999. Human capital and social capital: The rise of secondary schooling in America, 1910–1940. *Journal of Interdisciplinary History* 29 (4): 683–723.

2008. *The race between education and technology.* Cambridge: Harvard University Press.

Gosnell, Harold. 1935. *Negro politicians: The rise of Negro politics in Chicago.* Chicago: University of Chicago Press.

Gotham, Kevin F. 2000. Racialization and the state: The housing act of 1934 and the creation of the Federal Housing Administration. *Sociological Perspectives* 43 (2): 291–317.

2001. A city without slums – Urban renewal, public housing, and downtown revitalization in Kansas City, Missouri. *American Journal of Economics and Sociology* 60 (1): 285–316.

Great showing made by the colored voters, 1921. *Atlanta Independent,* March 10.

Green, Donald P., Bradley Palmquist, and Eric Schickler. 2002. *Partisan hearts and minds: Political parties and the social identities of voters.* New Haven: Yale University Press.

Greenberg, Carl. 1964. Prop. 14 wins by big edge. *Los Angeles Times,* November 4.

Greene, Suzanne E. 1979. Black republicans on the Baltimore city council, 1890–1931. *Maryland Historical Magazine* 74 (3).

Griffith, Ernest. 1927. *The modern development of city government in the United Kingdom and the United States.* London: Oxford University Press.

Guyer, Bernard, Mary Anne Freedman, Donna Strobino, and Edward. J. Sondik. 2000. Annual summary of vital statistics: Trends in the health of Americans during the 20th century. *Pediatrics* 106 (6): 1307–17.

Gyourko, Joseph, Albert Saiz, and Anita Summers. 2008. A new measure of the local regulatory environment for housing markets: The Wharton residential land use regulatory index. *Urban Studies* 45 (3): 693–729.

Habyarimana, James, Macartan Humphreys, Daniel N. Posner, and Jeremy M. Weinstein. 2007. Why does ethnic diversity undermine public goods provision? *The American Political Science Review* 101 (4): 709–25. www.jstor .org/stable/27644480.

2009. *Coethnicity: Diversity and the dilemmas of collective action.* New York: Russell Sage Foundation.

Haidt, Jonathan. 2001. The emotional dog and its rational tail: A social intuitionist approach to moral judgment. *Psychological Review* 108 (4): 814–34.

Haines, Michael R. 2001. The Urban Mortality Transition in the United States, 1800–1940. NBER Historical Working Paper No. 134. www.nber.org/ papers/h0134.

Hajnal, Zoltan. 2007. *Changing white attitudes toward black political leadership.* Cambridge: Cambridge University Press.

2009. Who loses in American democracy? A count of votes demonstrates the limited representation of African Americans. *American Political Science Review* 103 (1): 37–57.

2010. *America's uneven democracy: Race, turnout, and representation in city politics.* New York: Cambridge University Press.

Hajnal, Zoltan L., and Jessica Trounstine. 2013a. What underlies urban politics? Race, class, ideology, partisanship, and the urban vote. *Urban Affairs Review* 50 (1): 63–99.

2013b. Identifying and understanding perceived inequities in local politics. *Political Research Quarterly* 66 (2): 1–15.

Hall, Jaquelyn Dowd. 2005. The long civil rights movement and the political uses of the past. *The Journal of American History* 91 (4): 1233–63.

Hamilton, Bruce. 1975. Zoning and property taxation in a system of local governments. *Urban Studies* 12: 205–11.

Hamilton, David L., and Mark P. Zanna. 1972. Differential weighting of favorable and unfavorable attributes in impressions of personality. *Journal of Experimental Research in Personality* 6: 204–12.

Hand, Bill. 2014. About Jim Crow and Cedar Grove cemetery. *Sun Journal,* February 9.

Harris, David R. 1999. Property values drop when blacks move in, because...: Racial and socioeconomic determinants of neighborhood desirability. *American Sociological Review* 64 (3): 461–79.

Hartman, E. T. 1925. Zoning and democracy. *Social Forces* 4 (1): 162–5.

Hays, Samuel P. 1964. The politics of reform in municipal government in the progressive era. *The Pacific Northwest Quarterly* 55 (4): 157–69.

Hayward, Clarissa. 2009. Urban space and American political development: Identity, interest, action. In *The city in American political development,* ed. Richardson Dilworth: 141–53. New York: Routledge.

2013. *Americans make race: Stories, institutions, spaces.* New York: Cambridge University Press.

Helper, Rose. 1969. *Racial policies and practices of real estate brokers.* Minneapolis: University of Minnesota Press.

Helzner, Gerald. 1968a. What happened to Parkside? Negroes sought good homes, found disappointment. *Courier-Post*, March 6.

    1968b. Parkside in race for survival: Area has gone down hill in 5 or 6 years. *Courier-Post*, March 7.

Hersh, Eitan D., and Clayton Nall. 2016. The primacy of race in the geography of income-based voting: New evidence from public voting records. *American Journal of Political Science* 60 (2): 289–303.

Hetherington, Marc J., and Jonathan Weiler. 2009. *Authoritarianism and polarization in American politics.* New York: Cambridge University Press.

Hilber, Christian A. L. 2011. The economic implications of house price capitalization: A survey of an emerging literature. *Spatial Economics Research Centre*, Discussion Paper 91.

Hillier, Amy E. 2005. Residential security maps and neighborhood appraisals: The home owners' loan corporation and the case of Philadelphia. *Social Science History* 29 (2): 2007–221.

Hirsch, Arnold. 1983. *Making the second ghetto: Race and housing in Chicago 1940–1960.* Chicago: University of Chicago Press.

Hobbs, Frank, and Nicole Stoops. U.S. Census Bureau, Census 2000 Special Reports, Series CENSR-4. 2002. *Demographic trends in the 20th century.* Washington, DC: U.S. Government Printing Office.

Holliday, A. C. 1922. Restrictions governing city development: Zoning for use. *The Town Planning Review* 9 (4): 217–38.

Hopkins, Daniel J. 2009. The diversity discount: When increasing ethnic and racial diversity prevents tax increases. *Journal of Politics* 71 (1): 160–77.

Hopkins, Daniel J., and Katherine T. McCabe. 2012. After it's too late: Estimating the policy impacts of black mayoralties in U.S. cities. *American Politics Research* 40 (4): 665–700.

House of Commons Research Paper. 1999. *A century of change: Trends in UK statistics since 1900.* Social and General Statistics Section, House of Commons Library, Research Paper 99/111.

Hoxby, Caroline. 2000. Does competition among public schools benefit students and taxpayers? *Annual Review of Political Science* 90 (5): 1209–38.

Huckfeldt, Robert. 1986. *Politics in context: Assimilation and conflict in urban neighborhoods.* New York: Agathon Press.

Huckfeldt, Robert, and John D. Sprague. 1995. *Citizens, politics, and social communication: Information and influence in an election campaign.* New York: Cambridge University Press.

Hurwitz, Jon, and Mark Peffley. 1997. Public perceptions of race and crime: The role of racial stereotypes. *American Journal of Political Science* 41 (2): 375–401.

Hurwitz, Robert. 1949. Constitutional law: Equal protection of the laws: California anti-miscegenation laws declared unconstitutional. *California Law Review* 37 (1): 122–9.

Hutchings, Vincent L., and Nicholas A. Valentino. 2004. The centrality of race in American politics. *Annual Review of Political Science* 7: 383–408.

Iceland, John. 2004. The Multigroup Entropy Index (also known as Theil's H or the Information Theory Index): www.census.gov/housing/patterns/about/mul tigroup_entropy.pdf.

Iceland, John, and Rima Wilkes. 2006. Does socioeconomic status matter? Race, class, and residential segregation. *Social Problems* 53 (2): 248–73.

Ickes, Harold L. 1935. The place of housing in national rehabilitation. *The Journal of Land & Public Utility Economics* 11 (2): 109–16.

Iyengar, Shanto, and Sean Westwood. 2014. Fear and loathing across party lines: New evidence on group polarization. *American Journal of Political Science* 59 (3): 690–707.

Jackman, Mary R. 1994. *The velvet glove: Paternalism and conflict in gender, class, and race relations.* Berkeley: University of California Press.

Jackson, Kenneth T. 1987 [1985]. *Crabgrass frontier: The suburbanization of the United States.* New York: Oxford University Press.

Jargowsky, Paul A. 1996. Take the money and run: Economic segregation in U.S. metropolitan areas. *American Sociological Review* 61 (6): 984–98.

2013. *Concentration of poverty in the new millennium: Changes in prevalence, composition, and location of high poverty neighborhoods.* Century Foundation and Rutgers Center for Urban Research and Education.

Jensen, Noma. 1948. A survey of segregation practices in the New Jersey school system. *The Journal of Negro Education* 17(1): 84–8.

Johnson, Charles. 1932. *Negro housing; report of the Committee on Negro Housing, Nannie H. Burroughs, chairman.* Eds. John M. Gries and James Ford. Washington, DC: The President's Conference on Home Building and Home Ownership.

Johnson, Rucker. 2015. Long-run impacts of school desegregation and school quality on adult attainments. NBER Working Paper no. 16664.

Jones-Correa, Michael. 1998. *Between two nations: The political predicament of Latinos in New York City.* Ithaca: Cornell University Press.

2000. The origins and diffusion of racial restrictive covenants. *Political Science Quarterly* 115 (4): 541–68.

Kahneman, Daniel. 2003. A perspective on judgment and choice: Mapping bounded rationality. *The American Psychologist* 58 (9): 697–720.

Kahneman, Daniel, and Amos Tversky. 1979. Prospect theory: An analysis of decision under risk. *Econometrica* 47 (2): 263–92.

Katz, Bruce. 1998. Brookings' Beyond City Limits: A new metropolitan agenda: www.metroforum.org/articles/katz_071998.html.

Katznelson, Ira. 1981. *City trenches: Urban politics and the patterning of class in the United States.* New York: Pantheon Books.

Katznelson, Ira, and Margaret Weir. 1985. *Schooling for all: Class, race, and the decline of the democratic ideal.* New York: Basic Books.

Kaufmann, Karen. 2004. *The urban voters: Group conflict and mayoral voting behavior in American cities.* Ann Arbor: University of Michigan Press.

Kellogg, John. 1982. The formation of black residential areas in Lexington, Kentucky, 1865–1887. *Southern Historical Association* 48 (1): 21–52.

Kendi, Ibram X. 2016. *Stamped from the beginning: The definitive history of racist ideas in America*. New York: Nation Books.

Kennedy, John F. 1963. *Public papers of the President of the United States, John F. Kennedy, containing the public messages, speeches, and statements of the President, January 1 to December 31, 1962*. Washington, DC: United States Government Printing Office. http://name.umdl.umich.edu/4730892.1962.001.

Kennedy, Lawrence W. 1992. *Planning the city upon a hill: Boston since 1630*. Amherst: University of Massachusetts Press.

Key, Vladimer O. 1949. *Southern politics in state and nation*. New York: A. A. Knopf.

Keyssar, Alexander. 2000. *The right to vote: The contested history of democracy in the United States*. New York: Basic Books.

Kinder, Donald. 1998. Attitude and action in the realm of politics. In *Handbook of Social Psychology*, 4th ed., eds. Daniel Gilbert, Susan Fiske, and Gardner Lindzey: 778–867. New York: Oxford University Press.

Kinder, Donald R., and Lynn Sanders. 1996. *Divided by color: Racial politics and democratic ideals*. Chicago: University of Chicago Press.

Kinder, Donald R., and David O. Sears. 1981. Prejudice and politics: Symbolic racism versus racial threats to the good life. *Journal of Personality and Social Psychology* 40 (3): 414–31.

Kinder, Donald R., and Nicholas Winter. 2001. Exploring the racial divide: Blacks, whites, and opinion on national policy. *American Journal of Political Science* 45 (2): 439–56.

Klar, Samara. 2014. Partisanship in a social setting. *American Journal of Political Science* 58 (3): 687–704.

Knauss, Norman. 1929. 786 municipalities in United States now protected by zoning ordinances. *The American City* 40 (June): 167–71.

Knight, Charles. 1927. *Negro housing in certain Virginia cities*. Richmond, VA: The William Byrd Press.

Knoll, Katharina, Moritz Schularick, and Thomas Steger. 2014. No price like home: Global house prices, 1870–2012. *Federal Reserve Bank of Dallas Globalization and Monetary Policy Institute*, Working Paper #208.

Koch, O. H. and Fowler. 1928. *A city plan for Austin, Texas*. City of Austin: ftp://ftp.austintexas.gov/GIS-Data/planning/compplan/1927_Plan.pdf.

Kohl, Sebastian. 2014. *Homeowner nations or nations of tenants: How historical institutions in urban politics, housing finance, and construction set Germany, France, and the US on different housing paths*. Cologne: International Max Planck Research School on the Social and Political Constitution of the Economy.

Konvitz, Milton R. 1947. *The constitution and civil rights*. New York: Columbia University Press.

Kousser, J. Morgan. 1974. *The shaping of southern politics: Suffrage restriction and the establishment of the one-party south, 1880–1910*. New Haven: Yale University Press.

Kraft, Patrick W., Milton Lodge, and Charles S. Taber. 2015. Why people "Don't trust the evidence": Motivated reasoning and scientific beliefs. *Annals of the American Academy of Political and Social Science* 658 (1): 121–33.

Kraus, Neil. 2000. *Race, neighborhoods, and community power: Buffalo politics, 1934–1997*. Albany: State University of New York Press.

Kruse, Kevin. 2005. *White flight: Atlanta and the making of modern conservatism*. Princeton: Princeton University Press.

Kruse, Kevin Michael, and Thomas J. Sugrue. 2006. *The new suburban history*. Chicago: University of Chicago Press.

Krysan, Maria. 2002. Whites who say they'd flee: Who are they, and why would they leave? *Demography* 39 (4): 675–96.

Krysan, Maria, Reynolds Farley, and Mick P. Couper. 2008. In the eye of the beholder: Racial beliefs and residential segregation. *Du Bois Review* 5 (1): 5–26.

Kuklinski, James H., and Paul J. Quirk. 2000. Reconsidering the rational public: Cognition, heuristics, and mass opinion. *Elements of Reason: Cognition, Choice and the Bounds of Rationality*: 153–82.

Kuklinski, James H., Paul J. Quirk, Jennifer Jerit, and Robert F. Rich. 2001. The political environment and citizen competence. *American Journal of Political Science* 45 (2): 410–24.

Kunda, Ziva. 1990. The case for motivated reasoning. *Psychological Bulletin* 108 (3): 480–98.

Lafortune, Julien, Jesse Rothstein, and Diane Whitmore Schanzenbach. 2016. School finance reform and the distribution of student achievement. National Bureau of Economic Research Working Paper Series, No. 22011: www.nber.org/papers/w22011.

Lasker, Bruno. 1920a. The issue restated. *The Survey* 44.

1920b. Unwalled towns. *The Survey* 43.

Lassiter, Matthew. 2006. *The silent majority: Suburban politics in the sunbelt South*. Princeton, NJ: Princeton University Press.

Lau, Richard R. 1985. Two explanations for negativity effects in political behavior. *American Journal of Political Science* 29 (1): 119–38.

Lau, Richard R., and David P. Redlawsk. 2001. Advantages and disadvantages of cognitive heuristics in political decision making. *American Journal of Political Science* 45 (4): 951–71.

Lee, Barrett, Glenn Firebaugh, Stephen Matthews, Sean Reardon, Chad Farrell, and David O'Sullivan. 2008. Beyond the census tract: Patterns and determinants of racial segregation at multiple geographic scales. *American Sociological Review* 73(5): 766–91.

Lee, Don. 2015. Segregation continues to decline in most U.S. cities, census figures show. *Los Angeles Times*, December 3.

Leeper, Thomas J., and Rune Slothuus. 2014. Political parties, motivated reasoning, and public opinion formation. *Political Psychology* 35: 129–56.

Lees, Martha A. 1994. Preserving property values? Preserving proper homes? Preserving privilege? The pre-Euclid debate over zoning for exclusively private residential areas, 1916–1926. *The University of Pittsburgh Law Review* 56: 367–439.

Leighley, Jan E., and Arnold Vedlitz. 1999. Race, ethnicity, and political participation: Competing models and contrasting explanations. *The Journal of Politics* 61 (4): 1092–114.

Leonard, Elizabeth. 2010. State constitutionalism and the right to health care. *Journal of Constitutional Law.* 125: 1325–406.

Leonnig, Carol. 1989. Cherry Hill pays price for prosperity. *Philadelphia Inquirer*, September 10.

Levine, David D. 1941. The case for tax exemption of public housing. *The Journal of Land & Public Utility Economics* 17 (1): 98–101.

Levine, Katherine. 2012. *Divided regions: Race, political segregation, and the fragmentation of American metropolitan policy.* PhD Dissertation. Government and Social Policy, Harvard University.

Levine, Phillip, and David Zimmerman. 1999. An empirical analysis of the welfare magnet debate using the NLSY. *Journal of Population Economics* 12: 391–409.

Lewis, Charles F. 1937. Some economic implications of modern housing. *The American Economic Review* 27: 188–95.

Lieberman, Matthew D., Darren Schreiber, and Kevin N. Ochsner. 2003. Is political cognition like riding a bicycle? How cognitive neuroscience can inform research on political thinking. *Political Psychology* 24 (4): 681–704.

Linder, Forrest, and Robert Grove. 1947. *Vital statistics rates in the United States 1900–1940.* Washington, DC: United States Government Printing Office.

Litwack, Leon F. 1961. *North of slavery; the negro in the free states, 1790–1860.* Chicago: University of Chicago Press.

Lodge, Milton, and Ruth Hamill. 1986. A partisan schema for political information processing. *The American Political Science Review* 80 (2): 505–20.

Lodge, Milton, Kathleen M. McGraw, and Patrick Stroh. 1989. An impression-driven model of candidate evaluation. *The American Political Science Review* 83 (2): 399–419.

Lodge, Milton, and Charles S. Taber. 2000. Three steps toward a theory of motivated political reasoning. In *Elements of Reason*, eds. Lupia Skip, Mathew McCubbins, and Samuel Popkin: 183–213. Cambridge University Press.

  2007. The rationalizing voter: Unconscious thought in political information processing. *SSRN Electronic Journal*: 1–46.

Logan, John. 2011. *Separate and unequal: The neighborhood gap for blacks, Hispanics and Asians in metropolitan America.* US2010 Project.

Logan, John, and Harvey Molotch. 1987. *Urban fortunes: The political economy of place.* Berkeley, CA: University of California Press.

Logan, John R., and Brian J. Stults. 2011. *The persistence of segregation in the metropolis: New findings from the 2010 census.* US2010 Project.

Logan, John R., Weiwei Zhang, and Miao David Chunyu. 2015. Emergent ghettos: Black neighborhoods in New York and Chicago, 1880–1940. *American Journal of Sociology* 120 (4): 1055–94.

Loury, Glenn. 2002. *The anatomy of racial inequality.* Cambridge, MA: Harvard University Press.

Lublin, David, and Katherine Tate. 1995. Racial group competition in urban elections. In *Classifying by race*, ed. Paul Peterson: 245–61. Princeton, NJ: Princeton University Press.

Lupia, Arthur, and Mathew McCubbins. 1998. *The democratic dilemma: Can citizens learn what they need to know?* New York: Cambridge University Press.

Luttmer, Erzo F. P. 2001. Group loyalty and the taste for redistribution. *Journal of Political Economy* 109 (3): 500–28.

Mabee, Carleton. 1968. A negro boycott to integrate Boston schools. *The New England Quarterly* 41 (3): 341–61.

Macedo, Stephen. 2003. School reform and equal opportunity in America's geography of inequality. *Perspectives on Politics* 1(4): 743–55.

Mahan, Brent L., Stephen Polasky, and Richard M. Adams. 2000. Valuing urban wetlands: A property price approach. *Land Economics* 76 (1): 100–13.

Marcuse, Peter. 1995. Interpreting "public housing" history. *Journal of Architectural and Planning Research* 12 (3): 240–58.

Margo, Robert A. 1992. Explaining the postwar suburbanization of population in the United States: The role of income. *Journal of Urban Economics* 31 (3): 301–10.

Marschall, Melissa, and Paru R. Shah. 2007. The attitudinal effects of minority incorporation examining the racial dimensions of trust in urban America. *Urban Affairs Review* 42 (5): 629–58.

Martins-Filho, Carlos, and Okmyung Bin. 2005. Estimation of hedonic price functions via additive nonparametric regression. *Empirical Econometrics* 30 (1): 93–114.

Massey, Douglas S., and Nancy A. Denton. 1987. Trends in the residential segregation of blacks, Hispanics, and Asians: 1970–1980. *American Sociological Review* 52 (6): 802–25.

1988. The dimensions of residential segregation. *Social Forces* 67 (2): 281–315.

1998. *American apartheid: Segregation and the making of the underclass.* Cambridge, MA: Harvard University Press.

Massey, Douglas S., and Zoltan L. Hajnal. 1995. The changing geographic structure of black-white segregation in the United States. *Social Science Quarterly* 76 (3): 527–41.

Mather, Mark, Kelvin Pollard, and Linda A. Jacobson. 2011. *Reports on America: First results from the 2010 census.* Washington, DC: Population Reference Bureau.

Mazur, Christopher, and Ellen Wilson. 2011. US Census Bureau, 2010 Census Briefs. *Housing Characteristics: 2010.* Washington, DC: US Government Printing Office.

McAdams, Richard H. 2008. Beyond the prisoner's dilemma: Coordination, game theory and the law. *Southern California Law Review* 82: 209–58.

McCarty, Nolan, Jonathan Rodden, Boris Shor, Chris Tausanovitch, and Christopher Warshaw. 2018. Geography, uncertainty, and polarization. *Political Science Research and Methods.* doi.org/10.1017/psrm.2018.12.

McClain, Charles. 1996. *In search of equality: The Chinese struggle against discrimination in nineteenth-century America.* Berkeley: University of California Press.

McClosky, Herbert, and John Zaller. 1984. *The American ethos: Public attitudes toward capitalism and democracy.* Chicago: University of Chicago Press.

McConahay, John B. 1982. Self-interest versus racial attitudes as correlates of anti-busing attitudes in Louisville: Is it the buses or the blacks? *The Journal of Politics* 44 (3): 692–720.

McCormick, Erin. 2017. Rise of the yimbys: The angry millennials with a radical housing solution. *The Guardian*, October 2: www.theguardian.com/cities/2017/oct/02/rise-of-the-yimbys-angry-millennials-radical-housing-solution.

McDermott, Rose. 2002. Experimental methods in political science. *Annual Review of Political Science* 5: 31–61.

McDonald, Terrence J. 1986. *The parameters of urban fiscal policy: Socioeconomic change and political culture in San Francisco, 1860–1906*. Berkeley: University of California Press.

McDonald, Terrence J., and Sally K. Ward, eds. 1984. *The politics of urban fiscal policy*. Beverley Hills, CA: SAGE Publications, Inc.

McWilliams, Carey. 1964. *Brothers under the skin*. Boston: Little, Brown.

Meckel, Richard. 1990. *Save the babies: American public health reform and the prevention of infant mortality, 1850–1929*. Baltimore: Johns Hopkins University Press.

Meffert, Michael F., Sungeun Chung, Amber J. Joiner, Leah Waks, and Jennifer Garst. 2006. The effects of negativity and motivated information processing during a political campaign. *Journal of Communication* 56 (1): 27–51.

Mendelberg, Tali. 2001. *The race card: Campaign strategy, implicit messages, and the norm of equality*. Princeton, NJ: Princeton University Press.

Mercer, Jonathan. 2005. Prospect theory and political science. *Annual Review of Political Science* 8 (1): 1–21.

Merritt, Keri Leigh. 2016. Land and the roots of African American poverty. *Aeon*, March 11: https://aeon.co/ideas/land-and-the-roots-of-african-american-poverty.

Meyer, Stephen Grant. 2000. *As long as they don't move next door: Segregation and racial conflict in American neighborhoods*. Lanham, MD: Rowman & Littlefield.

Michener, Jamila. 2017. Social class as a racialized experience. *The Forum: A Journal of Applied Research in Contemporary Politics* 15 (1): 93–110.

Mieszkowski, Peter, and Edwin S. Mills. 1993. The causes of metropolitan suburbanization. *Journal of Economic Perspectives* 7 (3): 135–47.

Miguel, Edward. 2004. Tribe or nation? Nation building and public goods in Kenya versus Tanzania. *World Politics* 56 (3): 327–62.

Miguel, Edward, and Mary Kay Gugerty. 2005. Ethnic diversity, social sanctions, and public goods in Kenya. *Journal of Public Economics* 89 (11–12): 2325–68.

Miler, Kristina C. 2009. The limitations of heuristics for political elites. *Political Psychology* 30 (6): 863–94.

Miller, Gary. 1981. *Cities by contract: The politics of municipal incorporation*. Cambridge, MA: MIT Press.

Miller, Joanne M., Kyle L. Saunders, and Christina E. Farhart. 2015. Conspiracy endorsement as motivated reasoning: The moderating roles of political knowledge and trust. *American Journal of Political Science* 60(4): 824–44.

Miller, Warren E., and Merrill Shanks. 1996. *The new American voter.* Cambridge, MA: Harvard University Press.

Mitchell, Dona Gene. 2012. It's about time: The lifespan of information effects in a multiweek campaign. *American Journal of Political Science* 56 (2): 298–311.

Mollenkopf, John. 1994. *Phoenix in the ashes: The rise and fall of the Koch coalition in New York.* Princeton, NJ: Princeton University Press.

Monchow, Helen C. 1928. The Cambridge zoning decision. *The Journal of Land and Public Utility Economics* 4 (3): 322–4.

Monkkonen, Eric H. 1988. *America becomes urban: The development of U.S. cities and towns, 1780–1980.* Berkeley: University of California Press.

Monkkonen, Pavo. 2016. *Understanding and challenging opposition to housing construction in California's urban areas.* Housing, Land Use and Development Lectureship and White Paper. UC Center Sacramento.

Muhammad, Khalil Gibran. 2011. *The condemnation of blackness: Race, crime, and the making of modern urban America.* Cambridge, MA: Harvard University Press.

Mummolo, Jonathan, and Clayton Nall. 2017. Why partisans don't sort: The constraints on political segregation. *The Journal of Politics* 79(1): 45–59.

Myrdal, Gunnar. 1944. *An American dilemma: The negro problem and modern democracy.* New York: Harper and Brothers Publishers.

Nall, Clayton. 2018. *The road to inequality: How the federal highway program created suburbs, undermined cities, and polarized America.* New York: Cambridge University Press.

   2015. The political consequences of spatial policies: How interstate highways facilitated geographic polarization. *Journal of Politics* 77 (2): 394–406.

National defense labor problems: The Weaver appointment. 1940. *The Crisis,* October.

Negro runs for Camden Council job. 1951. *Chicago Defender,* April 21.

Nelson, Thomas, and Donald Kinder. 1996. Issue frames and group-centrism in American public opinion. *The Journal of Politics* 58 (4): 1055–78.

Nelson, William. 1990. Black mayoral leadership: A twenty-year perspective. In *Black Electoral Politics,* ed. Lucius Barker. New York: Routledge.

Nelson, William, and Philip Meranto. 1977. *Electing black mayors: Political action in the black community.* Columbus: Ohio State University Press.

New Jersey State Data Center. 2000. New Jersey Population Trends 1790 to 2000. NJSDC-P2000–3. www.nj.gov/labor/lpa/census/2kpub/njsdcp3.pdf.

Nicholson, Stephen P. 2011. Dominating cues and the limits of elite influence. *The Journal of Politics* 73 (04): 1165–77.

   2012. Polarizing cues. *American Journal of Political Science* 56 (1): 52–66.

Nicolaides, Becky. 2002. *My blue heaven: Life and politics in the working-class suburbs of Los Angeles, 1920–1965.* Chicago: University of Chicago Press.

Nightingale, Carl. 2006. The transnational contexts of early twentieth-century American urban segregation. *Journal of Social History* 39(3): 667–702.

Nobles, Melissa. 2000. *Shades of citizenship: Race and the census in modern politics.* Stanford: Stanford University Press.

North, Douglas. 1990. *Institutions, institutional change, and economic performance*. Cambridge University Press.

Oates, Wallace E. 1969. The effects of property taxes and local public spending on property values: An empirical study of tax capitalization and the Tiebout hypothesis. *Journal of Political Economy* 77: 957–71.

1981. On local finance and the Tiebout model. *The American Economic Review* 71 (2): 93–8.

Objects of zoning explained. 1923. *The Cincinnati Enquirer*, November 18.

O'Connor, Thomas H. 1984. *Bibles, brahmins, and bosses: A short history of Boston*, 2nd ed. Boston: Trustees of the Public Library of the City of Boston.

Ogorzalek, Thomas. 2018. *Cities on the hill: Urban institutions in national politics*. New York: Oxford University Press.

Oliver, J. Eric, 1999. The effects of metropolitan economic segregation on local civic participation. *American Journal of Political Science* 43(1): 186–212.

2001. *Democracy in suburbia*. Princeton, NJ: Princeton University Press.

2010. *The paradoxes of integration: Race, neighborhood, and civic life in multiethnic America*. Chicago: University of Chicago Press.

Oliver, J. Eric, and Tali Mendelberg. 2000. Reconsidering the environmental determinants of white racial attitudes. *American Journal of Political Science* 44: 574–89.

Oliver, J. Eric, and Shang Ha. 2007. Vote choice in suburban elections. *American Political Science Review* 101(3): 393–408.

Oliver, J. Eric, and Janelle Wong. 2003. Intergroup prejudice in multiethnic settings. *American Journal of Political Science* 47 (4): 567–82.

Orey, Byron D'Andrea. 2001. A new racial threat in the new South? (A conditional) yes. *The American Review of Politics* 22: 233–55.

Orfield, Myron. 2002. *American metropolitics: The new suburban reality*. Washington, DC: Brookings Institution Press.

Owens, Michael. 2007. *God and government in the ghetto: The politics of church–state collaboration in black America*. Chicago: University of Chicago Press.

Pager, Devah and Hana Shepherd. 2008. The sociology of discrimination: Racial discrimination in employment, housing, credit, and consumer markets. *Annual Review of Sociology* 34: 181–209.

Paterson, Robert W., and Kevin J. Boyle. 2002. Out of sight, out of mind? Using GIS to incorporate visibility in hedonic property value models. *Land Economics* 78 (3): 417–25.

Peffley, Mark, Todd Shields, and Bruce Williams. 2010. The intersection of race and crime in television news stories. *Political Communication* 13 (3): 309–27.

Pendall, Rolf. 2000. Local land use regulations and the chain of exclusion. *Journal of the American Planning Association* 66 (2): 125–42.

Perry, Ravi. 2013. *Black mayors, white majorities: The balancing act of racial politics*. Lincoln: University of Nebraska Press.

Petersen, Michael Bang. 2015. Evolutionary political psychology: On the origin and structure of heuristics and biases in politics. *Political Psychology* 36: 45–78.

Petersen, Michael Bang, Martin Skov, Soren Serritzlew, and Thomas Ramsoy. 2013. Motivated reasoning and political parties: Evidence for increased processing in the face of party cues. *Political Behavior* 35 (4): 831–54.

Peterson, Paul. 1981. *City limits*. Chicago: University of Chicago Press.

Pinderhughes, Diane. 1987. *Race and ethnicity in Chicago politics: A reexamination of pluralist theory*. Urbana: University of Illinois Press.

Plotnick, Robert D., and Richard F. Winters. 1985. A politico-economic theory of income redistribution. *The American Political Science Review* 79 (2): 458–73.

Pommer, Richard. 1978. The architecture of urban housing in the United States during the early 1930s. *Journal of the Society of Architectural Historians* 37 (4): 235–64.

Poterba, James M. 1997. Demographic structure and the political economy of public education. *Journal of Policy Analysis and Management* 16 (1): 48–66.

Power, Garrett. 1983. Apartheid Baltimore style: The residential segregation ordinances of 1910–1913. *Maryland Law Review* 42 (2): 289–328.

Preston, Benjamin L., Johanna Mustelin, and Megan C. Maloney. 2013. Climate adaptation heuristics and the science/policy divide. *Mitigation and Adaptation Strategies for Global Change* 20 (3): 467–97.

Proposed zoning system as it would apply to Fitchburg is debated. 1923. *Fitchburg Sentinel*, October 17.

Prowell, George. 1886. *The history of Camden County New Jersey*. Philadelphia: L. J. Richards and Co.

Puleo, Stephen. 1994. From Italy to Boston's north end: Italian immigration and settlement, 1890–1910. Graduate Master's Thesis, History. University of Massachusetts Boston.

Putnam, Robert. 2007. E pluribus unum: Diversity and community in the twenty-first century. *Scandinavian Political Studies* 30 (2): 137–74.

Quadagno, Jill S. 1994. *The color of welfare: How racism undermined the war on poverty*. New York: Oxford University Press.

Qualify and vote for bonds. 1921. *Atlanta Independent*, February 24.

Rabin, Yale. 1990. Expulsive zoning: The inequitable legacy of Euclid. In *Zoning and the American dream: Promises still to keep*, eds. Charles Haar and Jerrold Kayden. Chicago: American Planning Association Planners Press.

Rabinowitz, Howard N. 1974. From exclusion to segregation: Health and welfare services for southern blacks, 1865–1890. *Social Service Review* 48 (3): 327–54.

——— 1978. *Race relations in the urban South, 1865–1890*. New York: Oxford University Press.

Rabinowitz, Joshua L., David O. Sears, Jim Sidanius, and Jon A. Krosnick. 2009. Why do white Americans oppose race-targeted policies? Clarifying the impact of symbolic racism. *Political Psychology* 30 (5): 805–28.

Racial zoning by private contract. 1928. *The Virginia Law Register* 13 (9): 526–41, www.jstor.org/stable/1108328.

Rahn, Wendy M. 1993. The role of partisan stereotypes in information processing about political candidates. *American Journal of Political Science* 37 (2): 472–96.

Rahn, Wendy M., and Thomas J. Rudolph. 2005. A tale of political trust in American cities. *Public Opinion Quarterly* 69 (4): 530–60.

Rappaport, Jordan. 2005. *The shared fortunes of cities and suburbs*. Federal Reserve Bank of Kansas City: www.kansascityfed.org/publicat/econrev/pdf/3q05rapp.pdf

Reardon, Sean, Chad Farrell, Stephen Matthews, David O'Sullivan, Kendra Bischoff, and Glenn Firebaugh. 2009. Race and space in the 1990s: Changes in the geographic scale of racial residential segregation, 1990–2000. *Social Science Research* 38(1): 55–70.

Reardon, Sean F., and Glenn Firebaugh. 2002. Measures of multigroup segregation. *Sociological Methodology* 32 (1): 33–67.

Reardon, Sean F., and Ann Owens. 2014. 60 years after *Brown*: Trends and consequences of school segregation. *Annual Review of Sociology* 40: 199–218.

Reardon, Sean F., John T. Yun, and Tamela McNulty Eitle. 2000. The changing structure of school segregation: Measurement and evidence of multiracial metropolitan-area school segregation, 1989–1995. *Demography* 37 (3): 351–64.

Reber, Sarah. 2005. Court-ordered desegregation – Successes and failures integrating American schools since *Brown versus Board of Education*. *Journal of Human Resources* 40 (3): 559–90.

Redlawsk, David P., ed. 2001. You must remember this: A test of the on-line model of voting. *Journal of Politics* 63 (1): 29–58.

    2002. Hot cognition or cool consideration? Testing the effects of motivated reasoning on political decision making. *The Journal of Politics* 64 (04): 1021–44.

    2006. *Feeling politics: Emotion in political information processing*. New York: Palgrave Macmillan.

Redlawsk, David P., Andrew J. W. Civettini, and Karen M. Emmerson. 2010. The affective tipping point: Do motivated reasoners ever "get it"? *Political Psychology* 31 (4): 563–93.

Reed, Adolph Jr. 1999. *Stirrings in the jug: Black politics in the post-segregation era*. Minnesota: University of Minnesota Press.

    2016. The post-1965 trajectory of race, class, and urban politics in the United States reconsidered. *Labor Studies Journal* 41(3): 260–91.

Reed, Adolph Jr., and Merlin Chowkwanyun. 2012. Race, class, crisis: The discourse of racial disparity and its analytical discontents. *Socialist Register* 48: 149–75.

Report cites snag in public housing. 1952. *New York Times*, April 13.

Rhode, Paul W., and Koleman S. Strumpf. 2003. Assessing the importance of Tiebout sorting: Local heterogeneity from 1850 to 1990. *American Economic Review* 93 (5): 1648–77.

Rice, Roger L. 1968. Residential segregation by law, 1910–1917. *The Journal of Southern History* 34 (2): 179–99.

Ringelstein, Kevin Lang. 2015. Residential segregation in Norfolk, Virginia: How the federal government reinforced racial division in a southern city, 1914–1959. MA Thesis, History, Old Dominion University.

Riordan, Kevin. 1996. Portrait of Elijah Perry unveiled at City Hall. *Camden Courier Post*, February 2.

Robbins, Ira S. 1937. A brief summary of the Wagner Steagall housing bill. *The Compass* 18 (7): 4–5.

Robinson, Charles Mulford. 1916. *City planning: With special reference to the planning of streets and lots*. New York: The Knickerbocker Press.

Rodden, Jonathan. 2010. The geographic distribution of political preferences. *Annual Review of Political Science* 13: 321–40.

2011. The long shadow of the Industrial Revolution: Political geography and the representation of the left. Unpublished book manuscript: web.stanford .edu/~jrodden/wp/shadow.pdf.

Roediger, David. R. 1991. *The wages of whiteness: Race and the making of the American working class*. London: Verso Press.

2005. *Working toward whiteness: How America's immigrants became white: The strange journey from Ellis Island to the suburbs*. New York: Basic Books.

Roithmayr, Daria. 2014. *Reproducing racism: How everyday choices lock in white advantage*. New York: New York University Press.

Rose, Mark, and Raymond Mohl. 2012 [1979]. *Interstate: Highway politics and policy since 1939*. Knoxville: The University of Tennessee Press.

Ross, Stephen L. 2008. Understanding racial segregation: What is known about the effect of housing discrimination. Economics Working Papers. Paper 200815: digitalcommons.uconn.edu/econ_wpapers/200815.

Rothstein, Jesse. 2007. Does competition among public schools benefit students and taxpayers? A comment on Hoxby (2000). *American Economic Review* 97 (5): 2026–37.

Rothstein, Richard. 2017. *The color of law: A forgotten history of how our government segregated America*. New York: Liveright Publishing Corporation.

Rothwell, Jonathan T. 2011. Racial enclaves and density zoning: The institutionalized segregation of racial minorities in the United States. *American Law and Economics Review* 13 (1): 290–358.

Rothwell, Jonathan T., and Douglas S. Massey. 2009. The effect of density zoning on racial segregation in U.S. urban areas. *Urban Affairs Review* 44 (6): 779–806.

Russell, Mary Faith. 1954. Segregated education in St. Louis: A study of monetary costs. *The Midwest Sociologist* 16 (1): 22–7.

S., C. C. 1925. Constitutional law: Right of municipal corporations to zone: A comprehensive system of use zoning is within the police power. *California Law Review* 13 (5): 417–20.

Sampson, Robert J. 2012. *Great American city: Chicago and the enduring neighborhood effect*. Chicago: University of Chicago Press.

Schelling, Thomas. 1971. Dynamic models of segregation. *Journal of Mathematical Sociology* 1: 143–86.

Schuman, Howard, and Lawrence Bobo. 1988. Survey-based experiments on white racial attitudes toward residential integration. *American Journal of Sociology* 94 (2): 273–99.

Schuman, Howard, Charlotte Steeh, and Lawrence Bobo. 1997 [1985]. *Racial attitudes in America: Trends and interpretations*. Cambridge, MA: Harvard University Press.

Schuster, Dana. 2016. Ivana Trump on how she advises Donald and those hands. *New York Post*, April 3.

Schwarz, Norbert, and Gerald L. Clore. 1983. Mood, misattribution, and judgments of well-being: Informative and directive functions of affective states. *Journal of Personality and Social Psychology* 45 (3): 513–23.

Sears, David. 1988. Symbolic racism. In *Eliminating racism: Profiles in controversy*, eds. Phyllis Katz and Dalmas Taylor. New York: Plenum Press.

Sears, David O., and Jack Citrin. 1982. *Tax revolt: Something for nothing in California*. Cambridge, MA: Harvard University Press.

Sears, David O., Carl P. Hensler, and Leslie K. Speer. 1979. Whites' opposition to "busing": Self-interest or symbolic politics? *American Political Science Review* 73: 369–84.

Sears, David O., Colette Van Laar, Mary Carrillo, and Rick Kosterman. 1997. Is it really racism? The origins of white Americans' opposition to race-targeted policies. *The Public Opinion Quarterly* 61 (1): 16–53.

Seek repeal of city ordinance. 1964. *Chicago Defender*, December 23.

Self, Robert O. 2003. *American Babylon: Race and the struggle for postwar Oakland*. Princeton, NJ: Princeton University Press.

Shah, Nayan. 2001. *Contagious divides: Epidemics and race in San Francisco's Chinatown*. Berkeley: University of California Press.

Sharkey, Patrick. 2013. *Stuck in place: Urban neighborhoods and the end of progress toward racial equality*. Chicago: University of Chicago Press.

Shaw, Todd. 2009. *Now is the time! Detroit black politics and grassroots activism*. Durham, NC: Duke University Press.

Sigelman, Lee, Timothy Bledsoe, Susan Welch, and Michael W. Combs. 1996. Making contact? Black-white social interaction in an urban setting. *American Journal of Sociology* 101 (5): 1306–32, www.jstor.org/stable/2782356.

Silver, Christopher. 1997. The racial origins of zoning in American cities. In *Urban planning and the African American community: In the shadows*, eds. June Manning Thomas and Marsha Ritzdorf: 23–42. Thousand Oaks, CA: Sage Publications.

Silver, Christopher, and John Moeser. 1995. *The separate city: Black communities in the urban South, 1940–1968*. Lexington, KY: University Press of Kentucky.

Silvotti, Bert. 1968. Groups seek ouster of Melleby: Urge state, U.S. probes of police force. *Camden Courier-Post*, June 21.

Sinclair, Betsy. 2012. *Peer networks and political behavior*. Chicago: University of Chicago Press.

Slothuus, Rune, and Claes H. de Vreese. 2010. Political parties, motivated reasoning, and issue framing effects. *The Journal of Politics* 72 (03): 630–45.

Smith, Tom, Peter Marsden, and Michael Hout. 1972–2014. *General social surveys*. Chicago: NORC, 2016.

Sniderman, Paul M., Richard A. Brody, and Philip E. Tetlock. 1991. *Reasoning and choice: Explorations in political psychology*. New York: Cambridge University Press.

Sniderman, Paul M., and Edward G. Carmines. 1997. *Reaching beyond race.* Cambridge, MA: Harvard University Press.

Snyder, Thomas, ed. 1993. *120 years of American education: A statistical portrait.* National Center for Education Statistics, US Department of Education.

Soss, Joe, Richard Fording, and Sanford Schram. 2011. *Disciplining the poor: Neoliberal paternalism and the persistent power of race.* Chicago: University of Chicago Press.

Spence, Lester. 2015. *Knocking the hustle: Against the neoliberal turn in black politics.* New York: Punctum Books.

Spencer Banzhaf, H., and Randall P. Walsh. 2008. Do people vote with their feet? An empirical test of Tiebout's mechanism. *American Economic Review* 98 (3): 843–63.

Stearns, Richard. Racial Content of FHA Underwriting Practices, 1934–1962. Jenkins Files Special Collections Department. Plaintiffs Exhibit 48 Case no. MJG 95–309, 1962): archives.Ubalt.Edu.

Still, Bayrd. 1948. *Milwaukee: The history of a city.* Madison, WI: State Historical Society of Wisconsin.

Stockbridge, Basil. 1938. "Low-cost housing": 1938 model. *The Journal of Land & Public Utility Economics* 14 (3): 327–9.

Stone, Clarence. 1989. *Regime politics: Governing Atlanta, 1946–1988.* Lawrence: University Press of Kansas.

Sugrue, Thomas. 1996. *The origins of the urban crisis: Race and inequality in postwar Detroit.* Princeton: Princeton University Press.

2015. It's not Dixie's fault. *The Washington Post,* July 17.

Taber, Charles S., Damon Cann, and Simona Kucsova. 2009. The motivated processing of political arguments. *Political Behavior* 31 (2): 137–55.

Taber, Charles S., and Milton Lodge. 2006. Motivated skepticism in the evaluation of political beliefs. *American Journal of Political Science* 50 (3): 755–69.

Tate, Katherine. 1994. *From protest to politics: The new black voters in American elections.* Cambridge: Harvard University Press.

Taub, Richard P., D. Garth Taylor, and Jan D. Dunham. 1984. *Paths of neighborhood change: Race and crime in urban America.* Chicago: University of Chicago Press.

Tausanovitch, Christopher, and Christopher Warshaw. 2014. Representation in municipal government. *American Political Science Review* 108 (3).

Taylor, Marylee C. 1998. How white attitudes vary with the racial composition of local populations: Numbers count. *American Sociological Review* 63: 512–35.

Teaford, Jon C. 1979. *City and suburb: The political fragmentation of metropolitan America, 1850–1970.* Baltimore: Johns Hopkins University Press.

Tebeau, Marc. 2003. *Eating smoke: Fire in urban America, 1800–1950.* Baltimore: Johns Hopkins University Press.

Tessin, Jeff. 2009. Representation and government performance. PhD Dissertation, Politics, Princeton University.

Theil, Henri. 1972. *Statistical decomposition analysis: With applications in the social and administrative sciences.* Amsterdam: North-Holland Publishing Company.

Thibodeau, Paul, Matthew M. Peebles, Daniel J. Grodner, and Frank H. Durgin. 2015. The wished-for always wins until the winner was inevitable all along: Motivated reasoning and belief bias regulate emotion during elections. *Political Psychology* 36 (4): 431–48.

Thomas, William P. 1949. Letter to the Editor. *Washington Post*, February 27.

Tiebout, Charles M. 1956. A pure theory of local expenditures. *The Journal of Political Economy* 64 (5): 416–24.

Tippett, Rebecca. 2014. *Mortality and cause of death, 1900 v. 2010:* demography .cpc.unc.edu/2014/06/16/mortality-and-cause-of-death-1900-v-2010/.

Tolbert, Caroline J., and Rodney E. Hero. 1996. Race/ethnicity and direct democracy: An analysis of California's illegal immigration initiative. *The Journal of Politics* 58 (3): 806–18.

Toll, Seymour I. 1969. *Zoned American*. New York: Grossman Publishers.

Torres-Rouff, David. 2013. *Before L.A.: Race, space, and municipal power in Los Angeles, 1781–1894*. New Haven: Yale University Press.

Tretter, Eliot M. 2012. *Austin restricted: Progressivism, zoning, private racial covenants, and the making of a segregated city*: hdl.handle.net/2152/21232.

Troesken, Werner. 2001. Race, disease, and the provision of water in American cities, 1889–1921. *Journal of Economic History* 61 (3): 750–77.

2004. *Race, water, and disease*. Cambridge, MA: MIT Press.

Troesken, Werner, and Randall Walsh. 2017. Collective action, white flight, and the origins of formal segregation laws. National Bureau of Economic Research Working Paper 23691.

Trounstine, Jessica. 2008. *Political monopolies in American cities: The rise and fall of bosses and reformers*. Chicago: University of Chicago Press.

2015. The privatization of public services in American cities. *Social Science History* 39(3): 371–85.

Trounstine, Jessica, and Melody Ellis Valdini. 2008. The context matters: The effect of single-member versus at-large districts on city council diversity. *American Journal of Political Science* 52(3): 554–69.

Turner, Wallace. 1964. Rightists in West fight housing act: Californians gain power in drive against integration. *New York Times*, May 10.

Tversky, Amos, and Daniel Kahneman. 1974. Judgement under uncertainty: Heuristics and biases. *Science* 185 (4157): 1124–31.

1986. Rational choice and the framing of decisions. *The Journal of Business* 59: S251.

United States Environmental Protection Agency. 2004. *Report to Congress: Impacts and control of CSOs and SSOs*. Washington, DC: Office of Water, EPA 833-R-04-001.

United States Housing Act of 1937 Pub.L. 75–412, 50 Stat. 888. 75th Congress. 1st sess. (1937): 896.

U.S. Supreme Court kills segregation laws. 1917. *Chicago Defender*, November 10.

Valentino, Nicholas A., Vincent L. Hutchings, and Ismail K. White. 2002. Cues that matter: How political ads prime racial attitudes during campaigns. *American Political Science Review* 96 (1): 75–90.

Van Hecke, M. T. 1929. Zoning ordinances and restrictions in deeds. *Yale Law Journal* 37 (4): 407–25.

Van Ryzin, Gregg G., Douglas Muzzio, and Stephen Immerwahr. 2004. Explaining the race gap in satisfaction with urban services. *Urban Affairs Review* 39 (5): 613–32.

Vigdor, Jacob L. 2004. Community composition and collective action: Analyzing initial mail response to the 2000 census. *Review of Economics and Statistics* 86 (1): 303–12.

Vigdor, Jacob, and Edward Glaeser. 2012. *The end of the segregated century: Racial separation in America's neighborhoods, 1890–2010*. Manhattan Institute, 66.

Vigdor, Jacob, Douglas Massey, and Alice Rivlin. 2002. Does gentrification harm the poor? Brookings-Wharton Papers on Urban Affairs. Brookings Institution Press.

Vogl, Tom S. 2014. Race and the politics of close elections. *Journal of Public Economics* 109: 101–13.

Wade, Richard C. 1967. *Slavery in the cities: The South 1820–1860*. New York: Oxford University Press.

Wagner-Steagall Act. 1937. *Documents of American history II M2010 1930s*.

Walls, Margaret, Carolyn Kousky, and Ziyan Chu. 2015. Is what you see what you get? The value of natural landscape views. *Land Economics* 91 (1): 1–19.

Warner, Sam Bass. 1987 [1968]. *The private city: Philadelphia in three periods of its growth*. Philadelphia: University of Pennsylvania Press.

Washington, Booker T. 1915. My views of segregation laws. *New Republic*, December 3.

Washington, Ebonya. 2006. How black candidates affect voter turnout. *The Quarterly Journal of Economics* 121 (3): 973–98.

Watson, Tara. 2009. Inequality and the measurement of residential segregation by income in American neighborhoods. *The Review of Income and Wealth* 55 (3): 820–44.

Weaver, Robert C. 1940. Racial policy in public housing. *Phylon (1940–1956)* 1 (2): 149, 156, 161.

1946. Housing in a democracy. *The Annals of the American Academy of Political and Social Science* 244: 95–105.

1948. *The Negro ghetto*. New York: Russell & Russell.

1956. Integration in public and private housing. *The Annals of the American Academy of Political and Social Science* 304: 86–97.

1968. *Weaver oral history*. LBJ Presidential Library: transition.lbjlibrary.org/files/original/6404ca478ed6c3848eedaaf380acdb45.pdf.

Weiss, Marc. 1987. *The rise of community builders: The American real estate industry and urban land planning*. New York: Columbia University Press.

West, Bernard. 1976. Black Atlanta: Struggle for development, 1915–1925. MA Thesis. Department of History, Atlanta University.

What a zoning law is and what it does. 1924. *The Tampa Tribune*, January 6.

Wheildon, L. 1947. Negro segregation. *Editorial research reports 1947* (Vol. II). Washington, DC: CQ Press. Retrieved from library.cqpress.com/cqre searcher/cqresrre1947110700

Whitnall, Gordon. 1931. History of zoning. *The Annals of the American Academy of Political and Social Science* 155 (2): 1–14.

Widestrom, Amy. 2015. *Displacing democracy: Economic segregation in America*. Philadelphia: University of Pennsylvania Press.

Williams, Barbara. 1966a. Camden segregation: A matter of choice? *Camden Courier Post*, June 6.

1966b. Volunteers for integration: You can't tell a good neighbor by color. *Camden Courier-Post*, June 9.

Wilson, Charles Erwin. 1947. *To secure these rights, the report of the President's Committee on Civil Rights*. New York: Simon and Schuster. www.trumanli brary.org/civilrights/srights2.htm.

Wilson, James Q. 1966. *Urban renewal: The record and the controversy*. Cambridge, MA: MIT Press.

Wilson, Rick K. 2011. The contribution of behavioral economics to political science. *Annual Review of Political Science* 14: 201–23.

Wilson, William J. 1987. *The truly disadvantaged: The inner city, the underclass, and public policy*. Chicago: University of Chicago Press.

Winsberg, Morton D. 1989. Income polarization between the central cities and suburbs of U.S. metropolises, 1950–1980. *American Journal of Economics and Sociology* 48 (1): 3–10.

Winter, Nicholas. 2006. Beyond welfare: Framing and the racialization of white opinion on Social Security. *American Journal of Political Science* 50 (2): 400–20.

Woodbury, Coleman. 1929. Some suggested changes in the control of urban development. *The Journal of Land & Public Utility Economics* 5 (3): 249–59.

Woodward, C. Van. 1955. *The strange career of Jim Crow*. New York: Oxford University Press.

Wright, Marion Thompson. 1953. New Jersey leads in the struggle for educational integration. *The Journal of Educational Sociology* 26(9): 401–17.

Yearly, Clifton K. 1970. *The money machines: The breakdown and reform of governmental and party finances in the north, 1880–1920*. Albany, NY: State University of New York Press.

Yinger, John. 1997. *Closed doors, opportunities lost: The continuing costs of housing discrimination*. New York: Russell Sage Foundation.

Zackin, Emily. 2013. *Looking for rights in all the wrong places: Why state constitutions contain America's positive rights*. Princeton, NJ: Princeton University Press.

Zaller, John, and Stanley Feldman. 1992. A simple theory of the survey response: Answering questions versus revealing preferences. *American Journal of Political Science* 36 (3): 579–616.

Zipp, Samuel. 2012. The roots and routes of urban renewal. *Journal of Urban History* 39 (3): 366–91.

Zuckerman, Alan, ed. 2005. *The Social Logic of Politics: Personal Networks as Contexts for Political Behavior*. Philadelphia: Temple University Press.

COURT CASES

Banks v. Housing Authority of the City and County of San Francisco; Cal App 2d, 120 *Banks v. Housing Authority of the City and County of San Francisco;* Cal App 2d (California Court of Appeals 1953).

Brown v. Board of Education of Topeka, 347 U.S. 483, *Brown v. Board of Education of Topeka,* 347 U.S. 483 (1954).

Brown v. Board of Education of Topeka, 349 U.S. 294 (1955).

Burton v. Wilmington Parking Authority, 365 U.S. 715 (1961).

Gayle v. Browder, 352 U.S. 903, 77 S.Ct. 145, 1 L.Ed.2d 114 (1956).

Holmes v. City of Atlanta 350 U.S. 879, 76 S.Ct.141, 100 L. Ed 776 (1955)

Johnson v. Virginia, 373 U.S. 61, 83 S.Ct. 1053, 10 L.Ed.2d 195 (1963).

Mayor of Baltimore v. Dawson, 350 U.S. 877, 76 S.Ct. 133, 100 L.Ed. 774 (1958), aff'g 220 F.2d 386 (4th Cir. 1955).

Muir v. Louisville Park. 1953.

Plessy v. Ferguson, 163 US 537, *Plessy v. Ferguson,* 163 US 537 (1896).

Rice v. Sioux City Memorial Park Cemetery, Inc. 349 U.S. 70 (1955).

Shay v. Delaware 122 N.J.L. 313, 316 (N.J. 1939).

Shelley v. Kraemer, 334 U.S. 1, *Shelley v. Kraemer,* 334 U.S. 1 (1948).

Simkins v. Cone Memorial Hospital, 211 F. Supp. 628 (M.D.N.C 1962).

State v. Gurry 121 Md. 534, *State v. Gurry* 121 Md. 534 (1913).

United States v. Certain Lands in the City of Louisville, 78 F.2d 684 (6th Cir. 1935).

Village of Euclid, Ohio v. Ambler Realty Co., 272 U.S. 365, *Village of Euclid, Ohio v. Ambler Realty Co.,* 272 U.S. 365 (1926).

Watson v. City of Memphis,, 373 U.S. 526 (1963).

Yick Wo v. Hopkins, 118 U.S. 356, *Yick Wo v. Hopkins,* 118 U.S. 356 (1886).

Index